Praise for *The Impact Cycle*
by Jim Knight

Coaching done well may be the most effective intervention designed for human performance. Jim Knight's work has helped me understand the details of how effective coaching can and should be done.

—**Dr. Atul Gawande,** Surgeon, Public Health Researcher,
and Author of *The Checklist Manifesto*
Brigham and Women's Hospital

I struggle to know the difference between a good coach and a good teacher. I have watched the coaching movement grow in education, with much of this impetus coming from the success of Jim Knight and his team. I have PhD students wanting to research coaching, I have read the books about John Wooden and Bob Knight, I have coached cricket for many decades, and my team is translating Visible Learning into action with some elite sports teams in Australia. It was only when I read this book that I started to understand that difference.

Good teaching for me means teachers who are to DIE for—great Diagnosis, excellent Implementation, and superb Evaluation. Great coaching adds fidelity of implementation (and my colleagues will love this, as it removes the nasty "DIE" acronym). The core of implementation are the PEERS goals: powerful, easy, emotionally compelling, reachable, and student-focused. All are based on high levels of trust and a dogged attention to "What are the next steps?" based on excellent analyses of what is currently happening. The data are similar: video, student voice, and student work, although I am envious of the level of sophistication professional coaching teams have in apps and data interpretation. Their granularity is movement by movement, with many great higher-order analyses which surely could make a huge difference in classrooms—if we only got over our fears about using data to help instruction.

This is a book by the master coach in practice and theory; it sums up the core notions of coaching, and it provides a richness for action and thought for all who want to bring the power of coaching into teaching. I am convinced.

—**John Hattie,** Laureate Professor, Deputy Dean of MGSE,
and Director of the Melbourne Education Research Institute
Melbourne Graduate School of Education

Jim Knight is one of the wise men of coaching. His well is deep, and he draws from it the best tools from practitioners, the wisdom of experience, and research-based insights. And he never loses the bigger picture: the point of all this is to have more impact in this life we're lucky enough to live.

—**Michael Bungay Stanier**
Author of *The Coaching Habit*

There is no one more passionate about improving every student's learning experience than Jim Knight, and in *The Impact Cycle*, Knight has done it again with another well-researched and immensely practical book. There are some great features here—the visual maps that introduce each chapter, the numerous checklists and templates, links to the companion website, helpful chapter summaries, and great recommended resources in the "Going Deeper" sections. This is a book which will be referred to often. Instructional coaches will be an even better resource for the teachers with whom they work as a result of reading and using this book.

—**John Campbell**, Executive Director
Growth Coaching International

In this very helpful book, Jim Knight builds on knowledge gained from more than two decades of assisting coaches to inspire and guide teachers to improve their instruction. Following his own advice to "stay curious," Knight continues to expand upon his coaching model to explicate new dimensions of the coaching relationship. Conversational and informative, this book will be a useful resource for any coach working in the field.

—**Dr. Megan Tschannen-Moran**, Professor of Educational Leadership
College of William and Mary, School of Education

The Impact Cycle is an essential read for instructional coaches. It is organized to take the reader through each stage of an Impact Cycle, providing a vision for how to coach for a deeper impact. It is filled with stories from the field, allowing the reader to walk in the shoes of other coaches. In the end, all coaching is about creating meaning and supporting teachers to reach their goals; this book supports coaches to do just that.

—**Diane Sweeney**, Consultant
Diane Sweeney Consulting

Continuous improvement is fueled by a focus on improving the quality of teaching and learning. *The Impact Cycle* provides educators with the strategies and the tools necessary to make that improvement a reality. I have had the opportunity to see how Jim Knight's model works firsthand and can attest to its effectiveness. The emphasis on effective partnerships with shared responsibility and ownership, combined with a goal-oriented coaching cycle, results in lasting and meaningful changes for teachers and students. This book shares a clear vision for powerful instructional coaching along with the specific steps to make that vision a reality. Knight's *The Impact Cycle* is essential reading for educators who are committed to real and lasting change.

—**Dr. Jadi Miller,** Director of Curriculum
Lincoln Public Schools

Once again, Jim Knight has earned his reputation as the reigning expert in instructional coaching. With his trademark clarity and heart, Knight manages to capture both the simplicity and complexity of coaching in an accessible, detailed, and nuanced framework for instructional coaches. Packed with insight, concrete examples, and practical tools, *The Impact Cycle* is an indispensable guide for coaches who want to make the biggest possible difference for students.

—**Nancy Love,** Director
Program Development at Research for Better Teaching in Action

I have had many opportunities to learn with and from Jim Knight. I've learned as a participant in his workshops, from reading his books, and from being on panels with him. Now *The Impact Cycle* adds to my skills and insights. Knight's vision of the coach as a partner who sets goals with the teacher, strategizes with and supports the teacher, and monitors changes with the teacher until the goal is met, will assist many instructional coaches in targeting their efforts. Student-focused goals will be a game changer in many coaching initiatives and guarantee that coach and teacher investment in teacher learning is impacting student learning.

—**Dr. Stephen Barkley,** Executive Vice President
PLS 3rd Learning

Jim Knight's books are essential for instructional coaches, and *The Impact Cycle* is an invaluable contribution on how to move teachers in their practice. With his trademark kindness and wisdom, Knight guides us yet again through the systems, processes, and paths of meaningful instructional coaching. New and experienced coaches will find many resources and ideas to add to their toolkit in this book.

—**Elena Aguilar**
Author of *The Art of Coaching*

This book is dedicated to my daughter Emily Joan Kelly. At a time when so many are turning away in fear from refugees who are suffering persecution, you are dedicating your life to finding safe homes for the many children, women, and men whose homelands are no longer safe. Your conversations with me make me smarter, your work inspires me, and every day I'm proud and grateful for what you do to make the world a better place for everyone.

JIM KNIGHT

THE IMPACT CYCLE

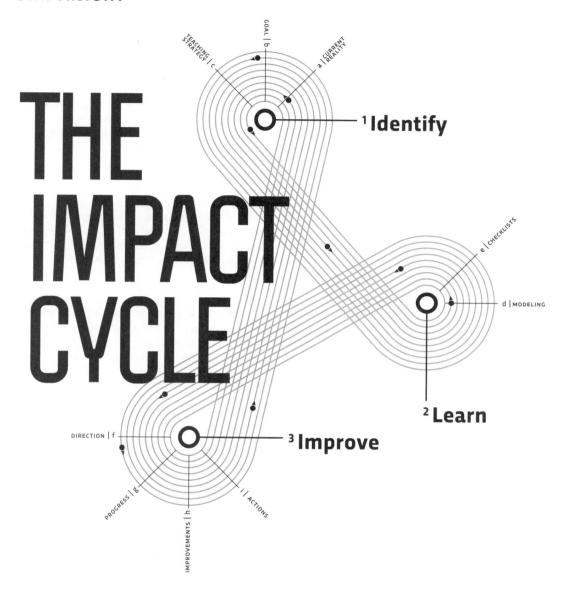

¹Identify

GOAL | b

a | CURRENT REALITY

TEACHING STRATEGY | c

e | CHECKLISTS

d | MODELING

²Learn

DIRECTION | f

³Improve

PROGRESS | g

i | ACTIONS

IMPROVEMENTS | h

WHAT INSTRUCTIONAL COACHES SHOULD DO
TO FOSTER POWERFUL IMPROVEMENTS IN TEACHING

CORWIN

A SAGE Publishing Company

FOR INFORMATION:

Corwin

A SAGE Company

2455 Teller Road

Thousand Oaks, California 91320

(800) 233-9936

www.corwin.com

SAGE Publications Ltd.

1 Oliver's Yard

55 City Road

London EC1Y 1SP

United Kingdom

SAGE Publications India Pvt. Ltd.

B 1/I 1 Mohan Cooperative Industrial Area

Mathura Road, New Delhi 110 044

India

SAGE Publications Asia-Pacific Pte. Ltd.

3 Church Street

#10-04 Samsung Hub

Singapore 049483

Program Director: Dan Alpert

Associate Editor: Lucas Schleicher

Senior Editorial Assistant: Katie Crilley

Production Editor: Melanie Birdsall

Copy Editor: Laurie Pitman

Typesetter: C&M Digitals (P) Ltd.

Proofreader: Caryne Brown

Indexer: Amy Murphy

Interior Designer: Anupama Krishnan

Marketing Manager: Maura Sullivan

Note From the Publisher: The author has provided video and web content throughout the book that is available to you through QR (quick response) codes. To read a QR code, you must have a smartphone or tablet with a camera. We recommend that you download a QR code reader app that is made specifically for your phone or tablet brand.

Cover design by Clinton Carlson

Additional editing and proofreading by Kirsten McBride and Stacey Blakeman

Printed in the United States of America

ISBN 978-1-5063-0686-5

This book is printed on acid-free paper.

17 18 19 20 21 14 13 12 11 10

CONTENTS

Visit the companion website at
resources.corwin.com/impactcycle
for videos and downloadable resources.

PREFACE

The Impact Cycle described in this book is a process coaches can use to partner with teachers to help them have a positive impact on students' learning and well-being. The three stages of the cycle—identify, learn, improve—are central to coaching and, I believe, are also central to something fundamental: our universal desire to get better. When we look deeply at the learning and growth coaches and teachers do together for students, we learn a lot about all forms of growth and learning.

The idea that we would study instructional coaching began in a conference room at the University of Kansas in 1996. My colleagues and I were discussing a grant we were leading that would study what impact, if any, inclusive teaching practices might have on students with learning disabilities who were taking technology classes. As we discussed our plans, one of us at the table said, "We all know that workshops aren't going to lead to real implementation. If we want teachers to use these strategies, we need to sit down one on one, explain them, model them in their classrooms, and observe and provide feedback. If we don't do that, nothing will change."

Then one of us at the table said what I suspect all of us were thinking: "If we know that's true for this project, why don't we provide that kind of support all the time?" On that day, the idea of instructional coaching as we describe it was born.

At first, we didn't call ourselves instructional coaches but rather learning consultants. We were staff developers who worked with teachers to help them learn inclusive teaching practices or learning strategies developed at the University of Kansas Center for Research on Learning. Then, in 1999, when we won the first of several Federal GEARUP grants to sponsor our work, we started using the term *instructional collaborator*. In these earlier years of our research work, we were stumbling toward an understanding of coaching. Then after our team gave a presentation about instructional collaborators, my colleague Mike Hock, now the director of the Center for Research on Learning, said what, looking back, should have been obvious to all of us. "You know, it would be helpful if you identified and described stages and steps to what you do. Then other people could do what you do, too."

Mike, as he often does, spurred us to action, and we began carefully studying what worked when we partnered with teachers. GEARUP provided funding for us to place instructional collaborators in all the middle and high schools in USD 501 in Topeka, Kansas, and each week, our team would meet for two hours on Friday afternoons to review (a) our goals for the previous week, (b) what had really happened, (c) what accounted for the difference, and (d) what we would do differently the next week.[1] Additionally, as a part of our research, we conducted a number of qualitative and informal quantitative studies to see what impact the coaches were indeed having.

In 2005, I submitted an article to the *Journal of Staff Development* that summarized what we were learning, changing our name from instructional collaborator to instructional coach, mostly because people always identified us as coaches when we described what we did. Two years later, I published a much more comprehensive description of what instructional coaches do with the release of *Instructional Coaching: A Partnership Approach to Improving Instruction* (2007).

The publication of *Instructional Coaching* introduced me to educators, coaches, researchers, and authors from around the world, and their

---

1. We borrowed our approach to reflective dialogue and group learning from the U.S. Army's After-Action Review, which is often discussed in learning organization literature. You can read about the After-Action Review in *The U.S. Army Leadership Field Manual* (2004). I also include a form for structuring After-Action Review discussions in my book *Instructional Coaching: A Partnership Approach to Improving Instruction* (2007) on page 131.

ideas definitely helped us refine our coaching cycle to make it simpler and more powerful. At the Center for Research on Learning, we were fortunate to receive additional funding from GEARUP, The Institute of Education Sciences, and The Poses Foundation to conduct studies that allowed us to further improve and simplify our approach to coaching. For the past five years, one particularly powerful approach to research for us has been a methodology we refer to as Lean-Design Research. Lean-Design combines strategies start-ups and design firms use to improve products or processes. I describe the Lean-Design Research methodology in the Appendix at the end of this book, starting on page 247.

We used Lean-Design, first with coaches in Beaverton, Oregon, and then with coaches from Othello, Washington, to continually improve the coaching cycle. Coaches would set goals with teachers, move through the coaching cycle, identify friction points within the cycle, and then partner with us to invent solutions, apply research, or apply ideas we gathered from coaching experts whom we interviewed. Each time we moved through the cycle, we got a little better, and the cycle got more powerful and easier to implement.

To deepen our knowledge, my colleagues and I also interviewed many instructional coaches from around the world, and I interviewed experts in fields such as coaching, feedback, and performance improvement, including Atul Gawande, Sheila Heen, Bob Garmston, and Christian van Nieuwerburgh. Coaches' comments and stories are included throughout this book to supplement the ideas we learned from our research. Similarly, where appropriate, I've included comments from my expert interviews. The result is the book you are reading right now.

The Impact Cycle is deceptively simple. It involves setting a goal, identifying a strategy to use to hit the goal, getting good at implementing the strategy, and then making adaptations until the goal is met. Hidden within that simplicity, though, is a lot that we have learned. Just the simple task of setting a goal, for example, requires different ways of getting a clear picture of reality so as to make sure the right issue is being addressed and strategies for ensuring the chosen goal is an important, powerful goal that matters to the teacher and students. Setting a goal also involves determining how to measure progress and how to be certain the goal has been hit. An instructional coach also needs a collection of strategies, a sort of playbook to draw from and to support teachers as they work toward their goal. And, goal setting is, of course, only one part of the Impact Cycle.

I wrote this book to recognize that coaching is both simple and complex, and I want to honor that simultaneous simplicity and

Video P.1

Crysta's Entire Impact Cycle—Complete

Video P.2

Cat's Entire Impact Cycle—Complete

resources.corwin.com/impactcycle

To read a QR code, you must have a smartphone or tablet with a camera. We recommend that you download a QR code reader app that is made specifically for your phone or tablet brand.

complexity by summarizing what we have learned to make it easier for instructional coaches to implement the Impact Cycle. The book can be read in different ways. You can jump to a section that you need today, say "identifying a clear picture of reality," or you can read it through page by page. You can stop and watch all of the supplemental videos as you work through the book, watching the coaching cycle unfold video by video, or you can watch the complete Impact Cycle in the elementary and secondary video examples linked in the QR codes to get an advance understanding of the cycle. There are also a lot of resources in the second half of the book to give you the tools you need to do this work, and there is a companion website at resources.corwin.com/impactcycle where you can download most of the forms in the toolkit.

I wrote *The Impact Cycle* with the sincere hope that it will help coaches help teachers make a difference in the lives of children. I think helping kids succeed is about the most important work that any of us can do. For that reason, I hope you will help us, too. If you learn something in applying this work, please let us know by writing us at hello@instructionalcoaching.com. We need to keep getting better, too.

ACKNOWLEDGMENTS

I would very much like to properly acknowledge all of the people who have contributed to this book in some way, but I feel compelled to admit that I am probably going to fail in that attempt. This book, perhaps more than any other, is so much the result of the hard work of dozens of other teachers, coaches, educators, researchers, authors, friends, family, colleagues, deep thinkers, and artists that inevitably, I'm sure, I will leave off naming people whose significant effort made this book possible. I am so indebted to so many that I watched Brian Greene's String Theory TED talk to see if there was some kind of cosmic analogy for interconnection I could use to describe how this book is so interwoven with the efforts of others, but I quickly realized that I'm not cut out for string theory. Perhaps my best strategy is simply to express my deep gratitude and admit, unfortunately, that there are many people who helped make this book possible and deserve recognition who, despite my best effort, will be accidentally omitted here. If you are one of those people, please know that I do truly appreciate your partnership with me in making these ideas become a reality not just in this book but, I'm happy to report, in many classrooms around the world.

Before I was a writer, I admit, I tended to skip acknowledgments. I just wanted to get to the good stuff, and I didn't bother to take the time for all of the thank-yous. Now that I am an author, however, I read acknowledgments with great interest because I know how important they are for those who write them. I've noticed, too, that families almost always come first or last in them. Families are mentioned in the places of greatest importance because families pay the greatest price when an author writes a book. My family is no different. I feel profoundly fortunate and grateful to my wife Jenny whose genuine, unwavering support of this work is one of the most important reasons I am able to write. Today, I'm thrilled that Jenny has become my co-author in so much of this work, writing the *Reflection Guide* for this and other books and working with me through all of our big ideas at the Instructional Coaching Group. Jenny is my soulmate, partner, and lover, but as we have grown together, she has become my co-laborer and thought partner. Together, we are trying to make the world a better place for people, especially children, and now there is something of Jenny's thinking in every word I write. I find it impossible, really, to say where her ideas end and mine begin—we just think and create together.

Most of my children are now grown and out changing the world for the better themselves. There were many times when I should have visited, called, or written when instead I was working on this book or out spreading the word about these ideas. They have accepted that this is just the reality of this life with Dad. What I am especially grateful for, though, is that now that my children are grown they are teaching me about making change happen, statistics, books to read, computers, or even how to write. I am so grateful to Geoff, Cameron, David, Emily, Ben, Isaiah, and Luke.

I am especially grateful to my parents. This has been a tough year because both Mom and Dad died while I was writing this book. Their belief in me and their unwavering determination that I get a university education are likely the main reasons this book exists. I loved them. I miss them. And, they inspire me to try to do good work and make what difference I can.

The research that was conducted in support of this book was done by many different people who all contributed a great deal. Most of what we've done started at the University of Kansas Center for Research on Learning, where I've been privileged to work on the study of coaching with many outstanding researchers and research assistants, including Barbara Bradley, Devona Dunekack, Irma Brasseur-Hock, Jake Cornett, Don Deshler, Marti Elford, Susan Harvey, Carol Hatton, Mike Hock, David Knight, Jackie Schafer, and Tom Skrtic. We especially learned an enormous amount from our coaches in Beaverton, Oregon, including Michelle Harris, Jennifer MacMillan, Lea Molczan, and Susan Leyden, and in Othello, Washington, including Denise Colley, Jerad Farley, Marci Gonzalez, Jackie Jewell, Jacee Martinez, and Jenn Perez.

Several experts, who had much better things to do than talk with me, took time out of their schedules to let me interview them as I was writing this book. Their ideas influenced my thinking, and their comments are included at different points. The experts I interviewed are John Campbell, a leading coaching expert in Australia; Bob Garmston, who founded cognitive coaching along with Art Costa; Atul Gawande, author of many books on improving performance, including *The Checklist Manifesto*; Sheila Heen, co-author of *Thanks for the Feedback*; and Christian van Nieuwerburgh, one of the leading coaching experts in the United Kingdom.

Many researchers and research assistants at the Impact Research Lab and the Instructional Coaching Group, the two organizations Jenny and I oversee, have also helped us validate, refine, and disseminate practices that support better teaching for better learning. I am particularly grateful to Brooke Deaton, LaVonne Holmgren, Marilyn Ruggles, Ruth Ryschon, Bill Townes, and Donna Wirth. The Instructional Coaching Group consultants Michelle Harris, Ann Hoffman, Tricia Skyles, and Conn Thomas have been outstanding presenters, and they teach us a great deal as they learn with their learning partners.

I worked with a great group of professionals to create this book, even before it was being shaped by my publisher. Andrew Benson, who has allowed me to work with him on many projects, did an outstanding job documenting the Impact Cycle on video as I moved through the cycle's stages with an elementary and a secondary teacher. I am also grateful to Austin Pulliam for his camera work as he worked with Andrew to create the video that is included throughout the book. Crysta Crum and Cathryn Munroe, the teachers featured in those videos, were simply wonderful learning partners, and I'm very grateful for the opportunity to partner with them. Clinton Carlson, my design partner for more than a decade, created a fabulous cover, and Kirsten McBride edited this book and made the text much clearer and less awkward. As I frequently say, I have never written a page that Kirsten couldn't improve. Stacey Blakeman did a great job of proofreading the final proofs of the text.

At my publisher Corwin, I am fortunate to know many people who started out as work partners but have now become friends. Dan Alpert, who has been my editor for more than a decade, has helped me maintain focus, redirected me when I've needed him to, given me wise counsel, and become a true friend especially when I have needed him the most. Dan took the time to listen to me with genuine empathy when I first realized I was about to lose my parents, and he gave me excellent advice when I told him I really didn't know what to do. There are so many other truly good people at Corwin whom I am also so grateful to have as colleagues and friends. That group includes, but is by no means limited to, Kristen Anderson, Melanie Birdsall, Katie Hann, Mayan McDermott, Lisa Shaw, Maura Sullivan, and Mike Soules. The Corwin consultants, who have spread the word about *The Impact Cycle*, *Better Conversations*, *Focus on Teaching*, and *High-Impact Instruction*, have done a fantastic job sharing the work, and they have also taught me an enormous amount when we've worked together. I'm very grateful to Laura Besser, Lindsey Deacon, Peter DeWitt, Lisa Dlablick, Jenni Donohoo, Ainsley Rose, and Kara Vandas.

Any book, of course, is the product of so many other ideas that an author has read or heard, and I can't begin to list everyone who has shaped my thinking. There are a small number of people, however, whom I must mention. Peter Block, Don Deshler (already mentioned above), Paulo Freire, Michael Fullan, Stephanie Hirsh, Joellen Killion, and Margaret Wheatley have all deeply shaped my thinking. I'm grateful to all of them and their ideas live in these pages.

I'm also grateful to many readers who gave me feedback as I was writing this book. Thank you to Sherri Barber, Lynn Barnes, Lynn Cole, Elizabeth Cotter, Lindsay Deacon, Peter DeWitt, Deborah Goodwin, Michelle Harris, Emily Joan Kelly, Joi Lunsford, Buffy Massey, Tricia McKale, Stacey Seik, Bill Sommers, LaTasha Timberlake, Kara Vandas, and Caryn Ziettlow.

Finally, I wrote *The Impact Cycle* mostly listening to jazz from the fifties and early sixties. I used my time writing this book as a chance to get to know Thelonious Monk, and I've become a real fan. I also deepened my appreciation for Coltrane, and I still list *A Love Supreme* as a desert island recording, even if it isn't the best background music for writing. My favorite writing music continues to be Bill Evans's *The Complete Village Vanguard Recordings, 1961*. I never grow tired of that music, and I don't think I ever will.

ABOUT THE AUTHOR

Jim Knight has spent more than two decades studying professional learning, effective teaching, and instructional coaching. He is a research associate at the University of Kansas Center for Research on Learning and the president of the Instructional Coaching Group and the Impact Research Lab.

Jim's book *Instructional Coaching: A Partnership Approach to Improving Instruction* (Corwin, 2007) popularized the idea of instructional coaching. Jim edited *Coaching: Approaches and Perspectives* (Corwin, 2009) and co-authored *Coaching Classroom Management* (Pacific Northwest Publishing, 2010). Jim's other books include *Unmistakable Impact: A Partnership Approach for Dramatically Improving Instruction* (Corwin, 2011), *High-Impact Instruction: A Framework for Great Teaching* (Corwin, 2013), *Focus on Teaching: Using Video for High-Impact Instruction* (Corwin, 2014), and *Better Conversations: Coaching Ourselves and Each Other to Be More Credible, Caring, and Connected* (Corwin, 2016).

Jim's articles on professional learning, teaching, and instructional coaching have appeared in journals such as *The Journal of Staff Development, Principal Leadership, The School Administrator, Kappan,* and *Educational Leadership.*

Frequently asked to lead professional learning, Jim has presented to more than 100,000 educators from six continents. He has a PhD in Education from the University of Kansas and has won several university teaching, innovation, and service awards. Jim also writes the Radical Learners blog.

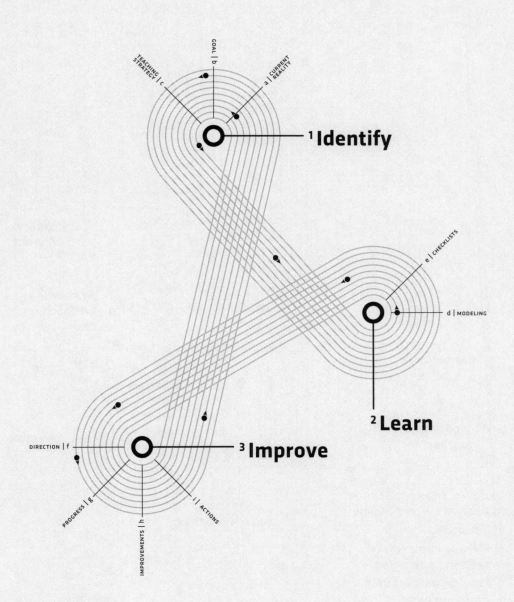

GOAL | b

TEACHING
STRATEGY | c

a | CURRENT
REALITY

¹ Identify

e | CHECKLISTS

d | MODELING

² Learn

DIRECTION | f

³ Improve

PROGRESS | g

IMPROVEMENTS | h

i | ACTIONS

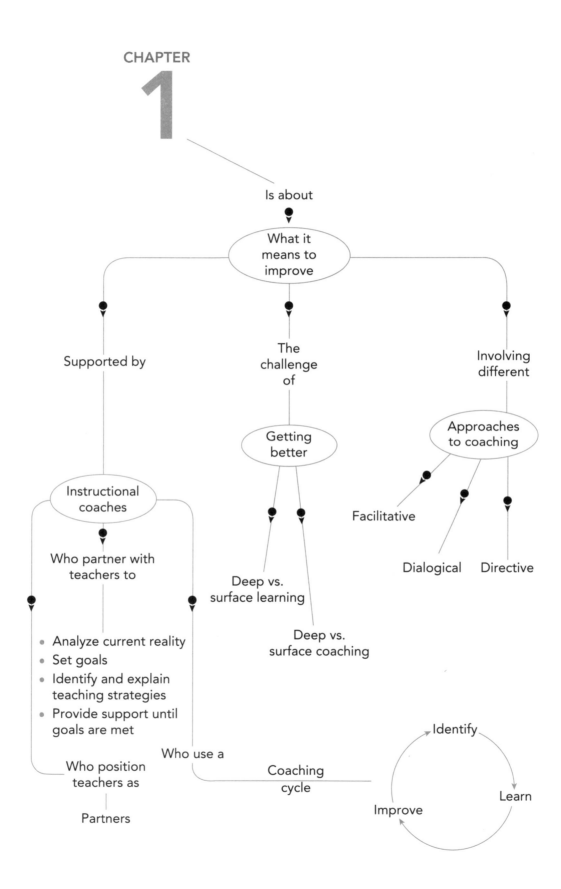

CHAPTER

1

Is about

What it means to improve

Supported by

The challenge of

Involving different

Instructional coaches

Getting better

Approaches to coaching

Who partner with teachers to

Facilitative

- Analyze current reality
- Set goals
- Identify and explain teaching strategies
- Provide support until goals are met

Deep vs. surface learning

Dialogical   Directive

Deep vs. surface coaching

Who use a

Who position teachers as

Coaching cycle

Identify

Partners

Improve   Learn

WHAT DOES IT MEAN TO IMPROVE?

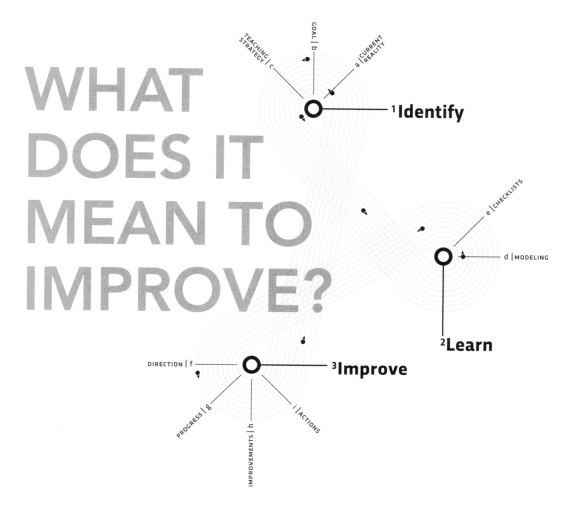

Like you, I've spent a lot of my life trying to improve. As I write this book, I'm trying to eat a cleaner diet, cut out sweets, and drop a few pounds (well, maybe 40!). I'm trying to be more present in conversations, trying to listen more than talk, and trying to focus and be more attentive. In the past year, I've watched about a dozen videos of myself presenting to various groups as part of my efforts to upgrade my skills, and I've been reading books about writing to try to improve the simplicity, utility, and (I hope) the beauty of my writing. Admittedly, I've also wasted a lot of time reading books about how to not waste time.

When it comes to trying to improve, I'm not alone. Your local bookstore or online retailer has stacks of books on dieting, relationships, leadership, money management, spiritual guidance, and self-help. Organizations in your community likely offer hundreds of courses on every topic from yoga, to iPad basics, to photography, to archery. Universities now offer thousands of online courses that anyone can take if they choose. Even Ivy League institutions such as Yale offer free online courses that are identical to the courses taught in traditional classrooms.

There are many ways to improve, and most of us try to do it the best way we know how. Increasingly, people are finding that one of the most powerful ways to improve is to partner with a coach. As Harvard researcher Atul Gawande has written, "Coaching done well may be the most effective intervention designed for human performance" (2011, p. 53).

For close to twenty years, my colleagues and I at the Kansas Coaching Project at the University of Kansas Center for Research on Learning, along with my colleagues at the Impact Research Lab in Lawrence, Kansas, have been studying one form of coaching—instructional coaching. This book describes what our research says about what instructional coaches should do and how they should interact with collaborating teachers to improve the quality of students' and teachers' lives to the greatest extent possible.

WHAT IS INSTRUCTIONAL COACHING?

Coaching is booming. There are life coaches, executive coaches, and performance coaches. There are coactive coaches, empathic coaches, and solution-focused coaches. There are image coaches, dating coaches, and even Twitter coaches. In other words, if you want to learn how to do something, you can find a coach to help you do it.

There are also many different types of coaches in education. For example, schools might employ cognitive coaches, literacy coaches, data coaches, content-focused coaches, technology coaches, behavior coaches, pedagogical coaches, and instructional coaches. Some approaches to coaching address many aspects of an educator's life. Others focus on a particular aspect of an educator's work, such as effective teaching to improve student learning, as in the case of instructional coaching. However, regardless of its focus, each approach is designed to help teachers improve.

Instructional coaches (ICs) partner with teachers to help them improve teaching and learning so students become more successful. To do this, ICs collaborate with teachers to get a clear picture of current reality, identify goals, pick teaching strategies to meet the goals, monitor progress, and

Instructional coaches partner with teachers to

o analyze current reality,

o set goals,

o identify and explain teaching strategies to meet goals, and

o provide support until goals are met.

problem-solve until the goals are met. At the Impact Research Lab, we define instructional coaching as follows: "Instructional coaches partner with teachers to analyze current reality, set goals, identify and explain teaching strategies to meet goals, and provide support until the goals are met."

Devona Dunekack, who has worked with me as an instructional coach since 1999, was prompted to try to define instructional coaching a few years ago when she was asked a question that many coaches hate: "Tell me, what is it that you do?" Devona's friend, who asked the question, was genuinely curious about Devona's work, and Devona did her best to explain her job, talking about how she worked with teachers and helped them improve their instruction.

Trying to understand, the friend, who was a nurse, then asked, "So, you're a trainer of trainers, isn't that right? You train teachers?"

"Well, in a way, I suppose," Devona answered, clarifying, "we help teachers improve what they do."

"We have them in nursing too," Devona's friend said. "I hate that."

"Why?" asked Devona, somewhat taken aback.

"Well, they show up, and we have to sit in a room all day and hear about stuff we already know. The sessions are boring, so we sit there and talk about the presenter's hairstyle or her shoes, but we have to go to remain certified. I hate that."

"I'd hate that too," Devona agreed. "But, what if your trainer of trainers met you on your floor, got to know you, and really listened to and affirmed you? What if you became comfortable telling her where you wanted to improve, and the trainer of trainers worked with you, showed you exactly how to improve in your chosen area by working with your patients, and then watched you and gave you helpful suggestions and support until you could easily do the new skill?"

"Oh, I'd love that," said Devona's friend.

"That's what I do," said Devona.

And that is what instructional coaches do. Shoulder to shoulder with teachers, ICs respectfully share teaching strategies that help teachers meet goals that they set. To accomplish this, we have found that instructional coaches are most effective when they do two things: (a) position teachers as partners so that coaching really is two teachers talking with each other

I think it's the perfect job. I have done some different things over the years, but coaching is where you get to put it all together. If you love children, love education, and have the mindset of always being a learner and wanting to try something new, then as an instructional coach, no two days are ever going to be alike. I love that. There may be some days where your calendar gets completely wiped out by a crisis or something unscheduled happens on your campus, but you've got to be there, be available, and be flexible enough to understand that not every day is going to go exactly the way that you planned it, but you're going to do your best.

—**Linda Zarsky**
Lead Instructional Coach for Lander
Wyoming, Independent School District

and (b) employ the high-impact actions within a coaching cycle, which I'm calling the Impact Cycle. Both are described below.

TEACHERS AS PARTNERS

How instructional coaches interact with others is as important as what they *do*. An instructional coach who sees herself as an expert and believes teachers simply need to buy into her good advice on what they did right or wrong is likely to encounter a lot of resistance.

Effective instructional coaches see teachers as professionals, which means they see teachers as the ultimate decision makers about what and how they learn. As I've emphasized over the years, we suggest that coaches guide their behavior by the set of Partnership Principles described in the box on the facing page.

When coaches act in ways that are consistent with the Partnership Principles, as opposed to a top-down approach, teachers do most of the thinking, and coaches and teachers work as equals with the goal of making a powerful, positive difference in children's lives.

The Partnership Principles[1]

Equality: In partnerships, one partner does not tell the other what to do; both partners share ideas and make decisions together as equals. Coaches whose interactions embody equality have faith that the teachers they work with bring a lot to any interaction, and they listen with empathy.

Choice: Taking away choice and telling others that they must act a certain way usually guarantees that they will *not* want to do what we propose. As the saying goes, "When you insist, they will resist." Coaches who act on the principle of choice position teachers as the final decision makers, as partners who choose their coaching goals and decide which practices to adopt and how to interpret data.

Voice: Conversation with a coach should be as open and candid as conversation with a trusted friend. When coaches follow the principle of voice, they expect to learn from their collaborating teachers, and the teachers they coach feel safe expressing what they think and feel. When coaches live out the principle of voice, teachers know that their opinion matters.

Dialogue: When people are partners, their conversation is often a dialogue, a conversation where everyone's ideas are shared through back-and-forth interactions. Coaches who foster dialogue balance advocacy with inquiry. They actively seek out others' ideas, and they share their own ideas in a way that makes it easy for others to share what they think. Dialogue helps instructional coaches set themselves up as thinking partners.

Reflection: Learning often involves the messy muddling through that we often refer to as reflection. As a result, when professionals are told what to do—and when and how to do it, with no room for their own individual thought—there's a good chance they will stop learning. Much of the pleasure of professional growth involves reflecting on what you're learning. When coaches collaborate with teachers by co-creating ideas in reflective conversations, teachers (and coaches) often find those conversations to be engaging, energizing, and valuable.

Praxis: People who engage in praxis apply knowledge and skills to their work, community, or personal lives. For example, a teacher who wants to increase student engagement by telling powerful stories, and then reads about stories and carefully considers how to use them during instruction, is engaged in praxis as I define it. When coaches act with the goal of praxis in mind, they make sure that coaching is productive, meaningful, and helpful to teachers and students.

Reciprocity: Reciprocity is the inevitable outcome of an authentic partnership. When coaches engage in dialogue, reflect, and strive for praxis with their collaborating teachers, they will be engaged in real-life situations and live out the old saying, "When one teaches, two learn." Partnership is about shared learning as much as it is about shared power.

---

1. See Chapter 2 in *Unmistakable Impact: A Partnership Approach to Improving Instruction* (Knight, 2011) for a detailed description of the Partnership Principles.

Top-Down	Partnership
Compliance	Commitment
People *outside* the classroom know what students need	People *inside* the classroom know what students need
One size fits all	One size fits one
Constructive feedback	Dialogue
Coach does most of the thinking	Teacher does most of the thinking
Judgmental	Non-judgmental
Teachers have lower status than coaches	Teachers have equal status with coaches
Accountable to leaders	Accountable to students

A COACHING CYCLE

The partnership approach is at the heart of the Impact Cycle that instructional coaches use with teachers. The Impact Cycle involves three stages: Identify. Learn. Improve. In this book, I dedicate most of the pages to describing this cycle.

We . . . have a small way of thinking about accountability. We think that people want to escape from being accountable. We believe that accountability is something that must be imposed. We have to hold people accountable, and we devise reward and punishment schemes to do this . . . These beliefs are so dominant in our culture that they are difficult to question, yet they are the very beliefs that keep us from experiencing what we long for.

—Peter Koestenbaum and Peter Block
Freedom and Accountability at Work:
Applying Philosophical Insights
to the Real World (2001, p. 3)

One coach who uses the Impact Cycle is Joi Lunsford, an instructional coach at Reeves-Hinger Elementary School in Canyon, Texas, just south of Amarillo. Joi collaborated with Melissa Kimbrough, an elementary teacher at Reeves-Hinger. All teachers in Joi's school were expected to set improvement goals, and Melissa sought out Joi because she wanted to increase the engagement of the students in her classroom. As Joi worked with teachers at Reeves-Hinger, word spread that the video goal setting that Joi did (how Joi describes the Impact Cycle) was a powerful way for teachers to figure out how to reach more children, so over time more and more teachers asked to partner with her.

To start the coaching process with Melissa, Joi offered to video record Melissa's class so Melissa could be sure they were focused on the right goal. To create the video, Joi used her iPhone to record some of the lesson. Then she shared it through the Teaching Channel's Video Collaboration Tool, Teams. Joi also gave Melissa the "Watch Your Students" and "Watch Your Self" reflection forms to fill out as she watched her video (copies of these forms are included in Chapter 2). Finally, Joi and Melissa watched the video separately and then got together to discuss the video.

"We set up a debrief meeting," Joi told me, "where we came together and went through the Identify Questions" (also included in Chapter 3). The Identify Questions,[2] which lie at the heart of the Impact Cycle, helped Joi be a more effective coach:

> The questions help me be a better listener and help me stay focused on what they [teachers] are thinking. The moment I start to give advice, I stop myself by going back to the questions because the teachers know what they want; they know what is bothering them. So if I just prompt them to reflect and to think about where they would like to focus, I do a much better job helping them set a meaningful goal that matters to them.

After they had moved through the Identify Questions, Melissa and Joi agreed that increasing student engagement would be a powerful goal. The video of Melissa's class had revealed that about half of the students were off task during small-group activities, so Melissa set a goal that 90 percent of her students would be on task during small-group activities.

To reach the goal, Joi suggested Melissa experiment with a strategy called "Chunking Instructions." To help Melissa learn the strategy, Joi did several things to help her learn how to chunk instructions so that her students would be more engaged. First, Joi recognized that Melissa might need to modify

---

2. Much more about these questions and how they were developed will be presented in Chapter 3.

the strategy or pick some other strategy if chunking didn't help her students hit their goal. As Joi explains, "Not every strategy works the first time. Some teachers love a strategy and it might work really well for them, but others might hate it or find that it doesn't work for their students." However, Joi has found that when she partners with teachers such as Melissa and helps them find a strategy that works for them, eventually they will hit their goal. In fact, only one teacher she has worked with in the past three years has not hit the goal.

Joi did many other things to help Melissa learn how to chunk instructions. For example, she shared a checklist through Google Drive, so she and Melissa could adapt the strategy as needed. "When I share a checklist with a teacher," Joi told me, "we go through the list together to make sure she's clear on it. Then when I share the checklist on Google Drive, I always say, 'Hey, I'm sending this to you so you can help us make it better.' It becomes a living document that improves with each new teacher learning the strategy and giving input."

Joi also deepens teachers' understanding of strategies by modeling or co-teaching. Like many others, Joi has found that "the most popular way for a teacher to see a strategy is to visit the classroom of a teacher on campus who's using the strategy effectively." Joi has also created a video library of strategies that she shares with teachers so that they can see what it looks like to implement a teaching strategy, like the chunking instructions strategy that Melissa used to increase engagement.

As it turned out, once Melissa incorporated the chunking instructions strategy, her students hit the goal of increased engagement quickly after a few modifications. When Joi recorded what she refers to as a "target video" to see how close Melissa's students were to the goal, it clearly showed that every student was engaged. Melissa's students had gone from 50 percent on task to 100 percent on task. As dramatic as the change was for Melissa's students, an even more dramatic change might have been experienced by Melissa. She went from being strongly opposed to coaching to enthusiastically praising it. At the end of her time working with Joi, she sent the following letter to her principal:

> *I would rather have my nose hairs tweaked out one by one than make a goal-setting video!* That is what was going through my mind for the past year or so regarding video goal setting. *Why would I want to have someone come into my classroom and film me as I struggle? What if they are judging me and think I'm a terrible teacher? I am so uncomfortable when people are in my classroom!* These deep-seated fears had kept me from one of the most valuable things I have ever experienced as a teacher. This year, out of pure need and frustration, I decided to give it a shot. I needed to see what was keeping my class from performing as I knew they should. I had tried everything I knew and I needed to figure

out the problem. Let me just say that I am now a believer. It was nothing that I thought it would be. I didn't even really notice Joi as she filmed my kids. When I watched the video, Joi helped me to set a goal, gave me some strategies to try, and I got to work. It has worked beautifully. The change in my kids and their performance is astounding. We still have a lot of work to do, but I have some valuable tools that I will use year after year. Video goal setting has gone from something I would never do, to something I will never *not* do. If I can do it, anyone can.

Melissa's students' success was great for students and great for Melissa, but successes like Melissa's also affect the entire school. When teachers at Reeves-Hinger heard about it, they became more and more interested in coaching. During Joi's first year, there were only eight teachers who, as Joi expressed it, "were brave and kind and let me use them as guinea pigs. You know, I learned a lot that first year." The second year, "word had spread throughout the grade levels and through friends, and more teachers were excited about getting involved to see if it would make a difference for them, too." As a result, in year two Joi had thirty teachers involved in coaching. "This year [her third year]," Joi told me, "we have forty-two teachers."

To summarize, the Impact Cycle that Joi employed involved three components. First, Joi and Melissa got a clear picture of reality through videotaping. Then, they identified the goal of 90 percent of students being on task and chose a teaching strategy that would help them reach the goal. We refer to this stage as **Identify**. Second, Joi used a checklist and modeled the strategy to make sure Melissa understood how to use the chunking instructions strategy. We refer to this stage as **Learn**. Finally, Joi and Melissa monitored progress toward the goal and made modifications to the teaching strategy until the goal was hit. We refer to this stage as **Improve**.

The Impact Cycle

Identify

Improve

Learn

THREE APPROACHES TO COACHING

The following three approaches to coaching are commonly used—facilitative, directive, and dialogical—each with its unique strengths and weaknesses. While the dialogical approach is the one used by ICs implementing the Impact Cycle, a short summary will be presented of all three.

Characteristic	Facilitative	Dialogical	Directive
Metaphor	Sounding board	Partner	Expert–apprentice
Teacher knowledge	Knows what they need to know to improve	Has valuable knowledge but may need other knowledge to improve	Must implement new knowledge to improve
Decision making	Teacher	Teacher	Coach
Approach	Does not share expertise	Shares expertise dialogically	Shares knowledge directly
Focus	Teacher	Student	Teaching practice
Mode of discourse	Inquiry	Balances advocacy with inquiry	Advocacy

FACILITATIVE COACHING

Facilitative coaches see collaborating teachers as equals who make most if not all decisions during coaching. As Sir John Whitmore has written in his influential book *Coaching for Performance: GROWing People, Performance, and Purpose* (2002), "The relationship between the coach and coachee must be one of partnership in the endeavor, of trust, of safety and of minimal pressure" (p. 20).

Facilitative coaches encourage coachees to share their ideas openly by listening with empathy, paraphrasing, and asking powerful questions. Additionally, facilitative coaches do not share their expertise or suggestions with respect to what a teacher can do to get better based on the assumption that (a) coachees already have the knowledge they need to improve, so a coach's role is to help them unpack what they already know and that (b) coaches who share their expertise with coachees may inhibit progress by keeping coachees from coming up with their own solutions. In other words, "The coach is not a problem solver, a teacher, an adviser, an instructor, or even an expert; he or she is a sounding board, a facilitator, a counselor, an awareness raiser" (Whitmore, 2002, p. 40).

Facilitative coaching can be used in all kinds of situations, so it has the potential to address issues that dialogical and directive coaching are not able to address. For example, facilitative coaching may be used to help a teacher get along with a difficult team member, to help a principal lead culture change in her school, or to help a student use his time more effectively.

In the classroom, facilitative coaching works best when the teachers being coached already have the knowledge they need to improve. It is less effective when teachers do not have the necessary knowledge to bring about the change they want to see. For example, a teacher who is struggling to create a learner-friendly classroom culture and who has not learned effective strategies for classroom management will likely need an instructional coach to help him master teaching behavioral expectations, reinforcing appropriate behavior, and correcting inappropriate behavior. Clearly, facilitative coaching would not be an appropriate approach in such a situation. Instead, the teacher would benefit from particular teaching practices such as those described in *The Art and Science of Teaching: A Comprehensive Framework for Effective Instruction* (Marzano, 2007), *The Skillful Teacher: Building Your Teaching Skills* (Saphier, Haley-Speca, & Gower, 2008), or *High-Impact Instruction: A Framework for Great Teaching* (Knight, 2013).

DIRECTIVE COACHING

In many ways, directive coaching is the opposite of facilitative coaching. That is, the directive coach's goal is to help coachees master a certain skill or set of skills. The directive coach and coachee relationship is similar to a master–apprentice relationship. The directive coach has special knowledge, and his job is to transfer that knowledge to the coachee. While the relationship is respectful, it is not equal.

In contrast to facilitative coaches who set their expertise aside when working with teachers, the directive coach's expertise is at the heart of this coaching approach. Since their job is to make sure teachers learn the correct way to do something, directive coaches tell teachers what do to, sometimes model practices, observe teachers, and provide constructive feedback to teachers until they can implement the new practice with fidelity.

Directive coaches work from the assumption that the teachers they are coaching do not know how to use the practices they are learning, which is why they are being coached. They also assume that teaching strategies generally should be implemented with fidelity, which is to say, in the same way in each classroom. Thus, the goal of the directive coach is to ensure fidelity to a proven model, not adaptation of the model to the unique needs of children or strengths of a teacher.

The best directive coaches are excellent communicators who listen to their coachees, confirm understanding using effective questions, and sensitively read their coachee's understanding or lack of understanding. Since the goal is high-quality implementation of a new practice, directive coaches need to especially be effective at explaining, modeling, and providing constructive feedback.

When teachers are committed to learning a teaching strategy or program, directive coaching can be effective. However, directive coaching tends to de-professionalize teaching by minimizing teacher expertise and autonomy, and, therefore, frequently engenders resistance. Telling teachers they have to do something a certain way whether they want to or not treats teachers more like laborers than professionals, and it often leads to resistance more than change.

The directive approach to coaching also often fails because it oversimplifies the complex world of the classroom. The unique, young human beings who attend our schools are too complex for one-size-fits-all approaches to learning. What teachers and students need is an approach to coaching that combines the facilitative coach's respect for the professionalism of teachers with the directive coach's ability to identify and describe effective strategies that can help teachers move forward. That approach is the dialogical approach.

I think you have to have a belief in and a passion for the importance of public education if you are working in a public school. It is not always an easy job, but it can be very rewarding. I hope that coaching is going to become standard operating procedure in our schools. I have worked with people that have said to me that they would never have implemented the targeted changes without my support. I really believe it is one of the single most important things that we could be doing to improve the quality of what is happening in our public schools.

—Janice Creneti
Instructional Staff Developer, FDLRS, Largo, Florida

DIALOGICAL COACHING

The facilitative coach focuses on inquiry, using questions, listening, and conversational moves to help a teacher become aware of answers he already has inside himself. The directive coach focuses on advocacy, using expertise, clear explanations, modeling, and constructive feedback to teach a teacher how to use a new teaching strategy or program with fidelity. The dialogical coach balances advocacy with inquiry.

Like a facilitative coach, a dialogical coach embraces inquiry, asking questions that empower the collaborating teacher to identify goals, strategies, and adaptations that will have an unmistakable impact on students' achievement and well-being. Dialogical coaches ask powerful questions, listen and think with teachers, and collaborate with them to set powerful goals that will have a powerful impact on students' lives. They employ a coaching cycle, like the Impact Cycle, that is driven by back-and-forth conversation about the current reality and the teacher's hoped-for reality in the classroom.

In contrast to facilitative coaches, dialogical coaches do not withhold their expertise. They work from the assumption that the issues teachers face in classrooms can often be better addressed if teachers look at what the research has identified as effective teaching strategies. Therefore, like directive coaches, dialogical coaches must have a deep understanding of teaching strategies they can share with teachers to help them improve. What separates them from directive coaches, however, is that they do not do the thinking for teachers; rather, they position teachers as decision makers.

Dialogical coaches do not give advice; they share possible strategies with teachers and let teachers decide whether they want to try one of them or some other strategy to meet their goals. Dialogical coaches partner with teachers to identify goals and teaching strategies and then describe strategies precisely, while also asking teachers how they want to modify the strategies to better meet students' needs. Then, they help implement the strategies and gather data on whether or not they lead to students hitting their goals. Dialogical coaches don't keep their ideas to themselves, but they realize that sometimes strategies have to be modified to meet students' needs and to align with teachers' strengths. They also understand that student-focused goals that matter to teachers are essential for effective coaching.

During dialogical coaching—in contrast to directive coaching—the standard for excellent implementation is not the coach's opinion but the goal itself. That is, if a teacher implements a strategy in a way that is radically different from how it was designed to be used, the coach doesn't take a top-down approach and tell the teacher how to teach the strategy with fidelity. Instead, she simply says, "Let's see if we can hit the goal." If the goal isn't hit, then teacher and coach can go back to the description and consider whether the strategy should be taught with greater fidelity.

Facilitative and directive coaching both involve conversation, but they do not involve dialogue. A dialogue is a meeting of the minds, two or more people sharing ideas with each other. It is not a dialogue if I withhold my ideas, and it is not a dialogue when I tell you what to do. It is a dialogue when I share my ideas in a way that makes it easy for others to share their ideas. A dialogue is thinking with someone. That is the approach we take when implementing the Impact Cycle, and the rest of this book provides a step-by-step description of how coaches can employ that cycle.

> *In a dialogue . . . nobody is trying to win. Everybody wins if anybody wins. There is a different sort of spirit to it. In a dialogue, there is no attempt to gain points, or to make your particular view prevail. Rather, whenever any mistake is discovered on the part of anybody, everybody gains. It's a situation called win-win, whereas the other game is win-lose—if I win, you lose. But a dialogue is something more of a common participation, in which we are not playing a game against each other, but with each other. In a dialogue, everybody wins.*
>
> —**David Bohm**
> *On Dialogue* (1996, p. 7)

DEEP LEARNING, DEEP COACHING

The purpose of coaching is to foster improvement. Therefore, if done well, coaching can be incredibly important since improvement stands at the heart of so much that matters in life. When we choose to learn and get better, on our own or with a coach, we open ourselves to a better life of healthier relationships, greater successes, deeper feelings of competence, and more vitality and growth. Not surprisingly, Edward Deci, one of the world's leading experts on motivation, identifies competence (along with autonomy and relationships) as one of the main factors in motivation. When we grow, improve, and learn, when we strive to become a better version of ourselves, we tap into something deep in ourselves that craves that kind of growth.

In one of my favorite quotations, Peter Senge writes about this desire for learning in *The Fifth Discipline: The Art and Practice of the Learning Organization* (1990):

> Real learning gets to the heart of what it means to be human. Through learning we re-create ourselves. Through learning we become able to do something we were never able to do. Through learning we reperceive

the world and our relationship to it. Through learning we extend our capacity to create, to be part of the generative process of life. There is within each of us a deep hunger for this type of learning. (pp. 13–14)

Coaching that is designed for impact taps into the "deep hunger for learning" that Senge describes. It is the motivating power of learning and changing for the better that has led thousands of teachers to feel positive and motivated after they have met their goals through coaching.

Joellen Killion, who has written extensively about coaching, distinguished between what she referred to as coaching light and coaching heavy. "Coaching light," Joellen wrote, "occurs when coaches want to build and maintain relationships more than they want to improve teaching and learning. From this perspective, coaches may act to increase their perceived value to teachers by providing resources *and* avoiding challenging conversations" (Knight, 2009, p. 22). In contrast, when coaches are "coaching heavy," they "work outside their comfort zone and stretch their coaching skills, content knowledge, leadership skills, relationship skills, and instructional skills. They are increasingly aware of the beliefs that drive their actions and reexamine them frequently" (p. 23).

Coaching heavy requires coaches to say "no" to trivial requests for support and to turn their attention to those high-leverage services that have the greatest potential for improving teaching and learning.

—Joellen Killion
"Coaches' Roles, Responsibilities, and Reach," in *Coaching: Approaches and Perspectives* (Knight, 2009, p. 23)

As I've worked with coaches, I've found Joellen's distinctions very helpful, and I've tweaked them slightly so they better address instructional coaching more specifically. Following Joellen's lead, I distinguish between surface coaching and deep coaching. When instructional coaches do surface coaching, similar to Joellen's "coaching light," they provide teachers with resources, offer supportive comments, model lessons, conduct quick observations, and share quick feedback. Surface coaching does not involve teachers in the deep work of setting student-focused goals and collaborating until those goals are met, and it usually involves only superficial reflection and little change.

When engaging in deep coaching, on the other hand, instructional coaches guide teachers through a reflective process that involves setting goals, identifying teaching strategies to be implemented to reach those goals, collaboration, and adaptation of teaching and learning until the goals are met. In short, deep instructional coaching uses the Impact Cycle.

At the receiving end of the distinction between deep coaching and surface coaching is the distinction I make between deep and surface learning. When we experience surface learning, we make minor adjustments, try something out for a while, but we don't really make significant steps forward. Deep learning, on the other hand, is learning that changes our assumptions about how we do what we do. Deep learning gets to the core of who we are. As such, deep learning should be the outcome of deep coaching.

Deep learning can happen in positive and negative ways. One of my deepest learning experiences occurred when I was in my early twenties. At the end of two years at university, my average grade was D- (that's just a tiny bit above an average of F!), and university officials wrote to inform me that I wouldn't be welcomed back for a third year. At twenty years old, I left school discouraged by my poor performance, but even more discouraged by my deep sense that I really wasn't capable of success. I had a bad case of what Martin Seligman has labeled "learned helplessness," a belief that I simply did not think I could be successful no matter what opportunities might present themselves.

I moved from my Ontario university to Jasper, Alberta, a tourist town in the Canadian Rockies, in large part to escape my growing belief that I was and always would be a failure. Once in the mountains, though, I quickly fell in love with the natural beauty, and I started to spend every free weekend hiking and then climbing in the backcountry. Looking at the mountains every day, I was drawn deeper and deeper into climbing. I felt compelled to improve, and I took courses on climbing safety, read every book I could find on mountaineering, rock climbed after work at the Rock Garden cliffs outside of town, and went out climbing almost every weekend with Peter Aman and Chris Dunlap, two experienced climbers who generously let me tag along.

For me, there was something powerful about learning how to climb, learning how to manage the carabiners, pitons, ropes, and other gear, and to feel a profound sense of accomplishment every time my friends and I reached the summit of another mountain. Each mountain I climbed changed me a little bit, and week-by-week I overcame my learned helplessness.

Climbing taught me that I could control my life. I went back to university with a new identity, and the second time around I learned to be a successful student, ultimately winning a hard-to-get Canadian Social Sciences and Humanities Research Council scholarship that funded my doctoral study of the partnership approach, which stands at the heart of my work on coaching. The truth is that I might not be writing this book if I hadn't moved to the Rockies and learned how to climb.

More recently, I had another deep learning experience. Four years ago, my wife, Jenny, and I were overjoyed to see our beautiful son arrive in our lives. Luke was born later in my life, and for many years I had dedicated most of my time to researching, writing, and consulting. Like many others who are deeply dedicated to their professional goals, I frequently worked eighty- and ninety-hour weeks, writing articles, books, and research proposals, traveling, presenting, attending meetings, consulting, and so forth.

Work seemed to be going well, and I felt encouraged to see my books and ideas shared. That success just encouraged me to do more work, and I came to believe that if I wasn't working, I was wasting my time. In fact, I'm ashamed to recall that when Jenny would ask me to help around the house or help with Luke, my pat response was, "That's not a good use of my time." I felt I needed to dedicate myself to improving the lives of students, even if that meant I had no time for the most important people in my life. I was convinced that the best way I could help my family was to work hard and provide for them. If I did that well, then I was a good family man.

Six months after Luke was born, my illusions about what "a good use of my time" was came crashing down. Jenny told me that we needed to talk. One evening after Luke was asleep, we sat down at the kitchen table and she told me that I was risking losing my new son, and not only that, I was risking losing her. I couldn't be an occasional dad and husband, she warned. "Your son," she said, "should be at least as important as your work. And, your wife should be, too."

Then, in the kindest and most compassionate way, Jenny pointed out all the events I had missed in Luke's and her life and all the things she had done when I was an absentee parent. Jenny was gracious when she listed off all I had missed, but she was also clear. My family should never be a waste of my time! Just the opposite: My family was the best use of my time. If I truly wanted to be a good father and husband, I would have to turn my life around.

Jenny's comments were painful to hear. Until that conversation, I thought I was being a good husband and father, but the truth was I had skipped the whole husband and father part completely. That night was one of the most difficult of my life, but it was also extremely important. Thankfully, I listened through the pain, and I recognized I had to change. I started to put boundaries on my work and travel time, and I have striven to make my family my top priority. I've learned that professional success without personal success is pretty hollow, and I've learned I have to live differently. For me, that was deep learning.

Learning to climb changed the story I told myself about who I was by showing me, again and again, that I could succeed and that I could control the outcomes of my life. The simple act of climbing to the summit of so many peaks convinced me, step by step, that I could be a success, that I wasn't doomed to a life of failure. Climbing gave me a more positive story for my life.

My conversation with Jenny was more difficult. I came face to face with the reality that I was not as good as I thought I was. I learned that if I wanted to be the father to Luke I imagined I was, I had to make some dramatic changes. When learning is difficult, when our positive story of ourselves has to change, consciously or unconsciously, we often choose ignorance over deep learning. All in all, life is a lot easier on the surface—choosing to assume everything is going just fine—than it is to go deeper and really see how we can improve. Deep learning, however, is one of the best ways to really improve.

These two experiences, one pleasant, the other painful, dramatically changed my life for the better. I include them here because I think they illustrate the central challenge at the heart of deep learning. Learning and change often appear to be difficult, but learning and change are essential. The good news is that learning and change often involve others who help us change—for me those people are my climbing partners and Jenny. For many teachers, that person is an instructional coach.

I think that we need profound growth in education because we have been very content with just teeny bits of growth. We have to figure out how to get more people engaged, and I think we are looking at the heart of change. We are all trying to figure out who we are, and realizing that what we thought was reality isn't reality, that who we thought we are isn't who we are, is a painful thing. You let go of this dream that you have and accept this painful reality. But that's how we become adults.

—Jean Clark
Administrator, Cecil County
Public Schools, Cecil County, Maryland

The Impact Cycle described in this book has been developed and refined to help instructional coaches help teachers experience deep learning. In turn, when teachers learn, they can guide students to experience the deep learning, which, as noted by Peter Senge in the quotation above, "gets to the heart of what it means to be human."

In the rest of this book, I will describe how coaches should interact with teachers and what they should do. For people learning how to do instructional coaching, this book provides a clear step-by-step process they can employ to help make deep learning really happen, and as a result, enable colleagues and their students to improve in clear, measurable ways.

The book is organized as follows:

Each chapter begins with a learning map depicting the key concepts in the chapter. Each chapter also contains these features:

Making It Real describes practical actions educators can take to turn the ideas in each chapter into actions.

To Sum Up provides a summary of each chapter.

Going Deeper introduces resources (mostly books) readers can explore to extend their knowledge of the ideas and strategies discussed in the chapter.

QR Codes are linked to videos illustrating the various parts of the instructional coaching cycle carried out by elementary teacher Crysta Crum and secondary teacher Cathryn Monroe in coaching conversations with me.

Finally, throughout the book you will find checklists that can be used to describe teaching strategies, gather data, plan coaching, and monitor progress toward goals.

The following is a brief description of the contents of the rest of the book.

Chapter 2, Identify: Getting a Clear Picture of Reality: The Impact Cycle involves three stages: Identify, Learn, Improve. In this chapter, I describe how to start the Identify stage of coaching by getting a clear picture of reality in the classroom using four approaches: student voice, student work, observation, and teacher evaluation data.

Chapter 3, Questions to Identify a PEERS Goal: After a teacher has gained a clear picture of reality, she is guided by the coach to identify a change for the better

Video 1.1

Introducing Crysta Crum

Video 1.2

Introducing Cat Monroe

resources.corwin.com/ impactcycle

she would like to see in her students—usually these changes are related to achievement (e.g., percentage of students proficient on formative assessments), behavior (e.g., number of disruptions per minute in a class), or attitude (e.g., percentage of students who report on exit tickets that they feel safe coming to school). We have found that the most effective goals are what we refer to as PEERS goals; that is, they are Positive, Easy, Emotionally Compelling, Reachable (they are measurable, and there is a strategy that can be implemented to hit the goal), and Student-Focused. I will describe PEERS goals in detail in Chapter 3. After setting a PEERS goal, teacher and coach identify a teaching practice, such as those identified in *High-Impact Instruction* (Knight, 2013), that the teacher will implement in an attempt to hit the goal.

Chapter 4, Learn: Once a teacher has chosen a strategy, she needs to implement it. In this chapter, I describe how to do that. We have found that if teachers are going to learn a new strategy, they first need to receive a clear explanation of the strategy. Then, they need to see a model or multiple models of the practice in action. The coach might go into the classroom and model the practice with students or model it when students are not in the room, if that is more appropriate. Coach and teacher could watch another teacher use the practice, or coach and teacher could watch a video of the target practice. To learn something new, you need to both hear about it and see it, and this chapter describes how to do that.

Chapter 5, Improve: Once a teacher has learned the chosen strategy or practice, she can set about implementing it to see if it hits the goal. This chapter describes how the coach and teacher monitor implementation of the practice as well as whether it leads to progress toward the goal. Additionally, the chapter describes how coach and teacher should talk about implementation and progress, and how decisions should be made about modifying the way a practice is implemented or pivoting to a new strategy in an attempt to hit the goal.

Instructional Coaches' Toolkit:

Strategies for Enrolling Teachers: In the past twenty years, coaches working with the Impact Research Lab have identified many different ways in which to enroll teachers in a coaching relationship while honoring the partnership philosophy. This section of the toolkit describes ways to enroll teachers in coaching and includes forms coaches can use during the enrollment part of coaching.

Data-Gathering Tools: Central to the improvement cycle is the gathering of data. Data are necessary for getting a clear picture of reality, for setting goals, and for monitoring progress toward goals. This toolkit provides tools coaches and teachers can use to gather data about learning and instruction.

Instructional Playbook: Instructional coaches support teachers in reaching their goals by helping them implement teaching strategies that they know will have a positive impact on students. To that end, they use a so-called instructional playbook consisting of a list of the teaching strategies instructional coaches share, a one-page summary of each strategy, and checklists that coaches can use to explain strategies to teachers. This section of the toolkit contains a model instructional playbook.

Strategies for Assessing Student Attitude: In many cases, teachers set goals that are related to students' attitudes and beliefs. For example, a teacher might want to know if students feel comfortable speaking in his classroom. This section of the toolkit contains forms teachers can use to gather data on what students think, feel, and believe.

Appendix: Lean-Design Research: The Impact Cycle results from a research model that my colleagues and I at the Center for Research on Learning refer to as Lean-Design Research. In this Appendix, I describe how we use this research methodology.

MAKING IT REAL

Coaches and other change leaders (especially principals and coaching supervisors) can make this chapter real by discussing what kind of coaching they want in their schools. Do they want surface coaching, where coaches work with larger numbers of teachers but have less impact, or do they want deep coaching, where coaches have much more impact but work with smaller numbers of teachers?

Change leaders responsible for coaching should also discuss whether they want facilitative, directive, or dialogical coaches. If they opt for dialogical coaches, usually because they believe coaches should foster better teaching for better learning, they should discuss and plan how instructional coaches can get the professional development they need so that they have deep knowledge of effective teaching strategies.

TO SUM UP

- We define instructional coaching as follows: "Instructional coaches partner with teachers to analyze current reality, set goals, identify and explain teaching strategies to meet goals, and provide support until the goals are met."

- Instructional coaches see teachers as professionals and, therefore, as equal partners in coaching, and they position teachers as the decision makers within the coaching process.

- The partnership approach involves seven principles: equality, choice, voice, reflection, dialogue, praxis, and reciprocity.

- The Impact Cycle involves three components:

  o Identify, during which coach and teacher collaborate to get a clear picture of current reality, identify a student-focused goal, and choose a strategy to try to hit the goal.

  o Learn, during which the coach ensures that the teacher learns the identified strategy by explaining it clearly, usually through the use of a checklist and by modeling the strategy so the collaborating teacher sees it being used before implementing it.

  o Improve, during which the teacher implements the teaching strategy and the coach and teacher monitor progress toward the goal, making adjustments as necessary until the goal is reached.

- Deep learning occurs when we make significant improvements in the way we go about doing something important, like teaching or raising a family.

- Deep learning is complicated by our identity, our lack of understanding of our current reality, and our mindset.

- Instructional coaches balance advocacy with inquiry, which means they adopt the partnership and inquiry approaches of facilitative coaching, while also sharing effective teaching practices in a dialogical way.

GOING DEEPER

In my previous books on coaching, *Instructional Coaching* (Knight, 2007), *Unmistakable Impact* (Knight, 2011), and *Focus on Teaching* (Knight, 2014), I have mentioned several books about coaching in schools, including Gary Bloom, Claire Castagna, Ellen Moir, and Betsy Warren's (2005) *Blended Coaching: Skills and Strategies to Support Principal Development*, Arthur Costa and Robert Garmston's (2002) *Cognitive Coaching: A Foundation for Renaissance Schools*, Jane Kise's (2006) *Differentiated Coaching: A Framework for Helping Teachers Change*, Joellen Killion and Cindy Harrison's (2006) *Taking the Lead: New Roles for Teachers and School-Based Coaches*, Stephen G. Barkley's (2010) *Quality Teaching in a Culture of Coaching*, Nancy Love's (2008) *Using Data to Improve Learning for All: A Collaborative Inquiry Approach*, Lucy West and Fritz Staub's (2003) *Content-Focused Coaching: A Foundation for Renaissance Schools*, Jan Miller Burkins's (2009) *Practical Literacy Coaching: A Collection of Tools to Support Your Work*, and Mare Catherine Moran's (2007) *Differentiated Literacy Coaching: Scaffolding for Student and Teacher Success*. Finally, *Coaching: Approaches and Perspectives* (Knight, 2008), contains chapters by several coaching authors discussing many of the coaching approaches listed here.

Additionally, three books are especially useful in explaining the practices we see effective instructional coaches using:

- Atul Gawande's (2010) *The Checklist Manifesto: How to Get Things Right* explains the importance of precise explanations of practices.

- Chip and Dan Heath's (2010) *Switch: How to Change Things When Change Is Hard* provides, among other things, an excellent description of what is required to begin and change initiatives like coaching.

- Joseph Grenny, Kerry Patterson, David Maxfield, and Ron McMillan's (2013) *Influencer: The New Science of Leading Change*, 2nd Edition explains the importance of modeling as a part of change and learning.

CHAPTER

2

Is about

Identifying a clear picture of reality

By using

By learning from

By reviewing data from

Video

Students

Observations

- Easy
- Free
- Powerful
- Cuts through perceptual errors
- Requires a culture of trust

Determining

- The desired form of feedback
- The purpose of the observation
- Which types of data will be gathered

- Everyone wants to be heard
- Informal conversations
- Interviews
- Writing prompts and exit tickets
- Student work

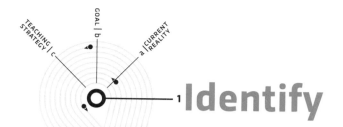

¹**Identify**

IDENTIFY

Getting a Clear Picture of Reality

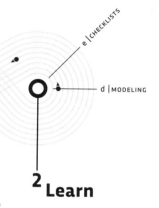

² **Learn**

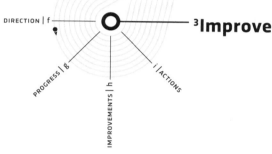

³**Improve**

> *The juxtaposition of vision (what we want) and a clear picture of current reality (where we are relative to what we want) generates what we call creative tension: a force to bring them together, caused by the natural tendency of tension to seek resolution. The essence of personal mastery is learning how to generate and sustain creative tension in our lives.*
>
> **—Peter Senge**
> summarizing Robert Fritz's theory of creative tension in *The Fifth Discipline: The Art and Practice of the Learning Organization* (1990, p. 132)

The Impact Cycle is a deceptively simple process consisting of three stages: Identify, Learn, Improve. The cycle positions collaborating teachers as the ultimate decision makers in a process that leads to powerful improvements in student learning and well-being. With a coach's help, teachers analyze video and student data, set powerful goals for the coaching cycle, identify what teaching strategies to implement to hit the goals, and problem-solve with their coach until goals are met. Instructional coaches who use the Impact Cycle understand that their main task within that cycle is to help teachers achieve their goals. Teachers, because they make the important decisions about what happens in their classrooms, see the Impact Cycle as a process designed to help them achieve their goals for their students.

I always feel a mixture of emotions when I start the Impact Cycle with a new teacher. I am excited to see what we will create and where our work together will take us—not knowing what we will create feels almost thrilling. But at the same time, I am also concerned, perhaps even worried, because I don't want to waste my partnering teacher's time. I am often a bit nervous because I wonder whether my skills and knowledge as a coach are up to the task of truly helping the unique person with whom I am about to partner. However, I feel deeply committed to the process of the Impact Cycle, since I have seen the power of coaching played out in cycle after cycle. I know that working to get better is one of the most important actions any of us can take, and our research and my experience have shown that when implemented effectively, the Impact Cycle will lead to important improvements for teachers and students.

When I was getting ready to coach the teachers featured in the videos that come with this book—Cat Monroe, who taught ninth-grade social studies at Free State High School in Lawrence, Kansas, and Crysta Crum, who taught fourth grade at Kennedy Elementary also in Lawrence—I felt my typical mixture of emotions. More than anything, I wanted to partner with Cat and Crysta to do something that would improve the lives of the children they taught—that was the thrilling part. At the same time, the fact that all of our conversations would be video recorded to illustrate the coaching cycle intensified everything just a little—the worrying part.

The Impact Cycle I applied when coaching Cat and Crysta, and described in this book, is highly structured. Coaches using the cycle move through three specific stages, ask particular questions, and guide teachers through specific actions in each stage. And yet the cycle is always different. We move through the steps and stages of coaching with the same kind of focused freedom that a jazz musician might bring to playing the melody of a song. Since each teacher and student is unique, each move through the cycle is different, and inevitably, like jazz musicians, we improvise. Thus, while the Impact Cycle is structured, it is also unpredictable. And like most important activities in life, because it is unpredictable, coaching can be exciting, challenging, enjoyable, and ultimately, profoundly worthwhile.

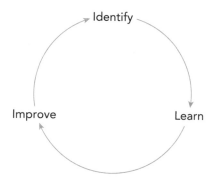

The Impact Cycle

Identify

Learn

Improve

GETTING A CLEAR PICTURE OF CURRENT REALITY

One of the major findings from our research is that, for many reasons, coaching likely won't succeed unless teacher and coach both clearly see what is happening in the classroom. For that reason, when I start the Impact Cycle,[1] I know that the collaborating teacher and I need to get a shared understanding of what is happening in the teacher's classroom. If we don't have a shared clear picture of reality, there is a danger that the focus of the coaching will be off target and a lot of time will be wasted on actions that have little impact on students. For example, a teacher who wants to implement cooperative learning, when a more important issue in her classroom is student behavior, may find that cooperative learning will not have a positive impact until students learn how to cooperate.

The focus that arises from having a clear picture of reality (and ultimately a goal) also saves teachers' and coaches' time. When teacher and coach understand the top priority for change in the classroom, they can address that priority with laser-like focus. That clear picture of reality also establishes a baseline for growth. In the same way athletes training for a race might keep track of how fast and how far they can run at the start of training so they can measure progress, teachers might get clear on student behavior, achievement, or attitude to monitor progress they make during coaching.

When people don't have a clear picture of reality, they tend to think that everything is going fine and don't see any need to change. The most

---

1. For information on how to enroll teachers in coaching, see The Coaches' Toolkit at the end of this book, pages 157–165.

important reason for wanting to get a clear picture of reality might be that it shifts teacher and coach out of talk and into action. One teacher who worked with instructional coach Stacey Cohen in Topeka, Kansas, after watching a video of her classroom, was so struck by her students' lack of engagement that she stayed up until the middle of the night reworking lesson plans with the goal of increasing engagement. A vivid understanding of reality can give us a vivid understanding of the need for change, and that desire to change is often the catalyst for powerful growth through coaching.

To see the classroom as it is, teachers need to appreciate (a) where there is room for improvement *and* (b) what is going well. Both aspects of reality are important. Often, as many educators have told me in interviews, teachers are their own worst enemies, seeing only what is not working. An entirely negative view of the classroom is no more accurate than an entirely positive view. While teachers shouldn't avert their attention from what isn't working, they also need to identify what is going well. Indeed, seeing what is going well may prove especially motivating for teachers.

When I talked with coaching expert Christian van Nieuwerburgh, he emphasized how important it is for teachers to see what is working:

> I like the slant to be on the preferred future—the desired future. This is what my ideal class would be—it's motivating and energizing to talk about that . . . What would I like to see? What's the ideal classroom? Therefore, what can I do to get closer to that? I like it also because it is putting responsibility where it belongs—with the coachee. When I work with educators sometimes there is a lot of finding the problems that the students are having, and that's not a very fruitful conversation. Two professional educators—I'd rather have them both talking about what is working.

An entirely positive view of reality is not enough, however. To grow, we need to see where we are and see it as completely as possible. As Bossidy and Charan (2004) wrote in *Confronting Reality: Doing What Matters to Get Things Right,* "To confront reality is to recognize the world as it is, not as you wish it to be, and have the courage to do what must be done, not what you'd like to do" (pp. 6–7). Instructional coaches can help teachers see the world as it is.

THE ILLUSION OF OBJECTIVITY

The reason most of us struggle to see reality clearly is that we look at life through an illusion of objectivity. We think that we see the world exactly

Common Perceptual Errors

Confirmation Bias: Our natural tendency to color our perceptions of reality by consciously or unconsciously seeking data that support our assumptions about the world around us.

Habituation: Our tendency to become desensitized to any experience, positive or negative, that we experience repeatedly.

Primacy Effect: Our tendency in our first experiences with someone or something to be biased in favor of a particular impression of that person or thing.

Recency Effect: Our tendency in our last experiences with someone or something to be biased in favor of a particular impression of that person or thing.

Stereotypes: Our tendency to prejudge people as having the characteristics of a group (often negative), which blinds us to the unique characteristics of individuals.

as it is, but the exact opposite is actually the case. We make our own meaning out of what we experience, including what we don't understand (in the classroom, a meeting, or coaching conversation), and as a result of these perceptual errors (such as those described in the box above), the meaning we create is often wrong.

In *No One Understands You and What to Do About It* (2015), Heidi Grant Halvorson explains how perceptual errors color our perceptions of reality: "The uncomfortable truth is that most of us . . . can't see ourselves truly objectively" (p. 4). For this reason, instructional coaches and teachers need to start by seeing through perceptual errors and getting a clear picture of reality.

We employ three different strategies to get a clear picture of reality in a teacher's classroom: (a) video recording, (b) learning from students, and (c) gathering observation data. Video is the easiest and most powerful strategy. It is powerful because it provides an objective perspective on a lesson, and it is easy because almost every teacher has a smartphone or some other device that can be used to record a class. Video is what Cat Monroe and I employed to identify current reality and ultimately set a goal when I coached her.

Video 2.1

Crysta Uses Video to Get a Clear Picture of Reality

resources.corwin.com/impactcycle

USING VIDEO TO GET A
CLEAR PICTURE OF REALITY

Cat Monroe divides her days at Free State High School in Lawrence, Kansas, between teaching social studies and being an instructional coach. For Cat, like most educators, teaching is much more than a job:

> If it was a job, I would come here for my contract hours from 7:50 to 3:50, and then I would check out and I would be done. But, it's my career, and it's something that I love, and I've always loved. I am here for the kids, to give them a rich and safe environment. I want to keep building and doing better. I feel that is my responsibility.

To create the videos that accompany this book, Cat and I moved through most parts of the Impact Cycle. We started by getting a clear picture of reality through viewing a video of one of Cat's lessons. Cat had learned about the power of video in her reflections on her lessons as a part of her coaching. The advantage of video, in Cat's words, is that "you get a bigger picture, an almost unbiased picture because you can look at every piece that is occurring."

Cat understood how powerful and helpful video recording lessons can be, but she also recognized that people can find it intimidating to watch video of themselves teaching. She related that when she was doing graduate work, one of her professors required teachers to video record their lessons and share them in the class. "I remember being more nervous about how I was going to look and sound than actually the quality of the lesson. Cat said, "Based on that experience, I tell teachers, 'It's going to be nerve-wracking the first time you hear and see yourself on video.' Some teachers are 100 percent for it, some teachers are only interested in me recording myself, and some are like, 'I don't care, let's go.' It's really interesting."

Starting the Impact Cycle by recording and watching a video of a lesson, as Cat and I did, is most commonly what happens during instructional coaching. Researchers have been describing the power of video to accelerate learning for decades. In athletics, video has become the athlete's most important learning tool, and not just for the pros—there are very few middle school football teams in the United States, for example, that don't watch video of their games. In education, we've known about the power of video at least since the 1960s when micro teaching was studied at Stanford University.

Video gives a teacher and coach a perspective on the classroom that cuts through perceptual errors. Our coaching research partners tell us that after teacher and coach have watched video of a lesson, the focus for coaching is often easy to identify.

Jackie Jewel, an instructional coach from Othello, Washington, summed up what many people have told us about using video during coaching:

> It's hard for people to watch themselves. It's hard for me to watch myself, but video has transformed everything. Sometimes teachers will come to me and say, "I think I really need to work on this," and then they watch their video and change completely, based on what they watched. When teachers stand in front of a classroom, they don't always have that perspective of what's really happening in their classroom. But when I set that video up in the back of their classroom, they can watch themselves, or look at a lesson through the kids' eyes, and can see what I see. You can't give them that picture without the video. I don't think I could coach without the video now.

Video is free, easy, and powerful, and once coaches start to use it, they may wonder how they ever made progress without it. However, if video recording is carelessly introduced to a school or individuals, it can do more damage than good.[2] Instructional coaches who plan to make video a part of their practice should consider several issues before beginning.

TRUST

We first experimented with video when we partnered with coaches from Beaverton, Oregon. As a part of our research,[3] the coaches made video a central part of their coaching. When we saw results through the use of video, I shared the results with many audiences. Inevitably, the first question asked was, "How did you get people to agree to video?" So, I asked the Beaverton coaches why teachers agreed to video; their answers were very helpful. "They did it because they trusted us," they said. "And if teachers don't want to do video, the problem probably isn't the video; the problem is a lack of trust."

---

2. *Focus on Teaching: Using Video for High-Impact Instruction* (Knight, 2014) offers an in-depth description of how to set up the use of video in schools.

3. To read about our research methods, please see the Appendix at the end of this book, starting on page 247.

What this means for schools is that a culture of trust needs to be in place for video to be embraced. For people to trust individuals or organizations, at least five factors need to be in place (Knight, 2015). We trust others who are (a) honest, (b) reliable, (c) competent, (d) warm, and (e) genuinely concerned about our best interests. If teachers do not want to be video recorded, chances are that one or more of these factors needs to be addressed, by either the coach or the school leaders. Of course, if teachers don't trust their school leaders or their coach, not much meaningful coaching is going to occur anyway.

CHOICE

Forcing teachers to record and watch video against their will most likely will lead to resentment or negative backlash. A better strategy is to propose video as one power tool for learning. Improvement is an expectation for every professional, but people will be enthusiastic about growth when they have control over how they improve.

Therefore, it is a good idea to give teachers options about how they use video to learn about the way they teach. For example, if a teacher is worried about who might see her video, the video could be recorded on her camera so that she can be certain she is the only one to see it. Or, if a teacher really doesn't want to see himself on video, his lesson could be recorded so that only students are recorded on the video (which might be especially appropriate for some learning activities). Additionally, if teachers are vehemently opposed to video, they might be offered the option of audio recording a lesson. While less data is captured in an audio recording, since teachers don't get to see themselves or their students, audio can be very helpful; in fact, in some cases, less data can actually help teachers focus their attention on something important—such as questioning.

OWNERSHIP

Teachers do not learn a lot from video if they do not feel psychologically safe. For that reason, teachers need to be the people who control how their video is used. Forcing teachers to share video of their lessons, or worse, forcing them to create video portfolios when they aren't comfortable watching themselves or sharing video of their lessons, is not treating them as professionals and may lead to strong negative reactions.

FILMING

Lessons can be recorded in many different ways. When instructional coaches are able to do the recording for teachers, they can turn the camera to the most important parts of the class during a lesson and likely provide teachers with especially useful video. I find it very helpful to do the recording because I learn a lot by being in the room. Watching a class on video without ever visiting the class is a bit like watching a game on TV vs. being at the game. There are certain dynamics in a classroom that a camera simply isn't able to pick up.

If the coach is not able to do the recording, other strategies can be used. For example, the camera can be put on a tripod or propped against a few books on a shelf and be used to record the lesson from a stationary position, preferably a position where the teacher and students will be recorded. Many educators have started to use Swivls, stationary devices that sit on tripods and that have a built-in slot where teachers can place their cameras. When using a Swivl to record themselves, teachers wear a sensor/microphone around their neck, and the device follows them as they move about the classroom. In addition to convenience, the sensor/microphone enables teachers to get better-than-average sound for their recordings.

When I coached Glenn McGlaughlan from Sydney, Australia, he told me that he asked a student who was interested in becoming a filmmaker to do his recording. As it turned out, the student got to practice with a camera, and Glenn got a very clear video of his lesson. Regardless of how the video is recorded, the truth is that video is so powerful that pretty much any approach to filming will be very useful.

Kind of Camera

In most cases, whatever kind of camera is available should work very well for teachers. Most educators we interviewed for *Focus on Teaching: Using Video for High-Impact Instruction* (Knight, 2014) reported that they used an iPad to record lessons. I use my iPhone. I deliberately purchased a phone with the largest memory so that I could use it to record many lessons. Cameras such as Go-Pros use a fisheye lens, which can give the viewer a bird's eye perspective that often includes the teacher and all students. Many other smartphones and tablets may be used to record lessons. The two most important considerations when choosing a camera are that it has enough memory for recording and that the microphone is sensitive enough to record voices well so that they can be heard clearly during playback.

Where to Point the Camera

Since the camera is gathering data for the teacher, the teacher should decide where the camera is pointed. Sometimes that decision is determined by what will be happening in a lesson. For example, if a teacher is interested in finding out how engaged students are during questioning, she might choose to have the camera focused on students. On the other hand, if a teacher is wondering whether or not her body language communicates presence, she likely would want the camera pointed at her. In general, when I record a lesson, I record the teacher when she is talking and the students when they are talking.

Length of the Recording

The challenge when recording a lesson is to get enough video so that teachers can really see what is going on in the classroom, but not so much video that the teacher won't have time to watch it. As a general guideline, I suggest recording at least 20 minutes, and if a lesson or class is less than 50 minutes recording the whole lesson. For most educators, watching anything more than 50 minutes takes too much time.

Full-time coaches can free up teachers to watch video recordings of their lessons by teaching a lesson in a teacher's class after they have recorded a lesson. For example, a coach might record a lesson in sixth hour and then teach a lesson in seventh hour so that the teacher can watch the video during a class while the coach teaches.

Moving forward, once a goal has been identified, all that needs to be recorded is the section of the lesson related to the goal. For example, if an elementary teacher wants to reduce the amount of time it takes for students to transition from one activity to another, all that needs to be recorded are the transitions.

WATCHING THE VIDEO

Although we initially thought that coaches should watch video with teachers after a lesson is recorded, we soon discovered that most conversations between coach and teacher when watching video together are so cautious and tentative as to be meaningless. Therefore, we suggest coach and teacher watch the video separately and then discuss it afterward. To help teachers get the most out of watching video of their lesson, we suggest coaches share the forms on pages 35–37.

HOW TO GET THE MOST OUT OF WATCHING YOUR VIDEO

Goal

Identify two sections of the video that you like and one or two sections of video you'd like to further explore.

Getting Ready

Watching yourself on video is one of the most powerful strategies professionals can use to improve. However, it can be a challenge. It takes a little time to get used to seeing yourself on screen, so be prepared for a bit of a shock. After a little time, you will become more comfortable with the process.

- Find a place to watch where you won't be distracted.

- Review the Watch Yourself and Watch Your Student forms to remind yourself of things to keep in mind while watching.

- Set aside a block of time so you can watch the video uninterrupted.

- Make sure you've got a pen and paper ready to take notes.

Watching the Video

- Plan to watch the entire video at one sitting.

- Take notes on anything that catches your attention.

- Be certain to write the time from the video beside any note you make so that you can return to it should you wish to.

- People have a tendency to be too hard on themselves, so be sure to also watch for things you like.

- After watching the video, review your notes and circle the items you will discuss with your coach (two you like, and one or two you would like to explore further).

- Sit back, relax, and enjoy the experience.

 Available for download at **resources.corwin.com/impactcycle**

WATCH YOUR STUDENTS

Date: _____

After watching the video of today's class, please rate how close the behavior of your students is to your goal for an ideal class in the following areas:

	NOT CLOSE						RIGHT ON
Students were engaged in learning (at least 90% engagement is recommended).	1	2	3	4	5	6	7
Students interacted respectfully.	1	2	3	4	5	6	7
Students talked about learning an appropriate amount of time.	1	2	3	4	5	6	7
Students rarely interrupted each other.	1	2	3	4	5	6	7
Students engaged in high-level conversation.	1	2	3	4	5	6	7
Students clearly understand how well they are progressing (or not).	1	2	3	4	5	6	7
Students are interested in learning activities in the class.	1	2	3	4	5	6	7

Comments:

 Available for download at **resources.corwin.com/impactcycle**

Copyright © 2018 by Corwin. All rights reserved. Reprinted from *The Impact Cycle: What Instructional Coaches Should Do to Foster Powerful Improvements in Teaching* by Jim Knight. Thousand Oaks, CA: Corwin, www.corwin.com. Reproduction authorized only for the local school site or nonprofit organization that has purchased this book.

WATCH YOURSELF

Date: _____

After watching the video of today's class, please rate how close your instruction is to your ideal in the following areas:

	NOT CLOSE						RIGHT ON
My praise to correction ratio is at least a 3-to-1 ratio.	1	2	3	4	5	6	7
I clearly explained expectations prior to each activity.	1	2	3	4	5	6	7
My corrections are calm, consistent, immediate, and planned in advance.	1	2	3	4	5	6	7
There was very little wasted time during the lesson.	1	2	3	4	5	6	7
My questions are appropriate for the learning occurring.	1	2	3	4	5	6	7
My learning structures (stories, cooperative learning, thinking devices, experiential learning) were effective.	1	2	3	4	5	6	7
I used a variety of learning structures effectively.	1	2	3	4	5	6	7
I clearly understand what my students know and don't know.	1	2	3	4	5	6	7

Comments:

Available for download at **resources.corwin.com/impactcycle**

Video and Students

When people are considering using video, they often ask me if video recording will distract students. The short answer is: no. Once learning begins, generally speaking, students are students, and they do what they would ordinarily do. Of course, there are exceptions, and I have worked with a few teachers who have asked me to come back and record another day because the camera tended to make students better behaved than usual, but in the vast majority of cases, the presence of a video camera will have little impact on students.

Why Teachers Should Be Recorded

Without question, the purpose of coaching is to improve student learning and well-being. However, that does not mean that video should record only what students do. While an enormous amount can be learned about student learning by watching video or a lesson, video is most powerful when the interactions between the teacher and students are recorded. No matter what kind of learning is taking place, the teacher shapes the learning, and, therefore, much can be learned by watching students and teachers. To record a lesson and not record what the teacher does, to me, is like recording a batter during a baseball game and not recording the pitcher. We learn more by seeing more, and the best way to learn about how we teach is to watch how we teach.

Big Ideas Related to Using Video as Part of Coaching

- Video is powerful, inexpensive, and easy to use.
- Most people won't agree to be recorded unless they trust their coach and their school.
- Everyone in a school should be committed to getting better, but that doesn't mean everyone needs to record their lessons.
- Teachers need to own their videos and control how they are used.
- Teachers should use whatever camera they have at their disposal.
- Teacher and coach should watch the initial video separately.
- The first video should be at least twenty minutes long.
- Recording a class probably won't change the way students behave.
- More is learned when video records the teacher and students.

LEARNING FROM STUDENTS

Sharon Thomas, a secondary English teacher from Elkton, Maryland, is one of the most accomplished educators I know. She has won numerous awards, including District Teacher of the Year, The Excellence in Education Award from Towson University, runner-up for state teacher of the year, and a pile of other awards for her work promoting literacy in Maryland. She is passionate about students, cares deeply about educators, and recognizes that teaching, done well, is an act of promoting social justice.

Sharon is at home in the classroom. She loves to teach, and her students love her. So it was a little surprising to Sharon when one year she encountered a group of students who presented her with a lot of behavior challenges. She was not used to having management issues, so she asked her instructional coach, Sherry Eichinger-Wilson, for help.

Sharon and Sherry agreed that Sherry would gather data in her classroom because Sharon believed her students were uninterested in learning. But after observing the class and gathering data, Sherry saw the class differently. Although she saw the same lessons and data that Sharon saw, Sherry wasn't sure that the students' behavior meant that they didn't like the learning or the class. Sherry proposed something different: "Why don't we ask the students what they think about the class?" As a result, they agreed that Sherry would interview a representative sample of students from the class.

Sherry met with students in a seminar room near their classroom, talking with each student individually for about ten minutes. She asked students what they thought about the class, what could be changed to make it better for them, and what they liked and didn't like about the way Sharon taught. "The kids," Sharon told me, "were positive and forthcoming. They liked the class and liked having choices. They wanted more choices, in fact."

The interviews showed Sharon that the management issues she was seeing had as much to do with her as they did with the kids. "I was letting the behavior of a few alpha dogs in class keep me from seeing that most students enjoyed learning and wanted more freedom. I realized there wasn't a conspiracy against me. They were just tired after lunch."

"When we encounter behavior problems, the tendency is to put the kids in lock-down," Sharon told me. "But, what I learned from the interviews made me more relaxed, and I was able to give students more choices, not fewer." If Sharon hadn't listened to her students, she might have acted in a way that would have made things worse. By listening, she learned, and ultimately her students learned more, too.

A major reason that interviewing students worked for Sharon was that her instructional coach, as Sharon told me, "is the gold standard for coaches." Her coach's openness, respect, and willingness to listen to students meant that Sharon could trust her and so could her students. "Sherry's demeanor," Sharon said, "led me to be willing to have her go and talk to the kids about me." Sherry's openness was also a major reason why Sharon's students were at ease telling Sherry information that ultimately led to much better learning experiences in school.

As Sherry and Sharon's experiences show, one powerful way to get a clear picture of reality in a classroom is to ask the students for their opinions about what they are experiencing. Even though students are the only people with firsthand knowledge of how learning is proceeding, they are infrequently consulted in many schools. Student voice is a powerful tool for professional growth that has been sorely underutilized.

Asking students about how learning is proceeding in a class has several advantages. First, students will give teacher and coach powerful information that can help them set goals and monitor progress. The most effective goals are student-focused goals, so it only makes sense that students should be asked for their opinion about learning goals. A second, very important, advantage is that by asking students for their opinions, teachers communicate their respect for students. In *Student Voice: The Instrument of Change* (2014), Russ Quaglia and Michael Corso describe how student voice can improve the way children experience school:

> When students believe their voices matter, they are more likely to be invested and engaged in their schools. When students believe teachers are listening to them, mutual trust and respect are likely to flourish. When students believe they are being heard and influencing decisions, schools become more relevant to students' lives and are more likely to be seen as serving their needs . . . In addition, students' insights, creativity, energy, and confidence offer important perspectives that can help schools improve. (p. 3)

We all want our voices to matter. We like giving our opinions and offering ideas. We want to be the subject of our activities, not the objects of someone else's.

—Russ Quaglia and Michael Corso
Student Voice: The Instrument of Change (2014, p. 2)

Unfortunately, although listening to students can be a powerful way of increasing motivation and learning, many students do not feel heard in schools. Quaglia and Corso's My Voice survey, given to 56,877 students in 2012–13, found that:

> Just 46% feel students have a voice in decision making at their school and just 52% believe that teachers are willing to learn from students (Quaglia Institute for Student Aspirations [QISA], 2013). In that same survey, even though nearly all students (94%) believe they can be successful and two thirds (67%) see themselves as leaders, less than half (45%) say that they are valued members of their school community. (2014, p. 2)

INFORMAL CONVERSATIONS

In many ways, coaches and teachers can do a better job of listening to students, some quite obvious and others more subtle. The most obvious way is to simply start asking students about their experiences in and outside class. Quaglia and Corso (2014) suggest that teachers make it a goal to talk to two students in every class each day about their experiences inside and outside school.

Questions for Daily Conversations With Students (in no particular order)

1. What's the best thing about coming to this class?

2. What's the worst thing about coming to this class?

3. What are you most excited about these days (sports, music, fashion, books, hobbies, games, work, etc.)?

4. How comfortable do you feel saying what you think in our class?

5. What could make this class more interesting for you?

6. Is this class too easy, too hard, or just right?

7. What should be changed in this school to make this a better school for you?

8. What do your friends say about our school?

Coaches and teachers can make learning from students a bit more formal by interviewing students about their learning experiences. Such interviews can happen at lunch, after school, or if it isn't too distracting, during class if students are working on group activities. This works best if students are interviewed one-by-one at the back of the class, in the hall, or in a nearby free room while class goes on.

Students can be interviewed in small groups or one-on-one, but we have found one-on-one conversations to be most helpful. When people (adults or children) talk in groups, they often modify what they say based on their concerns about what others in the group might think of their comments. When people speak one-on-one, they are much more candid. One-on-one conversations also provide more opportunities to build rapport and make connections with students.

Who should conduct the interviews? There are advantages to coaches interviewing students in that the interviews won't require any time of teachers, and students may be more candid about a class when they talk with someone other than the teacher. However, there are also advantages to teachers doing the interviews because when teachers talk with students, they can authentically listen, demonstrate empathy, and communicate their belief in their students. There is real power in one-on-one interactions.

Questions for Students in Grades 5–12

1. How would you say the class is going for you?

2. How engaged are you in class?

3. Tell me a bit about your goals for school, life, work.

4. What roadblocks are you encountering as you try to achieve your goals?

5. What can our class and our school do better to help you achieve your goals?

6. When do you feel comfortable speaking up in class? When do you feel uncomfortable speaking up in class?

7. What could be changed about our class to help you learn more?

8. What else can you tell me about how this class can become a better learning experience for you?

Questions for Students in Grades K-4

1. What do you like about school?

2. What don't you like about school?

3. What do you wish you could do more of in school?

4. Describe what the perfect school would look like for you.

5. What do your friends say about the school?

6. If you were the teacher, what would you change about the way things go in the class?

7. Is there anything you want to tell your teacher or the school principal about your class or school?

Whether interviews are conducted by teachers or coaches, the result should be that teachers have a clear understanding of how students perceive their class. To accomplish this, we suggest about 20 percent of students be interviewed, with particular attention paid to selecting students who can share the most helpful data. These are not necessarily the loudest students; in fact, it is important to talk with students who usually don't speak up in class along with more vocal students.

WRITING PROMPTS AND EXIT TICKETS

Some students find it easier to express their ideas in writing and may prefer to give written feedback about their experiences in the class. Writing prompts and exit tickets, described below, can also be used to monitor changes in school as they are easy to share with students. Teachers who want to know whether or not students feel psychologically safe in their classroom, for example, might ask students to write a journal entry or paragraph about what it feels like to be in the class. It is important that students understand that the task is meant to give them voices, and that they are to write honestly about what is on their minds, not try to write what they think their teacher wants to hear or what they think is clever. Students should be encouraged to share what they think.

Teachers can also give students exit tickets at the end of class with one question for students to answer. Any of the questions listed in this section or a question such as "How could today's lesson be changed to be more engaging for you?" could provide valuable information.

Exit Ticket

> How could today's lesson be changed to be more engaging for you?

In elementary classrooms where students might have difficulty expressing themselves in writing, teachers might use cards with emojis that students can check as a way of providing feedback. Teachers can ask students for their opinion on many different topics, but in particular, it is helpful to ask questions about how they are learning, about their attitudes, and about behavioral issues, such as their level of engagement or whether or not they feel respected by their peers and by adults in the school.

Emoji Form

Did you feel confident today?

LISTENING TO STUDENTS

Asking students what they think is a great start for motivating students, building relationships, and learning about the classroom, but the questions won't mean much unless students feel that they have been heard by their coach and teacher. This means that teachers and coaches need to make it very clear to students that they have been heard, that the students' opinions matter, and when possible, that what students say will be acted upon. Russ Quaglia and Michael Corso (2014) say this about listening:

> Listening to students takes time. . . . Yet at the same time, there is nothing more important we could be doing. Time sacrificed in the short run to listen to students pays off in the long run in the form of higher engagement, fewer student management issues, and greater student investment in the learning environment. One thing we have learned is that we must be purposeful in carving out time to listen to student voices (pp. 26–27).

Listening is vitally important, yet most of us do not listen very well. When I was conducting research for my book *Better Conversations: Coaching Ourselves to Be More Credible, Caring, and Connected* (2015), I asked people in nine countries to experiment with coaching using various communication habits. To do this, people video recorded conversations and then analyzed their conversations using self-coaching forms. One of our main findings was that the majority of people think they are better listeners than they are. A second finding was that people got better at listening when they practiced.

Teachers who want their students to feel heard (and shouldn't that be every teacher?) should work at becoming better listeners.[4] Teachers should also take time to share with students what they have heard to ensure that students understand that they have been heard. If students were asked to write or complete exit tickets, teachers might read out some of the students' responses. If students were interviewed, teachers might share some of the main themes from the interviews while protecting student anonymity. What matters most is that teachers respectfully thank students for their comments and refrain from sarcasm or defensiveness.

Once teachers have communicated that they have heard students, they need to communicate how they will act on what students said. For example, if students communicate that they'd like to have more debates during class, teachers need to explain how that will happen or why it can't happen. It is only when teachers ask, listen, and act that students can truly feel that they have been heard.

---

4. Readers can improve the way they listen by applying the self-coaching methods in *Better Conversations* (Knight, 2015), or just by video recording their interactions with students and making adjustments until they are content with their listening skills. Free forms for reflection on listening and empathy may be downloaded here: resources.corwin.com/node/28065/student-resources/chapter-3

Ask, Listen, and Act

Ask $\longrightarrow$ Listen $\longrightarrow$ Act

REVIEWING STUDENT WORK

One of the most powerful ways to get a clear picture of current reality is to review the work being done by students. The most obvious way to do this is for the coach and teacher to sit together and go through the most recent work done by students (e.g., written products, tests, assignments, homework, exit tickets) and identify students' strengths and weaknesses.

Coaches can also review student work separately and share their analysis with teachers. My colleagues and I did this a great deal in Topeka, Kansas, when we were sharing writing strategies with teachers. We would give students a writing prompt that was appropriate for a particular grade level or instructional focus (students might be asked to write six sentences, a paragraph, or a five-paragraph essay), and then we would analyze the writing according to specific criteria. For example, we might identify the percentage of complete sentences, the percentage of complicated sentences, the percentage of elements of a paragraph that were effectively used (topic sentence, details, transitions, concluding sentence), or apply a more sophisticated writing evaluation tool such as the 6+1 Trait® Writing Rubric (ideas, organization, voice, word choice, sentence fluency, conventions, and presentation).

When coaches analyze student work before sharing the results with teachers, they need to ensure that two issues are addressed. First, they must confirm that they are applying criteria that teachers see as most important. Second, they must ensure that they and their teachers have a shared understanding of every element of the criteria.

Coaches and teachers can gather data in other ways as well. The chart paper and marker method, sometimes used in mathematics classes, involves giving every student chart paper so that they can show their work as they complete classroom assignments. The coach can walk around the room and take notes on students' successes and roadblocks. Of course, teachers will also want to observe students when they are not interacting directly with students. When coach and teacher meet after the lesson, they can talk about what they saw students doing.

Coaches can also get information on students by quickly assessing students' reading skills as they sit next to them and ask them to quietly read a grade-level passage out loud for a minute. (More formal reading assessments can also be given.) Coaches can listen to students while they work on group activities, keeping a record of student comments. Additionally, coaches can talk quietly with students at their desks and ask them questions during class such as "What are you learning right now?" or "Why is this learning important?" When classroom management specialist Randy Sprick talked with me about coaching, he suggested that coaches could find valuable data for teachers by asking students to describe the expectations for their behavior during a particular activity.

Of course, teachers are always looking at student work, especially for grading. Instructional coaches can help by providing a second perspective and perhaps by gathering data (such as written assessments) that teachers don't have time to gather. Student work often provides a great point of departure for establishing student-focused goals for coaching.

OBSERVATION

My colleagues and I at The Instructional Coaching Group have had a long-term partnership with Lincoln Public Schools in Lincoln, Nebraska, spending our largest amount of time at Elliott Elementary School. We were asked to partner with the educators at Elliott in 2009, after the school experienced the mixed emotions that come with winning a Persistently Low-Achieving School grant. On the one hand, the school was awarded resources to help them move forward. On the other hand, they won those resources because the students in the school were not performing well. Elliott, I was told, was considered the sixth worst school in Nebraska at the time.

The students at Elliott brought complex challenges. Elliott had the most diverse student body and the most students living in poverty in Lincoln. To better meet the students' needs, Principal Jadi Miller, Coach and Project Manager Lynn Fuller, and Instructional Coaches Sy Settel and Sara Rose implemented a school improvement process designed to give teachers a voice in their professional development. All teachers were interviewed by a member of the school improvement team to ensure that they had an opportunity to shape the professional learning goals the school embraced. Then, every teacher had a chance to vote on the school's goal and veto it if they were not committed to hitting it[5] as a means of ensuring that everyone was committed to hitting the school's improvement target.

---

5. The process for improvement employed by Jadi Miller and the other educators at Elliott Elementary is described in Chapter 3 of *Unmistakable Impact: A Partnership Model for Dramatically Improving Instruction* (Knight, 2011).

An important part of Elliott's goal-setting process was data gathered in each teacher's classroom. We used a form similar to the comprehensive form included in this chapter. When we analyzed the data, we found, among other things, that students were involved in learning activities only 78 percent of the time. That is, for one out of every five minutes—22 percent of the time—students were not learning.

After Jadi Miller shared these data with the teachers, they agreed that they wanted to focus on decreasing transition time (the amount of time students took to hang up their coats, take out books, move from one activity to another, and so on) to increase instructional time. Jadi told me that she started to have nightmares about the number 22. But with the help of instructional coaches, who gathered data and collaborated with teachers around instructional changes, the school increased instructional time from 78 percent to 96 percent in an eighteen-month period.

When instructional time increased at Elliott, achievement scores on the state assessment for reading and writing also increased. The number of students who scored as proficient on Nebraska State Reading Assessment went from 50 percent to 69 percent between 2009–10 and 2011–12. Similarly, the number of students who scored as proficient on Nebraska State Mathematics Assessment increased from 56 percent to 68 percent between 2010–11 and 2011–12 (the mathematics assessment was not given in 2009–10).

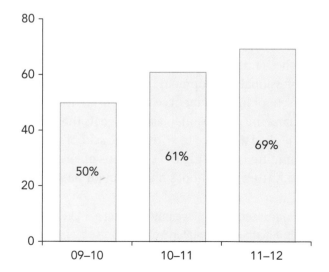

**Percent Proficient on
Nebraska State Reading Assessment**

Percent Proficient on
Nebraska State Mathematics Assessment

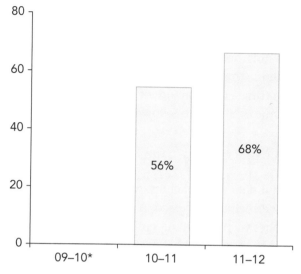

*Test not given in 09–10

The results were dramatic. Elliott went from being the "sixth worst school in Nebraska" to being featured in newspaper articles about school district successes. Students at Elliott were much more successful, and Jadi stopped having nightmares about the number 22.

I interviewed all of the teachers at Elliott at least twice, and they told me several reasons why the scores improved. Jadi was an inspiring leader and a very skilled project manager. Professional development was more relevant and worthwhile since teachers had a voice in decisions and a clear focus for their professional learning. The instructional coaches provided support that made it easier to make changes. Additionally, seeing the data about instructional time helped teachers understand what they needed to work on. "Until I saw the data," many teachers told me in various ways, "I never thought about transition time at all. When I saw the data, though, I knew I had to make a change." That is, data helped teachers see what they would not have seen otherwise. Data made the invisible visible, and as a result many more students became proficient.

The kinds of data gathered at Elliot can be gathered by any instructional coach. Observation data are not a replacement for video, student interviews, or student work. In fact, the coaches we partnered with in Oregon and Washington did not find observations to be the best way to help teachers get a clear picture of reality. Student comments, student work, and especially video were more compelling ways for teachers to get a clear picture of reality since they offered a direct, unfiltered picture of what happens in a classroom.

Nevertheless, data are essential for setting goals and measuring progress toward goals, and instructional coaches who want to be skilled in all aspects of their job must be able to gather observation data. Furthermore, since some teachers are not comfortable with video or do not see the benefit of interviewing students, the data gathered from observations provide a useful third option for getting a clear picture of reality. Conversations about data usually involve some or all of the following elements.

PRE-OBSERVATION CONVERSATION

When we talk about data with teachers, we ground the conversations in the Partnership Principles discussed in Chapter 1. This means that as instructional coaches we position our collaborating teacher as an equal who makes the decisions about what data will be gathered. We don't silence ourselves, but we share our ideas provisionally and clearly, so our collaborating teacher is comfortable sharing her ideas about data. Our work with a teacher is for the teacher and her students, and therefore, the teacher's wishes guide our actions in her classroom. To best serve teachers and students, we have found, as the checklist on the next page indicates, that a number of issues need to be clarified before we enter a teacher's classroom.

Take Notes

Some coaches find that taking notes helps them focus during conversations, whereas others find it distracting. I belong to the latter category, so whenever I feel notes are unnecessary, I opt for not taking them. Having said that, I must add that too much information is generally shared during the pre-observation conversation to be remembered without notes. For that reason, I created a simple form (see pages 52–53), coaches can use to take notes during the pre-observation conversation. Instructional coaches can use the form to guide the pre-observation conversation.

Form of Feedback

In *Thanks for the Feedback: The Science and Art of Receiving Feedback Well* (2015), Douglas Stone and Sheila Heen identify three kinds of feedback: appreciation, coaching, and evaluation. *Appreciation* is feedback that we receive when someone sees what we are doing well and expresses gratitude for our efforts. *Coaching* is feedback intended to help us get better at what we do. Finally, *evaluation* is feedback that tells us how we are doing compared to others or some standard.

CHECKLIST: PRE-OBSERVATION CONVERSATION

	✔
Take notes during the conversation.	
Determine the desired form of feedback—(a) appreciation, (b) coaching, (c) evaluation, or (d) some other form.	
Determine the purpose of the observation—(a) to get a clear picture of reality, (b) to establish a baseline for setting a goal, (c) to monitor progress toward a goal, or (d) some other purpose.	
Explain the different kinds of data that can be gathered.	
Determine which types of data will be gathered.	
Determine the location, date, and time for the observation.	
Determine whether or not it is OK for you to talk with students in the class.	
Ask, "Is there anything I need to know about particular students or this class in general?"	
Determine where you will sit and whether or not it is OK for you to move around the class.	
Ask, "Is there anything else you want to ask me that you haven't asked yet?"	
Determine how you will share data (e.g., face-to-face, via email).	
Identify when and where you will meet to discuss data.	

 Available for download at **resources.corwin.com/impactcycle**

OBSERVATION PLAN

What is the purpose of the visit?

To get a clear picture of reality _____

To establish a baseline for setting a goal _____

To monitor progress toward a goal _____

Some other purpose _____

What kind of feedback is desired?

Appreciation _____

Coaching _____

Evaluation _____

Some other form _____

What data will be gathered?

Time on task _____

Experience sampling _____

Ratio of interaction _____

Instructional and non-instructional time _____

Real learning index _____

Ratio of interaction _____

Corrections _____

Disruptions _____

Respectful interactions _____

Questions

- Open vs. closed _____
- Right/wrong vs. opinion _____

Level _____

Opportunity to respond _____

Correct academic responses _____

Different students responding _____

Teacher vs. student talk _____

Other _____

When will I visit the class?

Location _____

Date _____

Time _____

Should I talk with students?

Yes _____

No _____

Special information about students or the class:

Where should I sit?

Is it OK for me walk around the classroom during the lesson?

Yes _____

No _____

Is it OK for me to talk with students during the lesson?

Yes _____

No _____

Other information I should know:

How will I share data?

Face-to-face _____

Via email _____

Some other way _____

Next meeting:

When _____

Where _____

Coaches need to confirm what kind of feedback teachers desire. If teachers are looking for affirmation and appreciation and they receive coaching or evaluation, they likely will not be satisfied with the feedback. Instructional coaches should use the pre-observation conversation about kinds of feedback as an opportunity to explain that they are gathering objective data, not evaluating or judging the teacher. They can also explain that they will gather only the data that the collaborating teacher identifies as important.

Purpose of the Observation

While in most cases it is obvious what the purpose of the observation will be, coaches nevertheless should confirm that the purpose is to (a) get a clear picture of reality, (b) establish a baseline for setting a goal, (c) monitor progress toward a goal, or (d) accomplish some other purpose.

Explain the Different Kinds of Data

The most important part of the pre-observation conversation is likely the time when the coach explains the different forms of data that might be gathered. During this conversation, it is important that the coach makes it clear that the data to be gathered are for the teacher and her students and that, therefore, the teacher needs to determine what data she wants to see. Sometimes, it is necessary to explain each kind of data, especially if teachers have not worked with a coach previously. The first section in the

Data That Coaches Typically Gather

Time on Task: A measure of the percentage of students who are doing the learning that is proposed for them at different points during a lesson.

Experience Sampling: A way for students to communicate their level of engagement by circling a number on an engagement form every ten minutes.

Instructional and Non-instructional Time: A measure of the percentage of time when activities in the class are (a) related to learning and (b) not related to learning.

Real Learning Index: A global measure that combines time on task and instructional time.

Ratio of Interaction: A measure that compares the number of times teachers attend to students when students are behaving appropriately with the number of times teachers attend to students when students are acting inappropriately.

Corrections: A measure of how often teachers correct student behaviors that they have identified as ones that need to be corrected.

Disruptions: The number of times per ten minutes that students interrupt the teacher teaching or other students learning.

Respectful Interactions: The number of student interactions that demonstrate respect.

Type and Kind of Questions: The number of (a) open, (b) closed, (c) right and wrong, or (d) opinion questions asked by a teacher.

Level of Questions: The number of knowledge, skill, and big idea questions asked (or some other assessment of question levels such as Bloom's taxonomy).

Opportunities to Respond: The number of times students are prompted to respond to questions or other prompts, such as response cards, during a lesson.

Correct Academic Responses: The percentage of correct answers students give during a lesson.

Different Students Responding: The number of different students who respond during a class.

Teacher vs. Student Talk: The percentage of time that work in the classroom is mediated by the teacher compared with the percentage of time work is mediated by students.

Instructional Coaches' Toolkit at the end of this book provides an overview of the kinds of data coaches gather most frequently. The chart above summarizes the data provided in the toolkit.

Once the collaborating teacher feels she understands the types of data well enough to make an educated decision, she can communicate what data she wants the instructional coach to gather. Sometimes this is an easy decision; for example, when a coach is simply monitoring progress toward a goal and the coach and teacher are already clear on what data need to be gathered. At other times, the coach may have to scaffold the conversation, explaining data and why it might be helpful for the teacher to see the data. At all times, the teacher should be the decision maker when the coach works from the partnership perspective; however, the coach may need to help the teacher make an educated decision by explaining data and why it could be useful.

Determine Which Class/Hour You Will Visit

Teachers often want the coach to visit the class or lesson that is most likely to be a success. When I discuss the observation with teachers, I always suggest that I visit the class where we can learn the most. This might well be the class or lesson that is most successful, but it can also be the class or lesson that seems to be least successful. The data being gathered are for the teacher, so it only makes sense that he choose the class where data will be gathered.

Ask for Special Information About the Class or Individual Students

Sometimes a teacher may invite us to visit a particular class because she has a special concern about individuals or groups of students. For example, a teacher may want you to pay careful attention to a new student who frequently disrupts the class or students with special needs whom she wants to be fully integrated into learning activities. Instructional coaches can provide a helpful second perspective on students who are of special concern to the teacher.

Clarify What the Teacher Is Comfortable With You Doing While Observing

Before entering the classroom to gather data, coaches need to understand how the collaborating teacher would like them to gather data. Therefore, the coaches should ask the teacher where she would like them to sit, whether or not she is comfortable with them walking around the room while students are working, and whether or not she is comfortable with them talking with students during class. As visitors in teachers' classrooms, instructional coaches do not want to distract the teacher, so it is important that they confirm how the teacher would like them to act in their classroom.

Determine How Data Will Be Gathered

The way coaches gather data depends upon the focus of the observation. If a coach is gathering data to provide a teacher with a clear picture of reality, he may want to use a form such as the 20-Minute High-Impact Survey. At other times, a coach may want to use a specific form for one type of data, such as a form for recording and coding the type and level of questions (see page 185 in the Instructional Coaches' Toolkit for an example of this type of form). Finally, as I explain in the Instructional Coaches' Toolkit, a teacher's seating chart can be a great tool for gathering data such as time on task, ratio of interaction, corrections, different students answering questions, and so forth.

20-MINUTE HIGH-IMPACT SURVEY

COMMUNITY BUILDING

Time on Task

MINUTES	STUDENTS	ON TASK	% ON TASK
:10			
:20			

Ratio of Interactions

REINFORCING	CORRECTING

Expectations

CLEARLY POSTED OR STATED

( ) YES   ( ) NO

Respect

SHOWN TOWARD TEACHER
AND OTHER STUDENTS

( ) YES   ( ) NO

INSTRUCTION

Check which of the following teaching practices were present and record the number of minutes for each:

CHECK	PRACTICE/ ACTIVITY	MINUTES	CHECK	PRACTICE/ ACTIVITY	MINUTES
	Beginning routine			Transition time	
	Stories			Quizzes	
	Thinking prompts				
	Cooperative learning				
	Experiential learning				
	Labs				
	Seat work				
	Direct instruction				

Kinds of Questions

OPEN	CLOSED

Levels of Questions

KNOWLEDGE	SKILL	BIG IDEA

PLANNING, ASSESSMENT, LEARNING

	YES	NO
Teacher clearly states learning target for the lesson		
Teacher clearly describes success criteria for the student learning		
Teacher gathers data showing whether or not students are learning		
Teacher modifies teaching or learning to improve student achievement based on data gathered		

Available for download at **resources.corwin.com/impactcycle**

Before ending the pre-observation conversation, a few additional details should be addressed. The coach needs to confirm how she will share data with her collaborating teacher. We recommend that coach and teacher get together to discuss data whenever it is possible and necessary, but a teacher may want to see the data before a meeting, in which case data may be shared via email prior to a meeting. Coach and teacher also need to confirm when and where they will meet to discuss the data. Finally, before ending the conversation, a coach should ask, "Is there anything else you want to ask me that you haven't asked yet?"

PUTTING IT ALL TOGETHER

The most powerful approach for coaches to take, when time allows, is to combine two or all three ways of getting a clear picture of current reality. Thus, coaches could video record a lesson, interview students, and look at student work, or they could video record a lesson and teachers could analyze the video for some of the forms of data described here. Ultimately, teachers could learn to video record and study their own lessons, set goals, and work with coaches to implement new teaching practices until goals are met.

Regardless of the method teachers and coaches use, it is vital that teachers get a clear, objective picture of reality. Once teachers have a clear picture of reality, they can shift to the essential work of coach and teacher working together to make a positive change in students' (and usually teachers') lives.

MAKING IT REAL

If they are going to suggest to teachers that they use video to get a clear picture of reality, instructional coaches must use video to improve their own skills. Coaches can video record their coaching conversations to see how well they are implementing many of the strategies described throughout this book, such as the listening and questioning strategies described in Chapter 3. Additionally, coaches who give presentations can record their presentations, and coaches modeling teaching strategies can record their lessons. Something as simple as recording and reviewing a conversation with a spouse or child can be a powerful learning experience.

Coaches must also become highly skilled at gathering data reliably. A great way to do this is to watch videos of teachers with fellow coaches, gather data, and then compare what everyone records. Coaches should keep practicing and refining the way they gather data until everyone's scores are at least 95 percent the same. We've found it takes about two to three hours of practice to reliably gather such data as ratio of interaction, kinds and types of questions, and instructional vs. non-instructional time.

Using video is a great way to improve data-gathering skills since you can rewind the recording to discuss what was noted and why. However, some data, such as time on task, are difficult to see on video, so coaches will need to practice gathering that data with peers in cooperative teachers' classrooms.

TO SUM UP

- To get a clear picture of reality, teachers must appreciate (a) where there is room for improvement and (b) what is going well.
- Three strategies for getting a clear picture of reality are (a) video recording, (b) learning from students, and (c) gathering observation data.
- Video:
  - Video gives teachers and coaches a perspective on the class that cuts through perceptual errors.
  - Instructional coaches who plan to make video a part of their practice should take into consideration that a culture of trust must be in place for video to be embraced, that video should be a choice for teachers, and that teachers should own their recordings.

- Learning from Students:

  o Student voice is a powerful tool for professional growth that has been sorely underutilized.

  o All human beings want their voices to matter.

  o Teachers can learn from students in informal conversations, in interviews, and through writing prompts and exit tickets.

  o Review of student work is a powerful way to get a clear picture of reality.

- Observing a Lesson:

  o Though not the best way to get a clear picture of reality, observing can be helpful when teachers don't want to be video recorded and don't want students to be interviewed.

  o Gathering data is a necessary skill for coaches since data are often a big part of goal setting and measuring progress toward goals.

  o The pre-observation conversation needs to accomplish many things summarized in the Pre-Observation Planning Form.

GOING DEEPER

I learned about the importance of having a clear picture of reality and the creative tension that is at the heart of the Impact Cycle from Robert Fritz's book *The Path of Least Resistance: Learning to Become the Creative Force in Your Own Life*, first published in 1989.

Several books have deepened my understanding of the fallibility of our perceptions of reality. I like Heidi Grant Halvorson's *No One Understands You and What to Do About It* (2015), which offers a helpful summary of common perceptual errors and how they complicate effective communication. Michael Lewis's *The Undoing Project: A Friendship That Changed Our Minds* (2017) is, surprisingly, a page-turner about the theories of cognition developed through the friendship between Daniel Kahneman and Amos Tversky. Kahneman's own book on his theories about decision making is *Thinking Fast and Slow* (2011).

If you want to learn more about using video in schools, as I write this book, the only book I know of on that topic is my book, *Focus on Teaching: Using Video for High-Impact Instruction* (2014). Here I describe how video can be used by teachers who coach themselves, instructional coaches, teams, as well as principals and teachers in the midst of the teacher evaluation.

Dianne Sweeney's books *Student-Centered Coaching: A Guide for K–8 Coaches and Principals* (2010) and *Student-Centered Coaching at the Secondary Level* (2013) contain many excellent suggestions on how to use student work as the point of departure for goal setting during coaching.

Alexandra Horowitz's *On Looking: Eleven Walks With Expert Eyes* (2013) is like a course on observing. I think it can enhance the way anyone looks at the world. Douglas Stone and Sheila Heen's *Thanks for the Feedback: The Science and Art of Receiving Feedback Well* (2015) is a book about how to receive feedback, which is an important topic if you want to be a better learner. However, the book is also helpful for anyone who gives feedback, such as coaches.

CHAPTER

3

Is about

Goals that
make an impact

Because they
address

By coaches effectively

Surfaced through
use of the

Success factors

Asking questions

Identify Questions

- Powerful
- Easy
- Emotionally
  compelling
- Reachable
- Student-focused

- Let others do the talking.
- Pause to affirm before talking.
- Don't interrupt.
- Ask one question at a time.
- Ask for clarification.
- Ask, "And what else?"
- Assume people are doing
  their best.
- Be non-judgmental.
- Avoid leading questions.
- Avoid advice disguised as
  a question.

1. On a scale of 1–10, with 1 being the
   worst lesson you've taught and 10 being
   the best, how would you rank that lesson?
2. What pleased you about the lesson?
3. What would have to change to move
   the lesson closer to 10?
4. What would your students be doing
   differently if your class was a 10?
5. Tell me more about what that would
   look like.
6. How could we measure that change?
7. Do you want that to be your goal?
8. If you could hit that goal, would it really
   matter to you?
9. What teaching strategy can you use to
   hit your goal?
10. What are your next steps?

QUESTIONS TO IDENTIFY A PEERS GOAL

1 Identify

GOAL | b
TEACHING STRATEGY | c
a | CURRENT REALITY

2 Learn

e | CHECKLISTS
d | MODELING

3 Improve

DIRECTION | f
PROGRESS | g
IMPROVEMENTS | h
i | ACTIONS

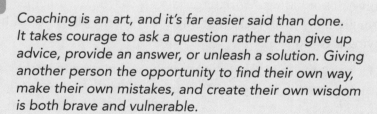

Coaching is an art, and it's far easier said than done. It takes courage to ask a question rather than give up advice, provide an answer, or unleash a solution. Giving another person the opportunity to find their own way, make their own mistakes, and create their own wisdom is both brave and vulnerable.

—**Brené Brown**
commenting on *The Coaching Habit*
by Michael Bungay Stanier (2016)

PEERS GOALS

Jackie Jewell is an instructional coach from Othello, Washington, who partnered with my colleagues and me at the Kansas Coaching Project at the University of Kansas Center for Research on Learning. Jackie was a highly successful coach; almost every teacher she worked with hit a powerful goal, but when I asked her to identify one coaching partnership that she was especially proud of, she chose her collaboration with Monica Ochoa.

Monica was a first-year teacher in Othello working to get her professional certification at Washington State University. She signed up for coaching when she heard Jackie give a brief presentation on the topic. Monica then sought out Jackie after her principal observed her class and suggested she work on ratio of interaction—increasing the amount of positive attention she gave students when they are working productively.

Monica was interested in working on ratio of interaction, and in an interview with me, she said that when she reached out to Jackie, "I really didn't know what to do. I came in really confused. There were so many things that I could do, but I just didn't know how it was going to unfold. Jackie kept telling me everything would be fine. Once she video recorded my lessons and took data, it started to become very clear for me."

Since Jackie was a partner with us at the Kansas Coaching Project, she ultimately participated in more than two weeks of professional development. Here she learned how to gather data, learned the teaching strategies in *High-Impact Instruction* (Knight, 2013), and most important, perhaps, she learned how to apply the Impact Cycle. Jackie's mastery of the knowledge and processes of coaching was further enhanced through her partnership with Dr. Marti Elford from the Kansas Coaching Project at the University of Kansas. Working as Jackie's coach, Marti helped Jackie move through many roadblocks that might have otherwise stopped her from moving forward.

So when Jackie met with Monica, she knew she would need to start by getting a clear picture of reality and then use that picture as a jumping off point for Monica to set a goal. Jackie's first step was to video record Monica's class for about twenty minutes and transfer the video to Monica's computer. She gave Monica the reflection forms included in Chapter 2 and went over them with Monica for a few minutes, as she wrote in her coaching journal, "to make sure she didn't have any questions about the video reflection forms."

Monica told me that hearing she was going to have to watch herself on video was "torture." "I was the first person to say I didn't want to work with Jackie because having to watch myself was one of my biggest fears." However, watching video of her lessons was, in Monica's words, "helpful." "Once I was able to look at my video, it all started to become clearer to me.

I thought the class wasn't listening to me, but when I watched the video, I saw that I had the students' attention and they were just fidgety. I had a lot of students who wanted to participate, wanted to speak out. So, it was good."

Monica had gone into coaching thinking she wanted to improve her ratio of interaction, but the video showed that there might be more important things for her to work on. Jackie offered to gather data in Monica's class. She observed her lessons, gathered data on time on task and ratio of interaction, and mapped how Monica's students were using their time (see the Instructional Coaches' Toolkit for more information on mapping instructional time). She also listened to students as they were working and wrote down the comments they made as they completed the various readers' workshop tasks.

It turned out that the biggest issue in Monica's class was that students were not on-task during readers' workshop, a part of the day when they worked in small groups to complete various tasks related to reading. Most students were not getting the tasks done during class and 75–100 percent of them had to stay late in class to complete their work and miss recess each day. Monica knew they should be getting the work done, but she didn't know how to get them to do it.

With the help of Marti Elford from our research center at the University of Kansas, Jackie learned to apply the Impact Cycle with a high-degree of fidelity with Monica and the other teachers she coached. Jackie used most of the methods for getting a clear picture of reality that I discussed in Chapter 2: video, observing lessons, and learning from students. Once she had gathered her data, she met with Monica to identify a goal, what we have come to refer to as a PEERS goal.

Our research on instructional coaching has led us to many insights into many success factors for coaching. For example, we have learned about the importance of modeling, effective questions, sound communication skills, the most helpful teaching strategies, how to explore data, and so forth. Our most important finding, however, is that goals are essential for coaching success. When teachers partner with coaches to set and meet measureable student goals, coaching improves instruction. When there is no goal, there is a real danger that coaching will have no lasting impact.

When I was conducting interviews for this book, I was excited to interview Bob Garmston who, along with Art Costa, originated the widely used Cognitive Coaching model. I wanted to explore the differences between cognitive coaching and instructional coaching, in particular, around the area of goal setting. Our research had revealed that goal setting is a vital part of coaching, and I wanted to run this by Bob. So, I asked him, "How important is goal setting in cognitive coaching? Can coaching be effective if there isn't a goal?" Bob's reply was to the point: "The short answer is no." I was in total agreement.

Bob then went on to give me two examples of why he saw goals as essential for coaching:

> First, a teacher must be clear about his or her goals, and the act of coaching should help the teacher clarify the goals. Everything else in the lesson rides on that. Coaching without a goal is like navigating without a compass.

> Relatedly, we have what we call a problem-resolving map in which we might work with someone who is distressed, whose efficacy is low. They can't figure out what to do. It might be an instructional issue, or it might be a situation with a colleague. In that conversation, we still focus on the goal, but we know that when a person is highly emotionally flooded, they often cannot identify a goal for themselves. But, we listen carefully. In essence, what we are doing is getting the person to express enough about what is going on with them without having the conversation going to the existing state rather than the desired state. So, when we believe that we understand a conceptual goal of where the person is, we state the goal. When we see the eyes light up and the body changes, we know we have hit pay dirt. Then we can start the conversation with the person about identifying resources to get them to their goal.

When our research team began to study goal setting, we started where many people start by asking teachers to set SMART goals, goals that are variously understood to be Specific, Measurable, Attainable (or Actionable/Assignable), Realistic (Relevant), and Timely (or Time Bound). However, as I studied the literature on goal setting, I came to believe that teachers and coaches can set better goals if they consider a different acronym, PEERS, which includes a few additional factors that are very important when setting goals. Teachers who create goals that address the PEERS factors will likely find that their goals will have more impact, and coaches who guide teachers to develop PEERS goals will likely find that their task—supporting teachers—becomes much easier. Once a teacher has a PEERS goal, coaching has a momentum of its own.[1]

We developed the PEERS goal framework over two years. I read widely in the field of goal setting and shared what I was learning with the coaches in Beaverton, Oregon, and Othello, Washington. Then, they tried out the

---

1. I introduced PEERS goals in my book *Focus on Teaching* (Knight, 2014). Here I include an updated version of what I first wrote in that book.

model and provided feedback on how it could be revised until we were satisfied we had a powerful model. Below, I describe the framework and some of the literature that informed its development.

POWERFUL

If a coach and teacher are going to spend the time it takes to hit a goal—in our experience, on average, five to six hours—they need to make sure the goal is worth the time they're going to invest. Educators who want to make an important difference in students' lives should sort through their possible goals by asking a simple question: "Will this goal make a real difference in students' lives?"

PEERS Goals
Powerful
Easy
Emotionally Compelling
Reachable
Student-Focused

As I explained in Chapter 2, to set a powerful goal, coach and teacher need to get a clear picture of reality by reviewing (a) video of the lesson, (b) the coach's observation data, (c) students' opinions gathered by interviews, (d) student work, or (e) some combination of these approaches. If a teacher does not have a clear picture of the reality of her classroom, she risks spending a lot of time pursuing a goal that ultimately has little impact on students' lives.

Such was the case with Monica Ochoa. Had she not seen a video of her lesson, she would have wanted to focus her efforts on increasing her ratio of interaction. But such efforts would not have brought about the changes she hoped for, because the video revealed that the more important area of concern in her class was that students did not understand what they were supposed to do during readers' workshop.

After they had watched the video and Jackie had shared what she had observed in the class, Monica identified that the real issue in class was that the students did not understand what they were supposed to do. That insight allowed her to set a goal that had the potential to have a real impact on her students' ability to read—that students would move from being on task 76 percent of the time to at least 90 percent of the time during readers' workshop. The ability to read fluently is one of the most important outcomes for students in elementary classrooms, and Monica knew her students wouldn't learn unless they were engaged. Her goal was a powerful one.

EASY

Powerful goals that are too complex to implement are not as helpful as powerful goals that are simply stated and therefore, easier to implement. Complex, confusing goals, no matter how much potential they have

Simplicity is the ultimate sophistication.

—Apple's 1977 brochure, from
Walter Isaacson's biography *Steve Jobs*

for positive change, often end up on the scrap heap of unrealized good intentions. Rather than leading people to flounder in complexity, simple goals describe a destination and the shortest path to the destination.

In his biography *Steve Jobs* (2015), Walter Isaacson wrote that, like many leaders in the field of design, simplicity was Steve Jobs's mantra. "It takes a lot of hard work to make something simple," Jobs told Isaacson, "to truly understand the underlying challenges and come up with elegant solutions." "Jobs," Isaacson wrote, "felt that design simplicity should be linked to making products easy to use." Even though simplicity wasn't easy to accomplish, Jobs's goal was to make designs and products that made users' lives easier.

Simple can be harder than complex: You have to work to get your thinking clean to make it simple. But it is worth it in the end because once you get there, you can move mountains.

—Steve Jobs
from *Business Week*, May 25, 1988

Like the designers Steve Jobs describes, coaches should also strive for the simplicity that makes it easier for teachers to hit their goals. The reality is that people are more likely to achieve goals that they think they can achieve. As Kerry Patterson and his colleagues write in *Influencer: The Power to Change Anything* (2008), "When it comes to altering behavior, you need to help others answer only two questions. First: Is it worth it? . . . And second, can they do this thing?" (p. 50). People will strive for a goal when they consider it worthwhile and when they believe they can hit it, and a powerful and easy goal is one people believe they can hit.

An instructional coach who desires to create simple and easy goals needs to think like a designer who is always striving for clarity. An effective instructional coach helps teachers identify the most important goals and the most efficient ways to realize them. As Greg McKeown has written in *Essentialism: The Disciplined Pursuit of Less* (2014), "It is about making the wisest possible investment of your time and energy in order to operate at our highest point of contribution by doing only what is essential" (p. 5). Coaches can also follow the advice of John Maeda, former president of Rhode Island School of Design, who wrote in *The Laws of Simplicity* (2006) that "simplicity is about subtracting the obvious, and adding the meaningful" (p. ix).

Monica's goal, as it turns out, was reasonably easy to achieve. Video recordings of lessons revealed that students were not resisting learning, that they actually were very interested in learning, but they simply didn't understand what they had to do. Since students didn't understand what they were to do, they didn't do anything. In her coaching conversation with Jackie, Monica set her goal as increasing the percentage of students who were on task to 90 percent simply by making sure students knew what they had to do.

EMOTIONALLY COMPELLING

Any change involves how people feel as much as it involves how they think, and instructional coaches or any other change leaders need to recognize the primacy of emotion in change. As Roger Fisher, one of the world's leading negotiation experts, wrote, "You cannot stop having emotions any more than you can stop having thoughts. At all times, you are feeling some degree of happiness or sadness, enthusiasm or frustration, isolation or engagement, pain or pleasure. You cannot turn emotions on and off like a light switch" (Fisher & Shapiro, 2005, pp. 9–10).

Similarly, in their book *Switch: How to Change Things When Change Is Hard* (2010), Chip and Dan Heath describe how reason and emotion are both essential for bringing about change. According to Heath and Heath, our emotions are like an unwieldy elephant that has to be reined in by our reason. "Our emotional side," they wrote, "is an elephant, and our rational side is its rider."

> Perched atop the Elephant, the Rider holds the reins and seems to be the leader. But the Rider's control is precarious because the Rider is so small relative to the Elephant. Anytime the six-ton Elephant and the Rider disagree about which direction to go, the Rider is going to lose. He is completely overmatched. (p. 7)

Coaches who want to help people set goals that they will be motivated to hit must speak to people's emotions as well as their reason. When people fail to change, it's usually not because they do not understand a problem. For example, smokers understand that cigarettes are unhealthy, but that doesn't make them quit. A goal that will compel people to act is one that people understand and feel (Heath & Heath, 2010).

When I spoke with Monica, she made it clear that she had chosen a goal that was emotionally compelling for her. She was deeply disappointed by her students' lack of engagement, and she wanted to turn her class around. "They tested me. My workshop time was a nightmare," Monica confessed. "I hated coming to work in the beginning because they were a very difficult class. I probably would have quit my job if I hadn't worked with Jackie," she added.

REACHABLE

Teachers and coaches also need to consider whether or not their goal, however admirable, is one that can actually be reached. A reachable goal is one that builds hope.

Shane Lopez, who was a researcher at the University of Kansas and the Gallup Organization, has been described as the world's leading expert on hope. In *Making Hope Happen: Create the Future You Want for Yourself and Others* (2014), Lopez writes that hope requires three elements. First, hope requires a goal that sets out an idea of "where we want to go, what we want to accomplish, who we want to be." Second, to feel hope, we need agency, "our perceived ability to shape our lives day to day . . . [our knowledge that] . . . we can make things happen." Finally, hope requires pathways, "plans that carry us forward."

Goals that move us to act must be clearly stated. "Clarity dissolves resistance," Heath and Heath write, and therefore they suggest that the most effective goals "provide a destination postcard—a vivid picture from the near-term future that shows what could be possible" (p. 76). Similarly, Heidi Grant Halvorson, associate director of the Motivation Science Center at Columbia University, describes "getting specific" as one of the most important aspects of goal setting:

> Taking the time to get specific and spell out exactly what you want to achieve removes the possibility of settling for less—of telling yourself that what you've done is "good enough." It also makes the course of action you need to take much clearer . . . Thousands of studies have shown that getting specific is one of the most crucial (though often overlooked) steps to take in reaching any goal. (2012, pp. 7–8)

A goal that fosters hope has a reasonable chance of being achieved because (a) teachers believe they can achieve it (agency) and (b) it includes a strategy or strategies that can help them achieve it (pathways). Increasing student achievement is an admirable goal, but it isn't a reachable goal unless teacher and coach can describe it clearly and identify a strategy that will help them reach the goal. Increasing achievement by decreasing non-instructional time from 22 percent to 5 percent by teaching students expectations for transitions, for example, is a more reachable goal because it describes a clear destination as well as the pathway that a teacher can take to get to the goal.

The best goals have a finish line (a clear, precise description of what will be different if a goal is hit), a yardstick (some way of measuring progress toward the goal), and a way to get to the finish line (a teaching or learning strategy that can make the change happen). Imprecise goals create frustration, but clearly described goals build hope and have the potential to lead to lasting, positive improvements in students' lives.

When Monica and Jackie set their goal, they had a precise goal in mind (90 percent time on task) and an additional goal that made the destination even more concrete for Monica. When they started working together, about twenty out of twenty-five of Monica's students were missing recess because they hadn't completed their work. Monica wanted to reduce that number to no more than three students missing recess and made that her second goal.

STUDENT-FOCUSED

Finally, effective goals are student- rather than teacher-focused. When teachers choose teacher goals ("I want to use graphic organizers at least twice a week"), they may implement a strategy to reach that goal but have no idea whether or not it made a difference for students. Additionally, no measure of excellence is built into the goal, with the result that people may implement the goal poorly and still meet the goal.

A student-focused goal, on the other hand, provides clear feedback on whether or not changes make a difference for students. Additionally, student-focused goals carry with them a built-in measure of quality. If a teacher ineffectively implements a teaching practice, it is unlikely that he will achieve the goal. The teacher will have to keep refining his use of the practice until he is able to implement it effectively, so that its use can lead to achievement of the goal.

The student-focused measureable goal for Monica's students was that an average of at least 90 percent of her students would be on task on average during readers' workshop time. Jackie helped Monica guide her students to the goal by clearly teaching the expectations for workshop activities. In almost all of its elements, Monica's goal was a PEERS goal.

CHECKLIST: PEERS GOALS

A PEERS GOAL IS	✔
Powerful: Makes a big difference children's lives.	
Easy: Simple, clear, and easy to understand.	
Emotionally Compelling: Matters a lot to the teacher.	
Reachable: Identifies a measureable outcome and strategy.	
Student-Focused: Addresses a student achievement, behavior, or attitude outcome.	

 Available for download at **resources.corwin.com/impactcycle**

QUESTIONS TO IDENTIFY A PEERS GOAL

Questioning is an essential part of all three stages of the Impact Cycle, so to better understand questioning, as I'll explain in more detail later in this chapter, I have interviewed coaching experts, read books and articles, and learned from the instructional coaches in Topeka, Kansas, Beaverton, Oregon, and Othello, Washington, who partnered with our research teams. I also learned quite a bit about questioning from a surprising source: our family doctor. When I was organizing this chapter, I visited Dr. Samantha Durland, and since she's always impressed me as an awesome

> *The skill of the coach is the art of questioning. Asking incisive questions forces people to think, to discover, to search.*
>
> **—Larry Bossidy and Ram Charan**
> *Execution: The Discipline of Getting Things Done (2002, p. 74)*

questioner, I asked her if she had any tips. She didn't disappoint me. Sam gave me some new ideas to ponder and reinforced many ideas that I had found as I studied the literature, during interviews, and with coaches. I left my appointment with my health on track and my notebook full of new ideas about questioning.

CREATING A WELCOMING ENVIRONMENT

One thing my doctor told me is that she is very intentional about trying to create a setting where people feel at ease right from the moment they enter her office so that they will be more likely to respond honestly to questions. Sam is designing a new clinic, and she told me that in the new setting, she's going to have people name their favorite song as part of the paperwork they fill in when they come to the clinic. Then when the patients come to the examination, Sam will have their song playing when they sit down for a visit. She will also have some soothing treats in the waiting area, like chilled water with cucumber slices, and she's even considering having certain scents piped into her facility, all with the goal of creating a space where people feel comfortable talking.

For Dr. Durland, the most important part of creating a welcoming environment is learning about her patients. The more she knows about what stresses or soothes them, the better she can respond to them in a way that puts them at ease, and the more open her patients will be to learning how to become healthier.

I've yet to meet an instructional coach who has figured out how to pipe sweet scents into a school (no matter how much they might want to), but coaches can do a lot to create a welcoming environment. As with Dr. Durland and her patients, the ability to put teachers at ease likely starts with learning about them. If coaches find out that a teacher likes chocolate (and who doesn't?), they might bring chocolate to a meeting. If teachers feel most at home meeting in their classroom, then coach and teacher can meet in the teacher's classroom. What matters is that the coach learns about collaborating teachers and does what he can do to put them at ease.

There are other simple things an instructional coach can do to put teachers at ease. For example, coaching should always take place in a setting where conversations are private. Teachers may be guarded if they are speaking where other teachers can hear them. To the best of their abilities, coaches also need to find places where coach

Creating a Welcoming Setting

Do everything you can to create a welcoming setting for coaching.

and teacher will not be interrupted. For example, a coach can put a do not disturb sign on the door to the room where coaching is occurring to keep people from interrupting. To get the best answers, coaches should do all they can to create welcoming environments for coaching conversations. Teachers who are on edge won't get as much out of coaching as teachers who are at ease.

BUILDING TRUST

Dr. Durland also told me that her questioning is effective only when her patients trust her. We have found the same thing again and again as we've studied coaching. When I went to Florida with a team of researchers to study some highly effective coaches, interview after interview emphasized that trust is critical for coaching.

I have written at length about trust in *Better Conversations: Coaching Ourselves and Each Other to Be More Credible, Caring, and Connected* (Knight, 2015). Here's a quick summary of the five factors that build trust.

First, people will trust you if you demonstrate a trustworthy character. A dishonest person will eventually be found out, and if people discover they have been lied to, they will have a hard time trusting again. Second, to foster trust, coaches should strive to be reliable. Coaches who do what they said they would do when they said they would do it are more likely to be trusted.

A third factor that influences trust is competence. We trust people who have the knowledge and skills to help us achieve our goals. For coaches, this means that getting better should always be a part of their game plan. Coaches should always be developing their coaching skills, content knowledge, and overall effectiveness. One way to do this is to apply and practice the Making It Real suggestions at the end of each chapter in this book. Coaches can improve their content knowledge by setting aside time to read, reread, summarize, synthesize, and describe the ideas and practices in the teaching manuals and books for the teaching strategies they share.

The fourth element in building trust is warmth. We are more likely to trust people who are warm toward us. We have found that coaches who do not demonstrate warmth, even when they possess expertise that could be extremely helpful for teachers, struggle to even get the coaching process started. Somebody who demonstrates warmth understands our needs and feelings, shares positive information frequently and effectively, listens,

Building Trust

1. **Character:** Are you honest, transparent, and non-judgmental? Do you need to change so that you can be more trustworthy?

2. **Reliability:** What can you say no to so that you have more time to be reliable? What rituals can you add to your daily routine (such as formal planning time, using reminders) so that you can be more reliable?

3. **Competence:** How can you increase your ability to help people realize their goals? Do you need to learn more teaching strategies or increase your depth of knowledge of the strategies you do share? Do you need to refine the way you employ the Impact Cycle?

4. **Warmth:** Do you need to improve the way you demonstrate empathy, make emotional connections, listen, and share positive information to encourage trust?

5. **Stewardship:** Do you need to change your outlook on life in some way so that you are less concerned with yourself and more concerned with others?

---

and builds emotional connections by making and responding to bids for emotional connection.[2]

Finally, the fifth element in trust is an attitude of stewardship or benevolence. We trust people who have our best interests at heart, and we hesitate to trust someone who seems to be primarily concerned with what's best for them. As one of the people we interviewed for my book *Better Conversations* (Knight, 2015) told me, "I have to know that a person is not going to screw me over if I am going to trust them."

LISTENING

If coaches don't listen effectively, it probably doesn't matter how they ask questions. Listening is such an essential communication skill that I have felt compelled to write about it in several other books (*Instructional Coaching*, *Unmistakable Impact* [Knight, 2007], *Better Conversations* [Knight, 2015]). My main point is always that good listening is primarily about authentically wanting to hear what the other person has to say and not about carefully

---

2. For more information on these and other effective communication habits, see my book *Better Conversations: Coaching Ourselves to Be More Credible, Caring, and Connected* (Knight, 2015).

1. Commit to listening.

2. Make sure your conversation partner is the speaker.

3. Pause and affirm before you respond to a comment.

4. Don't interrupt.

implementing a set of special listening techniques. If I am interested in another person's words and ideas and I genuinely care about what he or she has to say, I probably will be an effective listener.

When it comes to coaching, listening serves a practical purpose since coaches are thinking partners for collaborating teachers. For that reason, if coaches don't listen carefully, they will struggle to coach effectively. I describe listening as involving four elements. Good listeners (a) are committed to hearing what their conversation partners have to say, (b) keep their partners at the center of the conversation, (c) pause to affirm their partners before responding to their comments, and (d) make it a habit not to interrupt too frequently.

On some occasions, a coach may need to interrupt to encourage, empathize, or redirect. Tony Stotzfus, in *Coaching Questions: A Coach's Guide to Powerful Asking Skills* (2008) writes, "Part of your job as a coach is managing the conversation, so when you see a client bunny-trailing, interject with a question that brings things back to focus" (p. 15). For most coaches, however, the problem isn't failing to interrupt; it is a tendency to interrupt too often. All coaches can benefit from watching coaching conversations to see if their comments move the conversation forward or sidetrack the conversation.

One of the most helpful books I've read about questioning is not a coaching or a communication book but a book about research methods, Irving Seidman's *Interviewing as Qualitative Research: A Guide for Researchers in Education and the Social Sciences* (2013). I find Seidman's suggestions for researchers to be perfectly applicable to coaches.

Seidman proposes that researchers attend to three levels of listening during research interviews. First, interviewers must make sure they understand what a person is saying. I hope many of the suggestions in this chapter can help coaches do this more effectively. Second, Seidman suggests interviewers listen for the "inner voice" of the conversation partner, the real meaning in what people are saying, which often lies behind the actual words being spoken. Seidman, quoting George Steiner, contrasts the inner and outer voice. The outer voice, Steiner says, "always reflects an awareness of the audience" (p. 81). The outer voice, according to Seidman, "is not untrue; it is guarded" (p. 81) and often shows up in the cautious language people use. "Words like challenge and adventure," Seidman writes, "convey the positive aspects of a participant's grappling with a difficult experience but not the struggles" (pp. 81–82). The inner voice would reveal more about the difficult aspects of struggles. I believe the more collaborating teachers trust their coach, the more likely they are to speak from their "inner voice." As Susan Scott writes in *Fierce Leadership: A Bold Alternative to the Worst "Best" Practices of Business Today* (2009), "Listen for what is not being said as well as what is being said" (p. 142).

Finally, Seidman writes that interviewers need to remain aware of the process they engaged in as they listen. This means that coaches need to be aware of how much time is left for a particular conversation and how effectively they and their collaborating teacher are moving toward the targeted outcome for the conversation. This does not mean that the coach should rush through the coaching conversation to get to the outcome. Sometimes a coach who is paying careful attention to the coaching conversation may decide that the conversation is moving too fast and that it needs to slow down. What matters is that the coach listens to the collaborating teacher while also watching the process to make sure that the best chance for learning occurs.

> **Seidman's Three Levels of Listening**
> 1. What is said
> 2. The inner voice
> 3. The interview process

GETTING CLARITY

Another important aspect of questioning is for coaches to make sure that their questions are helping them clearly understand what a collaborating teacher is thinking. In everyday conversation, we often drift in and out, catching the main ideas of what is being said and missing some or sometimes a lot of the details. To be thinking partners, coaches must work hard to stay focused and understand exactly what a teacher is saying.

One way to get clarity is to ask only one question at a time so that it is easier for the collaborating teacher to formulate a well-organized, clear response and easier for the coach to understand the teacher. According to Jackie Walsh and Beth Sattes in *Leading Through Quality Questioning: Creating Capacity, Commitment, and Community* (2010), one of the most common errors questioners make is to ask "stacked" or "serialized" questions. The authors write, "Rather than posing a single question, we sometimes ask question after question, trying to clarify our own thinking. People don't know which question to think about when there is no clear focus" (p. 17).

Once they have asked a question, coaches need to give teachers the time to respond. This sounds so obvious, but what I've seen on video is that many coaches struggle to let their collaborating teachers finish their thoughts and often jump in to fill the silence rather than letting their teachers complete their thoughts. A better strategy is to do what Susan Scott suggests in *Fierce Conversations: Achieving Success at Work & in Life One Conversation at a Time* (2002), "Let silence do the heavy lifting" (p. 218).

A final simple but important piece of advice for coaches who want to clearly understand what their collaborating teachers are thinking is to ask questions whenever they are unsure of something a teacher has said. Sometimes we need to ask questions because, for whatever reason, we were distracted and lost track of the conversation. If that's the case, we should simply let the teacher know and say something like, "I apologize. I got distracted after you mentioned the new grading program, thinking about other people's experiences with the program. Could you go back to that part of the conversation and start over?"

A second clarifying question is to ask teachers to define any words or concepts that might be vague, imprecise, or open to multiple definitions. For example, if a teacher says he wants students to be more engaged, a coach will find it easier to think with the teacher by asking him to define *engagement*. A coach might prompt a collaborating teacher to explain what engaged students would look like by asking, "Can you paint a picture of engagement?" or propose more precise definitions such as Phil Schlecty's (2011) distinctions between noncompliance, strategic compliance, and authentic engagement. Creating a common understanding of words and concepts is an important way coaches get clarity on what teachers think.

Getting Clarity

Ask one question at a time. Give your conversation partner plenty of time to respond. Don't jump in right away when there is silence.

Ask additional questions whenever you need to backtrack, define words, or better understand anything your conversation partner is saying.

ASKING FOR MORE

Those who write about questioning often talk about the power of asking probing questions, but Seidman (2013) suggests that probing questions might not be the best:

I have never been comfortable with that word [probe]. I always think of a sharp instrument pressing on soft flesh when I hear it. The word also conveys a sense of the powerful interviewer treating the participant as an object. I am more comfortable with the notion of exploring with the participant than with probing into what the participant says. (p. 86)

In *The Coaching Habit: Say Less, Ask More, and Change the Way You Lead Forever* (2016), Michael Bungay Stanier offers a simple but powerful question for the mutual exploring suggested by Seidman. For Bungay Stanier, the "best coaching question in the world" is "And What Else?" (p. 56). He writes, "I know they seem innocuous. Three little words. But '**A**nd **W**hat **E**lse?'—the AWE question—has magical properties. With seemingly no effort, it creates more—more wisdom, more insights, more self-awareness, more possibilities—out of thin air" (pp. 57–58).

Since reading Bungay Stanier's *The Coaching Habit,* I have started asking this question, and it is indeed powerful. Having modified the question slightly, usually just asking, "What else?" I have found that there is almost always "something else," some important information, deeper insight, or better strategy for moving forward. Often, the best part of the coaching conversation happens after I ask, "What else?"

Asking for More

Rather than asking probing questions, ask "And What Else?"

LEARNING RATHER THAN JUDGING

In *Rising Strong: The Reckoning. The Rumble. The Revolution* (2015), Brené Brown tells about an encounter with a roommate she is forced to stay with when she travels to a conference to give a presentation. The story is powerful (equal parts gross and hilarious)—I'll let you read her book to get the full effect—but the result of this encounter prompted Brown to start obsessively asking everyone she meets a simple question, "Do you think, in general, that people are doing the best they can?"

After asking dozens of people this question, she eventually asked her husband, Steve, who, she writes, "as a pediatrician, . . . sees the best and worst in people" (p. 113). Steve takes a long time to think about how to answer the question but eventually answers, "I don't know. I really don't. All I know is that my life is better when I assume that people are doing their best. It keeps me out of judgment and lets me focus on what is, and not what should be.' His answer felt like truth to me. Not an easy truth, but truth" (p. 113).

Steve's answer feels like truth for instructional coaches, too. Judgment, as I have said many times, is a learning killer, and if teachers feel judged, they will not open up. When people feel judged, they don't feel comfortable sharing the kinds of thoughts and feelings that are necessary for learning. If coaches want teachers to share with them, they need to be careful to withhold judgment. The best way to do that is to assume that teachers are doing their best.

Learning Rather Than Judging

Assume people are doing their best.

Adopt a learner mindset.

Marilee Adams, in *Change Your Questions Change Your Life: 12 Powerful Tools for Leadership, Coaching, and Life* (2016), suggests that the best way to learn more from your questions is to reject a "judger mindset" and adopt a "learner mindset." "In every moment of our lives," Adams writes, "we're faced with choosing between the Learner Mindset path and the Judger Mindset path" (p. 39). Building on Adams's distinction, Michael Marquardt, in *Leading With Questions: How Leaders Find the Right Solutions by Knowing What to Ask* (2014), offers "specific suggestions that can help you coach others and adopt a learning attitude":

- Respond without judging the thoughts, feelings, or situations of other people.
- Consider yourself a beginner, regardless of experience.
- Avoid focusing on your own role (which can lead to a self-protective approach) and take the role of an outside observer, researcher, or reporter. [detach]
- Look at the situation from multiple perspectives, especially your respondents'.
- Look for win-win solutions.
- Be tolerant of yourself and others.
- Ask clarifying questions.
- Accept change as constant, and embrace it. (p. 110)

KEEPING OURSELVES OUT OF THE ANSWERS

When we ask questions, we also need to work hard not to shape our conversation partners' answers. Sometimes, the way we ask can subtly or not-so-subtly suggest the answer we want to hear, and, as a result, collaborating teachers may end up telling us what we want to hear rather than what they really think. Good questioners let the person answering the question speak his or her truth.

One way we shape others' responses is by asking leading questions. Leading questions are questions that contain our answer within them and therefore, "lead" or guide the responder to a particular answer. For example, if a teacher is asked, "You don't think those students were engaged, do you?" the teacher will recognize that the interviewer already has an answer in mind (the students weren't engaged) and that she would be disagreeing with the interviewer by saying anything other than what is proposed by the question.

We can also interfere with our conversation partner's ability to answer freely and candidly by asking questions that are advice disguised as a question, one of my own biggest weaknesses. Putting a question mark at the end of a suggestion doesn't stop a question from being advice. Asking, "Don't you think you should ask more open questions?" is only slightly different from saying, "I think you should ask more open questions." In either case, the coach is telling the teacher what to do and not coaching him or her.

Coaches who habitually ask questions in the way I suggest here will likely be very effective at questioning. However, coaches who spend the entire coaching conversation thinking about these suggestions could easily miss what collaborating teachers say. What then is a coach to do?

I suggest that coaches practice these skills until they become habits that don't require a lot of conscious thought. Journalist Charles Duhigg explains in his book *Habit: Why We Do What We Do in Life and Business* (2012) that a habit "is a formula our brain automatically follows" (p. 285), a "choice that we deliberately make at some point, and then stop thinking about, but continue doing every day" (p. 284).

The easiest way for coaches to turn these listening and questioning strategies into habits is to video record their coaching conversations and then review their questioning to see which habits they are adopting and which ones still need development. To help with this review, I've created the following questioning and listening checklist.[3]

---

3. Coaches can improve their communication skills by reading and applying the beliefs and habits described in *Better Conversations* (Knight, 2015). In the book, I explain how people can use video recordings of their conversations to improve the way they interact. You can download more than 30 forms to help you reflect on your communication habits at resources.corwin.com/knightbetterconversations.

✔ CHECKLIST: LISTENING AND QUESTIONING EFFECTIVELY

TO LISTEN AND QUESTION EFFECTIVELY, I	✔
Make sure my conversation partner does most of the talking.	
Pause and affirm before I start talking.	
Don't interrupt (except when it is very helpful).	
Ask one question at a time.	
Ask for clarification when I'm not certain what is being said.	
Ask, "And what else?"	
Assume people are doing their best.	
Am non-judgmental.	
Avoid leading questions.	
Avoid giving advice disguised as a question.	

 Available for download at **resources.corwin.com/impactcycle**

THE IDENTIFY QUESTIONS

Between 2009 and 2012, our research team partnered with instructional coaches Michelle Harris, Susan Leyden, Jennifer MacMillan, and Lea Molczan from the Beaverton, Oregon, School District. As partners in our Lean-Design Methodology,[4] the Beaverton coaches implemented early versions of the Impact Cycle, identified roadblocks encountered during implementation, helped us develop ways around the roadblocks, and then tried out the refined Impact Cycle, repeating the cycle as needed to get better and better.

As part of this process, our researchers at the University of Kansas and the coaches from Beaverton, Oregon, participated in three-day learning and problem-solving meetings two or three times a year in Kansas. During our time together, we would watch video of the coaches coaching, discuss what

---

4. For more information on our Lean-Design Research Model, please see the Appendix at the end of this book, starting on page 247.

was working, and identify what needed to be improved. Then, the coaches would return to Oregon and implement the changes so we could see how well they worked.

During our first learning and problem-solving meeting in 2009, we soon realized as we watched videos of coaching sessions that we needed to develop better questions to guide the Identify phase of coaching. As luck would have it, our meeting occurred about two weeks before the National Staff Development Council National Conference (NSDC) (now the Learning Forward Conference). I went to the conference with a clear agenda—I wanted to learn as much about questioning as I could, so I scheduled interviews with many of the leading coaching experts who all generously shared their best ideas about coaching.

I started my quest for questioning knowledge with a breakfast meeting with Bruce Wellman, author and co-author of a number of books on coaching and questioning, including *Data-Driven Dialogue* (2004) and *Mentoring Matters* (1994), when he happened to be in Kansas the week before the conference. Then, at the NSDC conference over lunches and coffees, I talked with the experts, including math coaching expert Lucy West, author of *Agents of Change* (2013) and *Content-Focused Coaching* (2003); questioning and coaching expert Steve Barkley, author of *Questions for Life* (2011b) and *Instructional Coaching With the End in Mind* (2011a); literacy coaching expert Cathy Toll, author of *The Literacy Coach's Survival Guide* (2006) and *The Literacy Coach's Desk Reference* (2007); and Joellen Killion, author with Cindy Harrison of *Coaching Matters* (2012) and *Taking the Lead: New Roles for Teachers and School-Based Coaches* (2006). I also participated in a daylong workshop led by communication expert Susan Scott, author of *Fierce Conversations* (2002) and *Fierce Leadership* (2009).

I took what I learned from these coaching experts and drafted a preliminary set of questions that the Beaverton coaches started to use as they moved through the Impact Cycle. I also reviewed and continue to review publications about questioning and coaching that informed this chapter. Over time, the coaches from Oregon and Washington and our research team developed, tested, and refined a list of questions that have proven to be very powerful in structuring conversations to identify a goal. When Jackie sat down with Monica to set a PEERS goal, the Identify Questions were at the heart of their conversation.

Instructional coaches use the Identify Questions to help teachers identify a PEERS goal. They ask the questions after the teacher has gained a clear picture of reality, either by watching video of the lesson, reviewing student work, learning about interviews with students, reviewing observation data,

The Identify Questions

1. On a scale of 1–10, with 1 being the worst lesson you've taught and 10 being the best, how would you rank that lesson?

2. What pleased you about the lesson?

3. What would have to change to move the lesso   10?

4. What would your students be doing differe   was a 10?

5. Tell me more about what that would look

6. How could we measure that change?

7. Do you want that to be your goal?

8. If you could hit that goal, would it   ?

9. What teaching strategy can you

10. What are your next steps?

Video 3.1

Crysta Answers the Identify Questions to Set a PEERS Goal

Video 3.2

Cat Answers the Identify Questions to Set a PEERS Goal

resources.corwin.com/impactcycle

or some combination of these methods. If a teacher watches video of the lesson, the questions would be the focus on the coaching conversation. If the coach needs to share data with the teacher, the questions would be asked after the information has been shared. Each question serves a specific purpose during the coaching conversation.

The questions are not to be asked robotically, the same way in each conversation. Instead, they are markers for a living conversation that is different every time, and most coaches eventually find other useful questions for their coaching conversations.[5] What matters is that coaches collaborate with teachers to identify goals that will have a powerful, positive impact on student learning and well-being. If the Identify coaching session ends with a PEERS goal, then whatever questions were asked proved successful. The Identify Questions we use and why we use them are described on the following pages.

---

5. A very helpful book on coaching questions is Tony Stoltzfus's *Coaching Questions: A Coach's Guide to Powerful Asking Skills* (2008).

1. On a scale of 1–10, with 1 being the worst lesson you've taught and 10 being the best, how would you rank that lesson? In our early years studying instructional coaching, we asked a simple question to break the ice: "How do you think the lesson went?" What we found, however, and what Joellen Killion confirmed when I interviewed her, was that this question rarely leads to useful information. For most people, the answer to the question "How did it go?" is "fine," "OK," "not too bad," or some other generic and meaningless phrase. We needed a different question to start the Impact Cycle.

When I spoke with Steve Barkley, he told me that he found scaling questions to be very helpful. Paul Jackson and Janine Waldman wrote in *Positively Speaking: The Art of Constructive Conversations With a Solutions Focus* (2011):

> The scale is a near-universal tool for measurement, used by doctors to ask patients to measure pain, teachers to rate achievement and on feedback questionnaires to show degrees of satisfaction. It's often used where 10/10 is the desired result and anything below that is not good enough. (p. 57)

Jackson and Waldman explain that scaling is "an effective tool for constructive conversations" because it helps people focus on "how they would like things to be," "helps elaborate their strengths," encourages "further change" by "measuring change," can be a "way of confirming progress" when repeated, and "is a means of deciding priorities and next steps" (p. 57).

Asking teachers to rank their lesson on a scale of 1–10 also signals to teachers that they are in charge of the coaching process. We want teachers to see that in our coaching conversations they are not passive recipients but the primary decision makers and thinkers—not watching the game, but making

> *Change has to come from within. It can't be dictated, demanded or otherwise forced upon people. A man or woman who does not wholeheartedly commit to change will never change.*
>
> —Marshall Goldsmith
> *Triggers: Creating Behavior That Lasts—Becoming the Person You Want to Be* (2015, pp. 7–8)

the plays. The instructional coach's genuine concern should be to listen, learn, and think with his collaborating teachers, not to use questions to direct teachers to some predetermined destination.

2. What pleased you about the lesson? Real learning is difficult if we don't have a clear picture of reality. As Jim Collins wrote in *Good to Great* (2001), to become great, "you must maintain unwavering faith that you can and will prevail in the end, regardless of the difficulties, AND *at the same time* have the discipline to confront the most brutal facts of your current reality, whatever they might be" (p. 13).

> *Positive thinking too easily becomes a form of medication. The more we have to remind ourselves to think positively, the more we are in the business of denying our despair at the struggles we see around us.*
>
> **—Peter Block**
> *The Answer to How Is Yes: Acting on What Matters* (2002, p. 88)

A purely rose-colored picture of reality probably won't lead to a better reality, so why would we prompt teachers to talk about what went well? The simple truth is that a negative view of reality is equally ineffective. Most of the coaches we've partnered with report that teachers who talk about their lessons are often much harder on themselves than anyone else would ever be. If teachers are going to get a clear picture of reality, then, it is important for them to see both what went well and what did not go well during their lesson. That is, pausing to consider what worked is at least as important as discussing what did not work.

The case for considering what is going well was powerfully stated by Martin Seligman and Mihaly Csikszentmihalyi in a landmark article about the field of positive psychology in a 2000 issue of *The American Psychologist*. The authors wrote, "Psychology is not just the study of pathology, weakness, and damage; it is about the study of strength and virtue" (p. 7). Their message is as clear for coaches as it is for psychologists: if we focus only on what has gone wrong, we might not see what is most important—what went well.

In instructional coaching, identifying what is going well can be a point of departure for getting better. In *High-Impact Instruction* (Knight, 2013), I tell the story of instructional coach Lea Molczan and reading specialist Jody Johnson, who were part of our coaching study with Beaverton, Oregon, Public Schools. Lea video recorded Jody teaching a lesson to her seventh-grade reading class, and afterward, Jody and Lea watched the video. When they watched the video separately, Jody and Lea both saw that it took students about eight minutes to settle in for the start of the lesson. Together, they set the goal for the students to be settled in to learn within three minutes of the bell. Since they were also were looking for what went well in the lesson, they noticed that although students were off task at the start of the lesson, they were very engaged and really enjoyed guided reading, largely because Jody was a master storyteller.

To hit the goal, Jody taught students expectations for the start of the class and shifted guided reading to the start of the class, telling students that guided reading would last ten minutes and that it would not start until they were ready. If it took them eight minutes to settle in, they would have only two minutes of guided reading. That simple shift changed everything about the class, and students actually settled in within two minutes. By taking advantage of what was going well, Jody added seven minutes of instructional time to each lesson. Spread across an entire year, that's more than a month of instruction.

Starting the class with students engaged changed the entire class. At the end of the year, all students showed great gains on the state reading test, and almost all students met proficiency even though none of the students, Lea told me, "had ever hit proficiency before." Because they had identified what was going well in the class to find a solution to their problem, Jody's students made more improvement than most would have considered possible.

3. What would have to change to move the lesson closer to a 10? It should be clear by now that the purpose of instructional coaching is not to perseverate on what is going wrong. During instructional coaching, we try to keep the focus on what can be done, not what isn't working. Thus, if a teacher says, "These students are so difficult to teach," instructional coaches should acknowledge the almost inevitable challenges of the emotionally complex creative work of teaching, but should also try to keep the focus on learning and improving perhaps by asking a question, "What would it look like if the students were acting in ways that promote their learning?"

The focus on a solution becomes clearer when coaches ask teachers to describe the change they want to see. Such questions ground the discussion in reality, while keeping the focus on a better possible future. Both issues are important because if the teacher jumps too quickly to a solution (I need to be more consistent correcting my students!), they may end up spending a lot of energy working hard to solve the wrong problem.

The goal of instructional coaching, then, is similar to the goal of solution-focused coaching as described by Paul Jackson and Mark McKergow in *The Solutions Focus: Making Coaching and Change Simple* (2013). Jackson and McKergow suggest a so-called miracle question:

> Suppose that tonight you go to bed—and you go to sleep as usual—and during the night a miracle happens—and the problem vanishes—and the issues that concern you are resolved—but you're asleep, so you don't know that the miracle has happened—so when you wake up tomorrow what will be the first things that tell you that the miracle has happened? How will you know that the transformation has occurred? (p. 32)

Within instructional coaching, the miracle question is asking the teacher, "What would have to change to make the lesson closer to a 10?" This question puts everyone's attention fully on the future and is a big step toward setting a goal. It also gives teachers an opportunity to consider what is most important to their students and to them. Additional questions can then flesh out exactly what the goal will be and how it will be achieved.

4. What would your students be doing differently if your class was a 10? While the overall structure and processes of education may appear to be fixed, the reality is that teachers are asked or told to change all the time. The trouble is that the changes they are asked to implement are too often good solutions to the wrong problem, like, as organizational change expert Peter Block says, throwing a fire extinguisher to a drowning person.

One common misguided solution is to focus on teaching strategies rather than student achievement and well-being. When teachers think about strategies rather than students' needs, they risk implementing a new practice that doesn't make much of a difference for students. A teacher who chooses to increase classroom structure and control when what his students really need is to understand why learning is relevant for them may find that, like the fire extinguisher tossed to the drowning person, his solution actually makes things worse, not better.

Asking "What would your students be doing differently if your class was a 10?" also helps people resist the #1 temptation facing all coaches: the temptation to give advice. In *The Coaching Habit: Say Less, Ask More, and Change the Way You Lead Forever* (2016), Michael Bungay Stanier writes that coaches find it difficult to learn to tame the "advice monster" and "stay curious" since "even if it is the wrong advice—and it often is—giving it feels more comfortable than the ambiguity of asking a question" (p. 60).

> You have the best of intentions to stay curious and ask a few good questions. But in the moment, just as you are moving to a better way of working, the Advice Monster leaps out of the darkness and hijacks the conversation. Before you realize what's happening, your mind is turned towards finding the Answer and you're leaping in to offer ideas, suggestions and recommended ways forward.
>
> —**Michael Bungay Stanier**
> *The Coaching Habit: Say Less, Ask More, and Change the Way You Lead Forever* (2016, p. 60)

Advice has its place, but there are at least two problems with advising rather than asking. First, when we give advice, we are doing the thinking for our collaborating teachers, which is problematic for all of the reasons mentioned in Chapter 2. Second, when we do all the thinking, we decrease our collaborating teachers' ownership of the solution and decrease their commitment to change. After solving teachers' problems for them, we shouldn't be surprised if they eventually tell us, "I did what you said to, and it didn't work."

A third false solution is to prematurely focus on numbers and achievement scores rather than student needs. Most teachers can't avoid achievement scores—they are an unpleasant part of the education environment, like mosquitoes at a picnic. However, if educators turn their eyes only toward student achievement scores, they could easily miss seeing what students really need. This question puts the attention of coach and teacher directly where it should be, on what's best for students.

5. Tell me more about what that would look like. In his book *The Coaching Habit* (2016), Michael Bungay Stanier says that the greatest coaching question in the world is the AWE question: "And what else?" The AWE question is also another way to "tame the advice monster," as Stanier notes, because by expanding the scope of the coaching conversation, it increases the likelihood that the true problem will be addressed.

In the Impact Cycle, the request to "Tell me more about what the change would look like" performs the same function as the AWE question. Before turning directly to the specific issues of pinning down a measurable goal and identifying strategies for hitting that goal, the AWE question provides teacher and coach an opportunity to look at the classroom from a broader perspective.

It also helps them get clearer on exactly what kind of change the teacher hopes to see in the classroom. Powerful coaching conversations can transform vague thoughts and feelings into concrete descriptions. Teachers might not know what they really want until they sit down with their coach and pin down just what the change should look like. A high school language arts teacher, for example, might say he wants students to be more engaged, but by answering this question, he might come to see that what he really wants is for his students to recognize how important writing is for their success and well-being in life. That clearer understanding of what the teacher wants for his students could lead to a much more effective strategy for moving forward.

6. How could we measure that change? For coaching to succeed, there has to be a finish line, and often that finish line involves a number. Numbers have limitations, and not all goals need to be numbers. What teachers and coaches need is a clear description of what will be different if a teacher meets a goal. Without that definition, without a destination for their coaching journey, coach and teacher risk wasting a lot of time going nowhere. Some way of identifying the endpoint for the coaching, therefore, is necessary, and often that endpoint is a number.

One advantage of quantifying the goal is that it can bring into focus some aspects of the classroom that might be otherwise overlooked. For example, teachers who watch videos of their lessons to pay particular attention to transition time, teacher talk vs. student talk, or the level of questions asked, may notice aspects of their lesson that otherwise they would have missed.

However, data are also important because they help teacher and coach assess whether or not what they are doing is making a difference. Like a stopwatch used to measure improvement in how fast someone runs, data help teacher and coach determine if the changes the teacher is implementing are moving students toward the goal. For this reason, regardless of what measure is identified, it must be one that can be taken frequently, at least once a week, so teacher and coach can see if they are on track. Data help coach and teacher ensure that they are on track and make adjustments when necessary (and adjustments are almost always necessary) so that the goal can be met. Coaching that relies on a measure that can be taken only once or twice a year is based more on wishful thinking than on effecting strategy and learning.

7. Do you want that to be your goal? It is not by chance that this question is seventh rather than first. Coach and teacher need to guard against too quickly jumping to a goal that seems to look the way a goal should look. The six preceding questions are designed to ensure that teachers choose a goal that will make a real difference for students and for them.

These questions are necessary because many teachers do not know what they want until they have reviewed video of their lessons and moved through these questions. As Michael Bungay Stanier (2016) writes, "We often don't know what we want . . . the question, 'But what do you really want?' will typically stop people in their tracks" (p. 112).

This question also clearly communicates that instructional coaching is for the collaborating teacher and his students. Coaching is an act of service, a way of helping others achieve their goals, and not something that teachers do to please their coach. Also, when teachers fully understand that coaching is guided by their desires and concerns, their interest in coaching increases.

It has to be their [teachers'] goal. When people set their goal, the coaching conversation kind of takes on a life of its own because they get really excited about it. You connect them back with their passion.

—Sue Woodruff
Instructional Coach and Educational
Consultant, Grand Rapids, Michigan

8. If you could hit that goal, would it really matter to you?

Before we turn to the practical discussion of how a teacher will achieve her goal, it is important to take a minute to ensure that the goal the teacher has chosen is one that she is convinced will be a great use of her time. Unless the teacher cares deeply about the goal, it simply will not be met. Instructional coaches should strive to help teachers identify a goal that is truly important to them. They should partner with teachers on the issue that is the thing teachers think about when they drive home from school, the concern that first pops into their head when they wake up in the morning.

One instructional coach from the Othello group I was coaching told me that she was struggling to get her teacher to identify a goal. "She [the collaborating teacher] doesn't want to set a goal for the whole class. This teacher won't stop talking about two students who are learning English and struggling in her class."

"Why don't you set a goal for those students?" I asked.

"Can I do that?" asked the coach. "Won't the other kids be missing out if she focuses on those two students?"

My response was, "If that's what your teacher is most concerned with, that should definitely be your focus, and I bet all students will benefit when you hit the goal."

The question, "If you could hit that goal, would it really matter to you?" is essential because people don't do the hard work necessary unless a goal matters to them deeply. As Heath and Heath write in *Switch* (2010), effective goals are "motivational," "inspirational," and they tap "into feeling." A goal shouldn't just be "big and compelling; it should hit you in the gut" (p. 76).

9. What teaching strategy can you use to hit your goal? This question is where instructional coaching parts company from many other approaches to coaching. Facilitative coaches, for example, work from the assumption that teachers have the knowledge they need to meet their goals and that, therefore, the role of the coach is to ask questions that help teachers understand what they must do. Instructional coaches, in contrast, work from the assumption that high-impact instructional practices may be needed to help teachers meet their goals.

Since instructional coaches frequently need to share teaching strategies with teachers, they must have a deep understanding of a small number of high-impact teaching practices. Often those practices are described in an instructional playbook such as the one included in the Instructional Coaches' Toolkit and described in Chapter 4. Such understanding is essential. If coaches are to help teachers hit their goals, they need to be prepared to share strategies that will help hit those goals. Indeed, given that billions of dollars have been spent on research identifying effective teaching, it seems almost criminal to ignore that research when coaching conversations are focused on instruction.

This does not mean, however, that coaches should move into a top-down form of communication, telling teachers what they should do to meet their goals. As I've emphasized throughout this book, if teachers don't make the majority of the decisions around their practice, if they aren't doing most of the thinking during coaching, they won't be embracing the solution. Teachers need to do the thinking and choosing, and instructional coaches need to make that easy for teachers.

I found an interesting analogy for the task the coach faces in an unlikely place, The Cheesecake Factory restaurant I visited while attending a conference with my wife, Jenny. When we sat down in the restaurant, we were handed the most detailed menu I have ever seen. The restaurant's website states that it offers over 250 different items. I found all those options impossible to sort through, and just when I was about to give up, our server showed up to help me make a choice. The server knew the menu inside and out, and he asked a few questions to determine what I might find tasty. Then, he pointed out a few options that seemed in line with what interested me. Never once did the server tell me what to do; he just helped me sort through the options so I was able to make my own choice.

In many ways, the work of an instructional coach is much like that of our server's at the restaurant. A coach needs to have a deep understanding of teaching strategies and must then help the teacher choose the best practices for her or his particular situation. To accomplish this, instructional coaches should withhold suggestions at first to see if their collaborating teachers know what teaching strategies to use to hit their goal. When teachers are unsure, a coach can explain some options that might be in line with the collaborating teacher's interests, explaining each option as a possibility, and making it clear that the teacher is only going to do what they choose to do.

An instructional coach collaborating with a teacher who wants to increase authentic engagement in her classroom, for example, could propose that engagement might increase if the teacher shifted to more open-ended questions, used thinking prompts to capture student attention, included more authentic learning activities so students could better see the relevance of their learning, or teach the learning and behavioral expectations more explicitly so that students knew what they were to do and how they were to do it.

There's a difference between having expertise and showing up as the expert. I think a coach has to be willing to be vulnerable and to say things like, "Let's try this and see what happens. I don't know how this is going to turn out. I think that's critical to building trust." It takes a certain amount of vulnerability to say that you don't have a guaranteed solution. You want to go in and you want to make their lives better. But our job is not to be fixers. Teachers are not broken and they don't need us to fix them. They need us to walk alongside them.

—Laurelin Andrade
Instructional Coach, Salem-Keizer
Public Schools, Salem, Oregon

When coach and teacher discuss the question, "What teaching strategy will you use to hit your goal?" the coach has to be intentional about ensuring that the conversation is a true dialogue. To encourage dialogue, instructional coaches balance advocacy with inquiry by fighting their desire to solve teachers' problems, by listening effectively, and by posing all ideas provisionally. To engage in dialogue means always to make room for the teacher's voice. However, this doesn't mean coaches silence their voices. A dialogue is two or more people thinking together, and the coach needs to be one of the brains involved in the conversation. Coaches just need to make sure they don't become the entire conversation.

Video 3.3

Crysta Identifies a Teaching Strategy to Use to Hit Her Goal

Video 3.4

Cat Identifies a Teaching Strategy to Use to Hit Her Goal

resources.corwin.com/impactcycle

10. What are the next steps? David Allen is probably our generation's leading expert on time management. The planning process he describes in his book *Getting Things Done: The Art of Stress-Free Productivity* (2002), often shortened to GTD, is embraced with the kind of zeal usually saved for rock stars. Central to Allen's GTD process is determining the next action. According to Allen, "When a culture adopts 'What's the next action?' as a standard operating query, there's an automatic increase in energy, productivity, clarity, and focus" (p. 236).

I have a personal mission to make "What's the next action?" part of the global thought process. I envision a world in which no meeting or discussion will end, and no interaction cease, with a clear determination of whether or not some action is needed—and if it is, what it will be, or at least who has responsibility for it. I envision organizations adopting a standard that anything that lands in anyone's "ten acres" will be evaluated for action required, and the resulting decisions managed appropriately. Imagine the freedom that would allow to focus attention on bigger issues and opportunities.

—**David Allen**
Getting Things Done (2002, p. 236)

The question "What are the next steps?" pins down the specific next actions that must be taken to move the coaching process forward and identifies when the actions will happen. Within the Impact Cycle, coach and teacher need to clarify when and where the next coaching sessions will occur and what will happen during those sessions.

In most cases, the next action following the Identify stage of instructional coaching is to determine when coach and teacher will meet so that the coach can explain the new teaching strategy to be implemented. Following that, coach and teacher should confirm how the collaborating teacher will get to see the new teaching strategy being used. (In Chapter 4, I explain that there are at least six ways that new teaching strategies can be modeled.) Coach and teacher should also discuss when the teacher will implement the strategy and when they will discuss how well the implementation went.

Next Actions After Identify

- Determine when coach and teacher will meet so coach can explain the new teaching strategies.
- Determine when modeling of the teaching strategy will occur.
- Determine whether or not teacher and coach will discuss modeling after it occurs (this a great idea, if time permits).
- Determine when the collaborating teacher will implement the new teaching strategy.
- Determine when coach and teacher will meet to discuss the successes and challenges of implementation.

When I'm leading professional development sessions for instructional coaches, I'm often asked whether I think coaches and teachers should identify the date when they will meet the goal. Others ask me how long I think it should take for a teacher to hit a goal.

With regard to the first question, we have found that setting a deadline for coaching is actually counterproductive. Certainly, coach and teacher should carefully plan when they will meet and what they will accomplish, but each coaching session is so unique that effective coaching rarely conforms to a set schedule.

In terms of how long it will take to hit a goal, we have found that, on average, coaching from start to finish requires 5–6 hours, but the crucial words here are "on average." Sometimes coaches and teachers can set and hit goals in 2–3 hours, but at other times hitting a goal takes much longer. A new teacher who feels overwhelmed by planning lessons, who is struggling to manage student behavior, and who likes a lot of support, will need a lot more time than an independent teacher with a lot of experience who wants her students to better understand how to compare and contrast.

Deciding on a set amount of time for coaching makes scheduling easier, and it likely feels reassuring at the start. However, for deep coaching, which involves a powerful goal that is clearly met, trying to squeeze the coaching into six weeks or stretching it out after a goal has been hit isn't as sensible as simply continuing coaching until the goal has been met.

MAKING IT REAL

For some reason, coaches sometimes hesitate to use the Identify Questions. When they eventually do, however, they tell me again and again that they can't believe how easily they guide themselves and their collaborating teachers to a PEERS goal. The truth is that to make this part of the Identify stage real, coaches just have to do it! As with swimming, this can't be learned only from a book; you've got to dive into the pool and swim.

One simple way to practice this process is for coaches to partner with other coaches. The coaches can video record a lesson and share the video with each other. Then, the partners can get together and use the questions with each other. This can involve two coaches or a group. Once coaches have coached another person, and have experienced being coached, it is sometimes easier for them to use the Identify Questions with teachers.

One of the most powerful ways coaches can improve their coaching skills is to video record their coaching conversations and use the Listening and Question checklist included here to review their video and improve their practice. To get really good at coaching, coaches should record and review at least one coaching conversation a week until they are totally satisfied with what they see themselves doing on video. Even then, coaches should continue to record and review video at least once each month—listening and questioning are that important for effective coaching.

TO SUM UP

- When teachers set PEERS goals, coaching gains a momentum of its own.
- PEERS goals are powerful, easy, emotionally compelling, reachable, and student-focused:
  - Powerful: Will this goal, when reached, make a big difference in students' lives?
  - Easy: Is this goal simple, clear, and easy to understand?
  - Emotionally Compelling: Does this goal really matter to the teacher?
  - Reachable: Has the teacher identified a measurable outcome and a strategy to meet that outcome?
  - Student-Focused: Is this goal about student achievement, behavior, or attitude rather than the teacher or a strategy?

- Since coaches are thinking partners with teachers, they must be skilled listeners and questioners. To listen effectively, coaches (and anyone else who wants to listen effectively) need to (a) commit to listening, (b) make sure their conversation partners are the speakers, (c) pause and affirm before responding, and (d) avoid interrupting.

- To question effectively, coaches should ask one question at a time, avoid leading questions, avoid giving advice disguised as a question, and use the other questioning strategies described in this chapter.

- Coaches can use the Identify Questions to help teachers develop PEERS goals:

  1. On a scale of 1–10, with 1 being the worst lesson you've taught and 10 being the best, how would you rank that lesson?
  2. What pleased you about the lesson?
  3. What would have to change to move the lesson closer to a 10?
  4. What would your students be doing differently if your class was a 10?
  5. Tell me more about what that would look like.
  6. How could we measure that change?
  7. Do you want that to be your goal?
  8. If you could hit that goal, would it really matter to you?
  9. What teaching strategy can you use to hit your goal?
  10. What are your next steps?

GOING DEEPER

My thinking about goal setting has been shaped by a number of writers and researchers. Two very helpful books are Chip and Dan Heath's *Switch: How to Change Things When Change Is Hard* (2010) and Heidi Grant Halvorson's little book *9 Things Successful People Do Differently* (2012). If you buy Grant Halvorson's book, I suggest you get the Kindle or iBook version, since she marshals numerous studies to support each statement she makes, and there are links back to the many studies in the eBooks.

Two other books that informed my thinking in this chapter are *Steve Jobs* by Walter Isaacson (2015) and *Making Hope Happen: Create the Future You Want for Yourself and Others* (2014) by Shane Lopez. Isaacson's biography of Jobs might seem like a strange book for coaches, and Jobs's personality as it comes through in this book doesn't reflect the partnership perspective at all, yet I found that this book deepened my understanding of creativity and design thinking. Jobs's views on simplicity have deeply influenced the way we see innovation at the Instructional Coaching Group.

Lopez's book on hope is wonderful and describes in many ways the work of coaches "making hope happen." It really helped me understand the complex activity of creating goals that foster hope.

I also read many books that helped me put together my ideas about questioning. Marilee Adams's *Change Your Questions Change Your Life*, 3rd Edition (2016) told in the form of a fable, is an easy-to-understand yet wise book about the power of mindset and how the questions we ask can improve our coaching and even shape the way we think. I found Warren Berger's *A More Beautiful Question* (2016) to be an inspiring description of the centrality of questioning within invention and problem solving. Michael Bungay Stanier's *The Coaching Habit* is a deceptively simple but powerful book that presents seven effective coaching questions and habits that I think would help just about any coach get better. Finally, Jackie Acree Walsh and Beth Dankert Sattes *Leading Through Quality Questioning* (2010) does a great job of summarizing the literature on questioning that any change leader might need to employ.

Video 3.5

Crysta's Identify Stage—Complete

Video 3.6

Cat's Identify Stage—Complete

resources.corwin.com/impactcycle

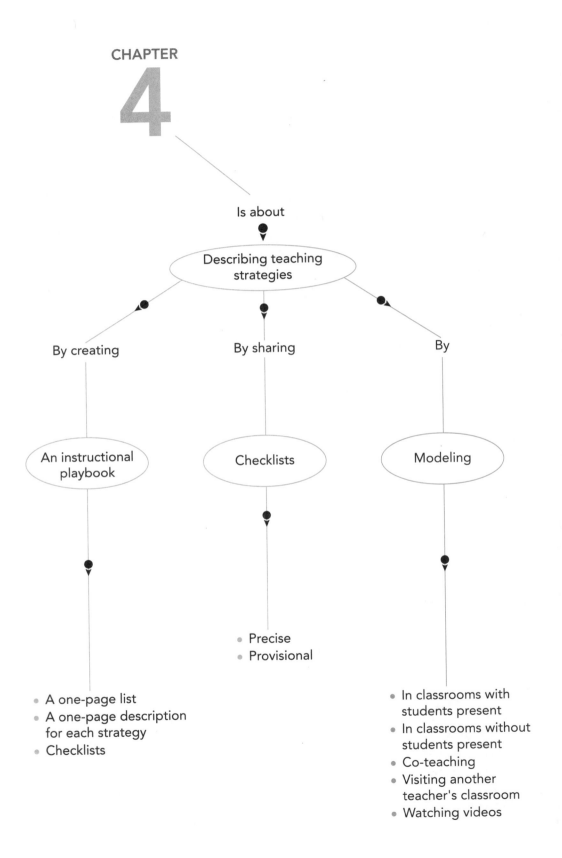

CHAPTER

4

Is about

Describing teaching strategies

By creating

By sharing

By

An instructional playbook

Checklists

Modeling

- Precise
- Provisional

- A one-page list
- A one-page description for each strategy
- Checklists

- In classrooms with students present
- In classrooms without students present
- Co-teaching
- Visiting another teacher's classroom
- Watching videos

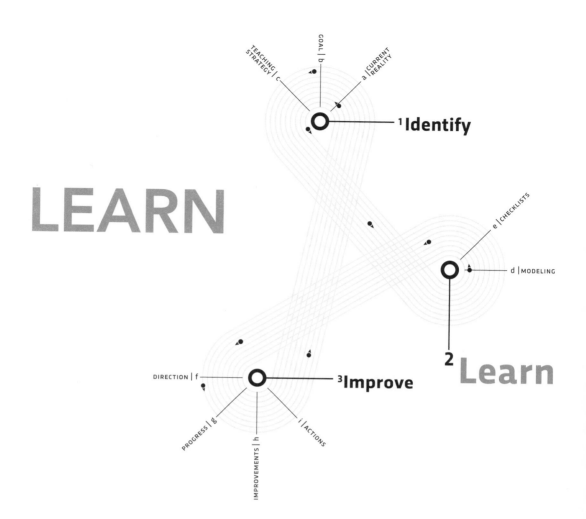

LEARN

¹Identify

- GOAL | b
- TEACHING STRATEGY | c
- a | CURRENT REALITY

²Learn

- e | CHECKLISTS
- d | MODELING

³Improve

- DIRECTION | f
- PROGRESS | g
- IMPROVEMENTS | h
- i | ACTIONS

DESCRIBING TEACHING STRATEGIES

I was drawn to become a professional developer for the same reasons that draw in many other people. I was using an instructional approach that I could see was working for my students, and I wanted others to have the chance to use what was working for me. Those practices were writing strategies for students with learning disabilities from the Strategic Instruction Model (SIM) developed at the University of Kansas (KU) Center for Research on Learning.

After watching my students learn how to confidently express themselves as writers, I decided I wanted to share the strategies with other teachers. I contacted KU to find out how to proceed, and I learned that to become a certified professional developer for SIM, I would need to complete a rigorous certification process. Motivated by the successes I saw my students experiencing, I decided to make the commitment to become certified as quickly as possible.

To become a SIM professional developer, I was required to read a few dozen research articles, gather extensive student portfolios that showed that my students had learned the writing strategies, and attend a weeklong training at KU. When I left the training, I took with me stacks of overheads depicting important information about the model, and I returned to my home in Toronto, inspired by my trainer, Dr. Fran Clark, to do my best to help other teachers use the strategies to help their kids succeed.

My good intentions did not lead to good professional development right away. Looking back, I shudder as I think about the first workshops I led. Feeling the heavy responsibility to do my job well because I knew what a difference strategies could make for students, I made the mistake of overwhelming my audiences with slide after slide of information. My earliest presentations really were death by overhead! In addition, by trying to say the last word on everything, I ended up presenting information that I had not yet had time to fully understand myself. Armed with hundreds of slides, on more than one occasion, I found myself staring at an overhead not knowing what to say about what I was presenting.

Fortunately (or perhaps unfortunately), my audiences didn't seem to notice, in part, no doubt, because I wasn't keeping them that engaged. My lack of deep knowledge produced a lack of participant engagement. When I wasn't clear, my audiences didn't listen. Although my goal was to help teachers reach more students, my own lack of clarity meant that my workshops probably didn't have any positive impact on children's lives.

My enthusiasm for effective instruction that is validated by research, and my understanding that I was ineffective sharing that instruction, brought me to KU, first to complete my dissertation on the Partnership Approach and then to study instructional consultants, who became instructional collaborators, who became instructional coaches. As a novice professional developer, I quickly learned that the effectiveness of professional developers is directly related to how well they know the material they share, and that insight has been firmly supported by my ongoing work with instructional coaches. As a result, I have come to believe that it is better for instructional coaches to know a few strategies well than to know a lot of strategies superficially. However, the most effective instructional coaches have both a broad understanding of a variety strategies they can share with teachers to help them the address the many unique needs of students and themselves *and* a deep understanding of each of those individual strategies. Instructional coaches, in other words, have wide and deep knowledge of teaching strategies.

We learned how important it can be for instructional coaches to have a broad and deep knowledge of strategies in our early years studying coaching in Topeka, Kansas. At first, our coaches shared only two sets of tools: (a) inclusive instructional practices for teachers and (b) learning strategies for students. We assumed that if teachers were more inclusive and students were better learners, positive results would naturally follow. However, we discovered that to meet all teachers' and students' needs, we had to offer teaching strategies that addressed other instructional issues. In particular, we needed teaching strategies that would increase student engagement and create safe learning environments. We also needed strategies for formative assessment so teachers could measure whether or not students were actually learning what was covered in class.

Our journey toward a comprehensive model for coaches has now gone on for more than fifteen years. My colleagues and I have reviewed hundreds of research articles, and I have learned from instructional experts who have deeply influenced my thinking. First, the work and mentoring of my colleagues at the KU Center for Research on Learning, Don Deshler, Jean Schumaker, Keith Lenz, Jan Bulgren, and Mike Hock, laid a deep foundation for my ongoing study of teaching. Randy Sprick taught me an enormous amount about classroom management, and he, Wendy Reinke, Tricia Skyles, Lynn Barnes-Schuster, and I eventually wrote a book together— *Coaching Classroom Management: Strategies and Tools for Administrators and Coaches* (2010)—that summarized a lot of that learning. Rick Stiggins also generously met with me on numerous occasions and taught me a great deal about formative assessment. I consumed his books, watched his videos with our team, and, thanks to him, gained a deeper knowledge of formative assessment (which Rick refers to as Assessment for Learning). More recently, other researchers such as Bob Marzano (see *The Art and Science of Teaching: A Comprehensive Framework for Effective Instruction*, 2007), Jay McTighe and Grant Wiggins (see *Understanding by Design*, 2005), and especially John Hattie (see *Visible Learning: A Synthesis of Over 800 Meta-Analyses Relating to Achievement*, 2008) have further deepened my knowledge.

As we tested and refined our set of teaching practices, we arrived at a framework that I first introduced in *Instructional Coaching: A Partnership Approach to Improving Instruction* (Knight, 2007). Our coaches have come to organize the strategies they share around the concept of the Big Four: (a) Content Planning, (b) Formative Assessment, (c) Instruction, and (d) Community Building. I expanded and deepened my description of the Big Four in my book *High-Impact Instruction* (Knight, 2013).

I revised the way I organize and describe the Big Four one more time after I met a corporate trainer for a major software firm on a flight into Chicago. She explained that her company creates what they refer to as playbooks, manuals that describe how organizations should best use her company's products. During that conversation, I realized that the concept of a playbook could be an excellent way to describe the set of teaching strategies that instructional coaches share with collaborating teachers. Since that day, I've been helping coaching teams develop instructional playbooks.[1]

INSTRUCTIONAL PLAYBOOKS

Instructional coaches help teachers improve student learning and well-being by improving teaching, so they must be able to clearly describe a set of teaching strategies teachers can use to hit their goals. The instructional playbook describes those strategies. I see an instructional playbook as a simple, short publication made up of three parts: (a) a one-page list of high-impact teaching strategies, (b) a one-page description for each of the strategies, and (c) checklists coaches need to use to describe the teaching practices contained in the playbook. I have included examples of the different parts of a playbook on the following pages. A complete example of an instructional playbook, based on *High-Impact Instruction* (Knight, 2013), is included at the end of this book, starting on page 189.

ONE-PAGE LIST

The first page in a playbook is a list of the teaching strategies described in the playbook. I suggest limiting the list to one page to keep the playbook from becoming overly complex and unwieldy. There is no special magic in the number one, however. The list doesn't have to be one page long, but if it goes beyond that length, there is a danger that it will describe more practices than coaches can understand deeply. Having a comprehensive list of strategies does not mean we need a long list; what matters is that the list contains high-impact teaching strategies that address many aspects of teaching, which for us is the Big Four.

Bill Jensen talks about the importance of one-page documents in his book *Simplicity: The New Competitive Advantage* (2000). He quotes Chief Knowledge Officer Kent Green, who notes that in his research and engineering firm, "People get focused through one-page tools. If you can

---

1. In *What Teachers Can Learn From Sports Coaches: A Playbook of Instructional Strategies* (2014), Nathan Barber also talks about the idea of an instructional playbook.

actually get everything on one page—and not just editing stuff out—that means the tool and the process caused you to reflect on what it is you want to do . . . If you limit the number of pages people have to explain themselves, it forces them to reflect first and think about what they're trying to do. That's very important" (pp. 52–53).

One simple but powerful way for a team of instructional coaches to clarify and deepen their knowledge of teaching practices is to come together to identify the teaching strategies that need to be on the one-pager. Additionally, coaches and leaders should come together at least once a year to consider how the playbook can be improved. A playbook is a living document, and as such it should only include teaching strategies that have clearly shown that they can help teachers hit their goals. If a strategy hasn't been used over an entire year, the team should consider removing it from the list.

ONE-PAGE DESCRIPTIONS OF TEACHING STRATEGIES

The playbook should also contain one-page descriptions for each of the teaching strategies listed in the playbook. Instructional coaches can share these summaries to help teachers gain a quick understanding of any strategies they are learning. Coaches can also share the one-page document

Sample One-Page Description of Teaching Strategies Based on *High-Impact Instruction*

1. Content Planning

Guiding Questions

Learning Maps

2. Formative Assessment

Specific Proficiencies

Assessments (checks for understanding, checklists, rubrics)

Modifications to Teaching and Learning

3. Instruction

Thinking Prompts

Effective Questions

Cooperative Learning

Stories

Authentic Learning

4. Community Building

Learner-Friendly Culture

Power With vs. Power Over

Freedom Within Form

Expectations

Witness to the Good

Effective Corrections

LEARNING MAPS

In One Sentence

- A graphic organizer depicting the essential knowledge, skills, and big ideas students are to learn in a unit.

Hattie Check

- Student expectations = 1.44; Teacher clarity = 0.75; Concept mapping = 0.75.

- Students can use learning maps to review and monitor their learning and confirm understanding.

- Learning maps are a form of a concept map teachers can use to ensure their lessons are clear.

What's the Point?

- Learning maps are powerful because the visual depiction of a unit keeps students and teachers on track.

- The map is an accommodation for students who struggle to take notes, and it structures the beginning and ending of lessons.

- Learning maps are living study guides that make connections explicit and that support repeated review.

How Are Learning Maps Used by Teachers?

- Teachers should spend twenty-five to forty minutes to introduce the unit through an interactive discussion of the map on the first day of a unit.

- Throughout the unit, the maps may be used as visual prompts for conversations around advance- and post-organizers.

- Learning maps can be used to introduce learning targets every day.

- Teachers should prompt students to record new information on their maps as it is learned.

- At the end of the unit, maps can be integrated into the unit review.

How Are Learning Maps Used by Students?

- Students use learning maps
  - to take note of key information,
  - to frequently review and clarify their learning, and
  - as points of departure for classroom dialogue.

with other teachers and administrators who might be interested in learning more about the teaching strategies being shared. Eventually, coaches will share more detailed information about the strategies through the use of checklists.

THE NEED FOR CHECKLISTS

The bulk of an instructional playbook is made up of checklists for each of the teaching strategies included. Checklists make it easier for coaches to clearly describe teaching practices. Effective instruction to improve students' lives is the focus of instructional coaching, and to be effective, instructional coaches must have a deep knowledge of that content. That deep knowledge doesn't come from a quick internet search or a TED Talk. Indeed, instructional coaches should read, reread, and reread again the books and articles that describe the teaching strategies they share, marking up their books with notes, sticky notes, and highlights, and creating their own checklists. Then, they need to refine their checklists by sharing them with other coaches and using them with teachers.

Not only do instructional coaches need to know their teaching practices inside out, but they also need to be able to communicate that knowledge clearly. Explaining teaching strategies is a deceptively complex interaction, and we have found that such explanations fail for at least four reasons. First, if a coach's description of a teaching strategy is too complex or disorganized, coach and teacher may become overwhelmed by all the details. When I started leading workshops, I was so intent on sharing everything I knew with my audiences that I ended up overwhelming them until they reached a kind of knowledge saturation point, and they couldn't take in any more information.

Second, if coaches don't have ways to assess whether their audiences understand what is being discussed, they may leave audiences behind. When I was first presenting, although my audiences were polite and nodded pleasantly as if they understood and were planning to apply everything I said, it turned out that they did not remember anything I said. Since I did not build in a way for my audiences to let me know whether or not they understood what I was saying, I just assumed they were with me, but, unfortunately, many times they were not.

A third problem is an extension of one of the ideas I've already discussed in detail: Most of us don't know what it looks like when we do what we do. From watching video of many coaches explaining teaching strategies (including myself), I have learned that coaches often think they are being clearer than they actually are.

One particular version of such false clarity is "the curse of knowledge," which, as Heath and Heath (2010) write, "is a natural psychological tendency that consistently confounds our ability to [communicate clearly]" (p. 19). The authors explain that "once we know something, we find it hard to imagine what it was like not to know it. Our knowledge has cursed us. And, it becomes difficult for us to share our knowledge with others, because we can't readily re-create our listeners' state of mind" (p. 20).

The final reason communication can break down involves the limitation of each learner's memory. When it comes to implementing new strategies, there are only so many things anyone can remember. A set of instructions that is too lengthy will be too difficult to recall and, therefore, will likely not be turned into action. As Heath and Heath (2010) note, "What looks like resistance is often a lack of clarity" (p. 17), and, therefore, "clarity dissolves resistance" (p. 72).

The challenges coaches face describing complex teaching practices can seem daunting, but our team learned early on that a partial solution to these challenges is something quite simple: checklists. As we were first experimenting with instructional coaching, we recognized that we had to deepen and focus our knowledge of the strategies we shared and simplify how we described them to teachers. Using checklists forced us to cut through complexity to the core and identify the essential elements of the strategies we described.

Checklists gave us a simple way to communicate the essential elements of teaching strategies. When we shared them with teachers, we learned to go through them line by line, stopping to confirm that teachers understood what we were describing and asking teachers for feedback on how they might want to adapt the strategy to better meet their students' needs or better exploit their strengths as teachers. Checklists also helped our team stay focused and thorough. We found that it was a lot easier to remember all of the elements of a teaching strategy when they were written on the page you and your collaborating teacher are discussing.

Finally, since checklists are short, expressing the most important parts of a teaching strategy concisely, we found that teachers could process and remember them better. We still give teachers articles, chapters, and books to read about the teaching strategies we share, but checklists are designed for action. When coach and teacher discuss a checklist, they are getting ready to do something new—a change that should have a positive impact on students' lives.

Effective Checklists

A few years after our team created checklists for the strategies we shared with teachers, Atul Gawande's book *The Checklist Manifesto: How to Get Things*

> We need a different strategy for overcoming failure, one that builds on experience and takes advantage of the knowledge people have but somehow also makes up for our inevitable human inadequacies. And there is such a strategy—though it will seem almost ridiculous in its simplicity, maybe even crazy to those of us who have spent years carefully developing ever more advanced skills and technologies. It is a checklist.
>
> **—Atul Gawande**
> *The Checklist Manifesto: How to Get Things Right*
> (2011, p. 13)

Right (2010) was published, providing further research to support our use of checklists. Gawande practices surgery at Brigham and Women's Hospital and is a professor at Harvard Chan School of Public Health. He also directs Ariadne Labs, a joint center for health system innovation of the Brigham and Harvard Chan, and is a staff writer for *The New Yorker,* among other things. In addition, he was named a MacArthur Fellow in 2006.

Gawande's books and *New Yorker* articles are about health care, but they are read widely by the general public because others see Gawande's struggle to be a better surgeon and help others get better at handling uncertainty and complexity as a universal struggle, not simply a health care concern. When Gawande writes, for example, that "we are now witnessing a global societal struggle to assure universal delivery of our know-how" in his article "Cowboys and Pit Crews" in the May 26, 2011, *New Yorker*, he is writing about health care, but people see it as their issue even when their field of endeavor is a long way from a surgical ward.

Gawande is particularly interested in how people get better at what they do, so it should not have surprised me that he would be interested in coaching. His office contacted me in 2011, and he and I talked soon after that. After we talked a few times over the telephone, we eventually spent a day together at Walton Middle School in Albemarle County, Virginia. His article, "Personal Best: Top Athletes and Singers Have Coaches. Should We?" describes that visit and much of what Gawande learned about coaching, talking with master performers such as Itzhak Perlman (who said that his wife is his coach) and, ultimately, getting his own coach to help him become a better surgeon. Of that coaching session, Gawande wrote, "That one twenty-minute discussion gave me more to consider and work on than I'd had in the past five years" ("Personal Best," 2011, p. 50).

Gawande invited me to Harvard to talk with his team about a study of coaching in India designed to improve the effectiveness of midwives in decreasing infant mortality. Central to those coaching efforts was a checklist that described exemplary practice. Like us, Gawande saw checklists as essential for some forms of learning. His book *The Checklist Manifesto: How to Get Things Right* (2010), which popularized the importance of the lowly checklist, had become a *New York Times* best seller. In *The Checklist Manifesto*, Gawande described a global study he led for the World Health Organization with four hospitals in high-income countries (Canada, United States, New Zealand, and United Kingdom) and four hospitals in low- or middle-income countries (India, Jordan, Philippines, and Tanzania).

What Gawande and his research team found was that the simple checklist could save thousands of lives and billions of dollars. In *The Checklist Manifesto*, he writes that "under conditions of complexity, not only are checklists a help, but they are required for success" (p. 79). Today, largely because of Gawande's research, hospitals around the world are adopting checklists, and so are instructional coaches.

To learn how to make effective checklists, Gawande met Daniel Boorman, who had spent two decades creating checklists for Boeing. Of Boorman, Gawande wrote, "Few have more experience translating . . . theory into practice . . . He has studied thousands of crashes or near crashes over the years, and he has made a science of averting human error" (p. 115). In his conversations with Gawande, described in *The Checklist Manifesto*, Boorman explained that there are good checklists and bad checklists:

> Bad checklists are vague and imprecise. They are too long; they are hard to use; they are impractical. They are made by desk jockeys with no awareness of the situations in which they are to be deployed. They treat the people using the tools as dumb and try to spell out every single step. They turn people's brains off rather than turn them on.
>
> Good checklists, on the other hand, are precise. They are efficient, to the point, and easy to use even in the most difficult situations. They also do not try to spell out everything—a checklist cannot fly a plane. Instead, they provide reminders of only the most critical and important steps—the ones that even the most highly skilled professionals using them could miss. Good checklists are, above all, practical. (p. 120)

Boorman spelled out other guidelines for writing checklists that are specifically designed to improve the performance of professionals doing

CHECKLIST: CREATING CHECKLISTS

AN EFFECTIVE CHECKLIST IS:	✔
Short, between five and nine items	
Focused, describing only the most critical and important steps	
Clear, with simple and precise wording	
Practical, easy to use, and to the point	
Concise, fitting on one page	
Easy to read, with no distracting clutter, color, or fonts	

Source: Based on Daniel Boorman's description in Atul Gawande's *The Checklist Manifesto.*

 Available for download at **resources.corwin.com/impactcycle**

their work (someone making a checklist for a family vacation, for example, doesn't need to follow these guidelines). For example, they shouldn't be too long. "A rule of thumb some use," Boorman told Gawande, "is to keep it between five and nine items, which is the limit of working memory" (p. 123). The checklist's "wording should be simple and exact" (p. 123). For Boorman, Gawande explains, "Even the look of the checklist matters. Ideally, it should fit on one page. It should be free of clutter and unnecessary color. It should use both uppercase and lowercase text for ease of reading. (He even went so far as to recommend using sans serif type like Helvetica)" (p. 123).

How Coaches Share Checklists

Once checklists are created, coaches share them with teachers to explain the new practices they are going to use to hit their goals. The challenge is for instructional coaches to go through checklists with teachers in a way that is just as dialogical and co-constructed as the conversations during the Identify stage of coaching. These dialogues should be engaging, stimulating (often fun) conversations about what is possible by the teaching strategy described by the checklist, not a boring, one-sided conversation where the coach just tells the teacher what to do. The temptation to simply tell teachers how to implement a strategy can be overwhelming, but if an instructional coach shifts to top-down communication, it can make it difficult for any real communication to occur.

To create conversations that are energizing and creative, I suggest coaches be "precise *and* provisional" when explaining teaching strategies. Coaches can be precise by systematically going through a checklist line by line with their collaborating teachers. They can be provisional by frequently asking teachers whether or not they want to modify the checklist and change how they will teach the strategy in their classroom. When teachers see each line on the checklist as a choice rather than an obligation, they are much more engaged in the conversation.

When I interviewed Atul Gawande about this very challenge, he told me that "any kind of systems improvement like coaching has an iterative nature to it. It has to be iterated because you are learning how to make it work. It's a discovery process. The checklist has to be adapted to the local environment. It's going to be different coaching in a small school in western Virginia vs. a huge, urban school in New York City."

There will always be some local customization of checklists, but what should a coach do if a collaborating teacher wants to change a strategy so dramatically that it bears little resemblance to the strategy as it is described in the literature? What should a coach do, in other words, if a teacher wants to butcher a practice—trying to do "I do it, We do it, You do it" by just doing the "You do it" part?

If a teacher wants to engage in what Anne Marie Palincsar has referred to as "lethal mutation," the coach should not sit idly by. A dialogue is a conversation between two people, and both voices are important. Coaches should not hesitate to share their thoughts; they just need to do so in a manner that leaves plenty of room for their collaborating teachers to share their views.

Dialogue genuinely enables people to learn together, so it is not about "my" opinion or "your" opinion; it is a mutual exploration. Coaches can foster dialogue by provisionally sharing ideas with such phrases as, "Tell me what you think about this," or "I'm wondering about . . . ," rather than telling the teacher, "You need to do it with fidelity." What is most important for the coach is not to buy into the idea that there is only one correct way to teach a strategy, which, as it turns out, always happens to be the way the coach would teach it. To the best of my knowledge, there is no one, perfect way to teach anything.

Instructional coaches should not lose sight of the goal to be learners as much as they are teachers. Often, the insights shared by collaborating teachers improve the way a strategy will be implemented. When Crysta Crumb and I went through a checklist for formative assessment, for example,

I think the most important thing is to build a trusting relationship with the people you are working with. Don't act like you have all the answers but that you are going to figure out an answer together. Share with them that you are a lifelong learner, or however you want to say it. If you try something and it works, great. If you try something and it doesn't work, nobody is going to get zinged for that. The only bad thing about trying something that doesn't work is continuing to do it. Be the person who says, "Let's work together to make things better for the kids."

—Deborah Mitchell
Instructional Coach, Metro Nashville Public Schools
Nashville, Tennessee

her suggestion that students practice with response cards before they use them for real was very helpful. Crysta knew her students and had valuable information to share.

Ultimately, if a teacher chooses to teach a strategy in a way that is likely to decrease its effectiveness, the final measure is the goal set by the teacher. Coaches do not have to determine what is good or bad practice; they can simply say, "Well, we have a goal. Let's see if your modified version of the strategy helps you hit the goal. If it doesn't, we can always come back and revisit the checklist."

The power of having a goal is that coaches don't have to be, as one coached called it, the "fidelity police." If a teacher wants to modify a practice, that is her decision as a professional. She knows her students best, and she is the one who will be using the teaching strategy. Further, if the teacher hits the goal, then whether she modifies the practice is irrelevant. Indeed, using her experience and understanding of students, she may have improved the practice. However, if the goal is not met, coach and teacher can revisit the checklist to see if the implementation of the practice needs to be refined to better meet the goal. That way, the coach does not end up being in the one-up position of telling the teacher what to do.

Video 4.1

Crysta Learns About Formative Assessment From a Checklist

Video 4.2

Cat Learns About Thinking Prompts From a Checklist

resources.corwin.com/impactcycle

How Many Checklists?

Coaches should share as many checklists as are necessary for a teacher to implement a new strategy effectively, but ideally that is a small number of checklists. For some teaching strategies, a coach might need to share only one checklist, but for others they may need to share several. For example, for learning maps, coaches probably need several checklists describing (a) the characteristics of effective maps, (b) how to create a map, (c) using maps on the first day of the unit, (d) using maps throughout the unit, and (e) using a map at the end of a unit. Example checklists follow.

Sample Learning Maps Checklists

 CHECKLIST: LEARNING MAP

A QUALITY LEARNING MAP:	✔
Answers all the guiding questions	
Has a starting map with only the core idea, paraphrase, and subtopics	
Has a complete ending map on no more than one page	
Shows connections through line labels	
Is organized according to the sequence of the learning in the unit	

 CHECKLIST: CREATING LEARNING MAPS

	✔
Identify the knowledge, skills, and big ideas and other information that needs to be in the map.	
Display everything by transferring information to sticky notes and putting it out where it all can be seen.	
Organize information into a map.	
Connect information using line labels.	
Refine the map by adding, subtracting, combining, and simplifying.	

CHECKLIST: INTRODUCING THE LEARNING MAP AND GUIDING QUESTIONS

	✔
The teacher spends twenty-five to forty-five minutes to thoroughly introduce the unit.	
Students complete their personal map in their own handwriting (at least partially).	
The teacher co-constructs the map with students.	
The teacher provides many opportunities for students to respond to learning so that learning is highly interactive.	
Students store their map in a place where it will be easy for them to retrieve it.	

CHECKLIST: DAILY USE OF THE LEARNING MAP AND GUIDING QUESTIONS

	✔
Students have their map open on their desk when the bell rings to start the class.	
Class begins with a review of the content covered up until the current point in the unit.	
The learning map is used to introduce the day's lesson.	
Students record new content learned on the learning map.	
Each day ends with a review of the material depicted on the learning map.	

(Continued)

(Continued)

CHECKLIST: END-OF-UNIT REVIEW WITH LEARNING MAP AND GUIDING QUESTIONS

	✔
Teacher and students have created a complete learning map by the end of the unit.	
The learning map should be integrated into the end-of-unit review.	
Teacher should prompt students to use the map to study for the end-of-unit test (when there is a test).	
Teacher should prompt students to keep their maps stored in an orderly, easy-to-find place in their notebooks.	
When returning students' tests, the teacher should clearly explain how the map would have helped students prepare for the test.	

MODELING TEACHING STRATEGIES

Early in our studies, teachers told us that it was not enough to hear about strategies; they also needed to see them in action. Teachers who weren't interested in implementing new teaching strategies weren't interested in watching us model teaching practices. However, when teachers committed to goals for improvement that mattered to them and their students and identified teaching strategies that they really wanted to implement, they wanted to see how teachers would implement them. Many teachers told us in various ways, "It would really help me to see this strategy before I have to do it."

As I report in *Instructional Coaching: A Partnership Approach to Improving Instruction* (Knight, 2007), teachers told us that they found modeling to be very helpful. Many teachers said that they would have "sunk" if their coach hadn't modeled the teaching strategies they were to learn. Amber Sheritt's comments about her experiences watching her coach Lynn Barnes Schuster model, which I first included in *Instructional Coaching,* are typical:

> She came in and modeled after I tried the Unit Organizer once, and. . . it was funny because I could see the look on the kids' faces. It was as if they were saying, "This is so not what you had us do." So I was like, OK, I'm learning, too. And it was wonderful. . . . The kids got the big picture. I could never have gotten that if it hadn't been modeled for me. *Never* could have gotten it. . . . Because even when she and I just talked about it, I thought OK, I'll do it if they make me do it, but I'm not going to do it after this because I can't see any benefit to it—because I didn't know how to use it. Then when I saw her . . . that was just like, wow! I look for that light in the kids' eyes. When Lynn came in and modeled for me, oh my God, the light just went on.

In *Instructional Coaching,* I describe modeling as coaches going into teachers' classrooms and demonstrating teaching strategies in front of teachers' students. Over time, we have learned from our coaching research partners in Oregon and Washington that coaches often need to adapt the way they model to better respond to the unique needs of teachers and their students. Specifically, we have found that modeling can occur in at least five ways: (a) in teachers' classrooms with their students present, (b) in teachers' classrooms without their students present, (c) co-teaching, (d) visiting another teacher's classroom, and (e) watching video. Each of these approaches is described next.

IN TEACHERS' CLASSROOMS WITH THEIR STUDENTS PRESENT

Instructional coaches model teaching strategies so that teachers will be able to implement them easily and effectively. For that reason, coaches do not need to teach an entire lesson; they only need to model the strategy the teacher is learning. In fact, teachers have told us they prefer that coaches do not teach the entire lesson because it can waste valuable instructional time, and, worse in many teacher's eyes, erode a teacher's authority with her students.

Modeling focused on a single teaching strategy feels completely different from a model lesson because it is usually only a small part of a lesson. Modeling how to share a learning map at the start of a lesson, for example, takes only a few minutes. When coaches come into teachers' classrooms to model, teachers can introduce coaches by telling students that they are collaborating with the coach and that the coach is going to try out a new strategy with the students and get some feedback. In this way, the coach is the person who appears to be getting the help, not the collaborating teacher. Coaches, like all teachers, can learn a great deal by watching video recordings of their model lessons. They may also ask their collaborating teacher to review the video of the lesson with them.

To prepare for the model lesson, coaches need to have a deep understanding of the teaching practice they are going to model. The purpose of the model, after all, is to show teachers one example of how a teaching strategy might be used, and a poorly delivered model might lead to a poorly taught teaching strategy.

While instructional coaches need to model teaching practices effectively, they should resist the temptation to spend several hours preparing an extra-special lesson that will dazzle the children. Doing that is not fair to the teacher who has only limited time since she is teaching many lessons and can't prepare a "dazzling" lesson for each hour. If a student turns to the coach after the model lesson and asks, "Could you be our teacher?" the odds are the teacher will hesitate to invite the coach back into a classroom. A better way is for coaches to provide a simple but clear demonstration of the teaching strategy, nothing more.

Prior to the model lesson, coach and teacher should discuss a few issues. First, they should review the teacher's behavioral expectations, so that the coach can reinforce them in the classroom. They should also confirm who will control students' behavior if students violate the expectations. It doesn't matter who does it, but it is important to have a plan in place if any student's behavior has to be addressed. Finally, coaches should ask the teachers about any students who have particular learning needs. Some students have needs that must be addressed so that they are able to get the most out of learning, and a model lesson can fall apart quickly if a coach doesn't have that information.

I have found it is helpful to have the children create name tents so I can use their names when I call on them. During the model, I also go out of my way to honor the collaborating teachers, complimenting them in front of students and deferring to their expertise throughout the model, asking, for example, "Mrs. Monk, you're the expert here, am I explaining this concept correctly?"

I like to video record modeling and share the video with teachers in case they wish to review the video before they implement the practice. If time permits, I get together with the teacher to watch and discuss the model lesson, maybe even reviewing the video together so we can talk about any issues that arose during the model.

IN TEACHERS' CLASSROOMS WITHOUT THEIR STUDENTS PRESENT

When a coach models in front of a teacher's students, teachers can learn a lot by seeing how the students respond to new teaching strategies. However, in some instances, teachers and coaches might agree that modeling should not occur in front of students. The most obvious reason might be that teachers are not ready to have a coach model in their classrooms and that they would be more comfortable watching the model without students in the room. If this is the case, the teacher's wishes should be respected.

In many other cases, teachers prefer to have a coach model when students are not in the classroom. This is especially true in elementary school classrooms when teachers are with the same group of students all day. In middle and high school, a coach can model with one group of students and later that same day, the teacher can try out the strategy with a different group.

We have also found that modeling in front of students is not effective when the teacher is working to meet a behavioral goal. If a teacher is trying to reduce disruptions from seventeen per ten minutes to three per ten minutes, for example, it might be difficult for a coach to get students' attention in the short time period of the model. Conversely, if the coach does get students' attention and controls the class when the teacher is unable to do that, the coach's success can make it more difficult for a teacher to manage students since the coach's success might point out to students the extent to which their teacher is struggling to maintain control. When it comes to behavior, the most effective modeling might be some of the other approaches described, especially visiting another teacher's class or watching video.

Video 4.3

Jim Models Using Response Cards in Crysta's Class

Video 4.4

Jim Models Using Open, Opinion Questions in Cat's Class

resources.corwin.com/ impactcycle

✔ CHECKLIST: I, WE, YOU DO IT

I DO IT	✔
Review the steps of the strategy.	
Explain how it will help them learn.	
Specify what they need to do.	
Think out loud.	
Problem solve.	
Address categories of error that arose in the previous day's work.	
WE DO IT	✔
Ask for strategy steps.	
Call on a variety of students to explain how to perform steps.	
Ask students to explain how they are thinking.	
Shape student responses.	
Encourage students with authentic praise.	
Evaluate student understanding.	
Reinstruct if necessary.	
YOU DO IT	✔
Let students perform independently.	
Give brief, specific, constructive feedback.	
Identify categories of error to discuss in the next day's session.	
Have students record their grade on their progress chart.	

 Available for download at **resources.corwin.com/impactcycle**

One of the advantages of modeling without students in the classroom is that the coach can stop at any time so coach and teacher can discuss the model. Pushing the "pause" button, so to speak, can provide an opportunity for teacher and coach to deepen their understanding by talking about why and how a checklist, such as the one on the facing page, would be translated into action in the classroom.

A coach who is modeling how to use the teaching strategy "I do it, We do it, You do it" as a way to teach students how to edit their writing, for example, should first ensure that the collaborating teacher has a copy of the checklist. During the model, the coach can pause at any point to discuss the importance of the review at the start or why teachers should explain what students will do. Coaches can also stop and redo the model if they are not confident that they modeled something effectively or stop to allow teachers to ask clarifying questions and take notes as they think about what the strategy will look like when they implement it.

To decide whether to model with or without students in the room, coaches and teachers need to consider one basic question: Will the advantages of watching students respond outweigh the advantages of being able to stop the model and discuss it? In some cases, the best solution is to do both. A coach can first model the strategy without students, then with students, and when the teacher feels confident about the strategy, she can try it on her own.

CO-TEACHING

Coaches also may not want to model in teachers' classrooms in front of students when they do not feel they have enough knowledge of the content students are learning. For example, I was once asked to model how to use a graphic organizer, Ed Ellis's *The Framing Routine* (2001), to help teach students learn how to draw a picture that includes a vanishing point. Since I didn't know that content, my collaborating teacher and I agreed we would co-teach the lesson. I showed students how to complete a graphic organizer that helped them take notes, and their teacher explained and demonstrated how to draw, including a vanishing point. Co-teaching, in this case, allowed me to model a teaching strategy and also provide an opportunity for the teacher to ensure that the correct content was taught.

To ensure that co-teaching succeeds, teacher and coach need to plan carefully what will happen during the lesson. I suggest erring on the side of too much planning rather than too little, maybe even using a simple form to plan their lesson, such as the one that follows.

CO-TEACHING PLANNING FORM

Date and Time:	October 20, 9:00–10:30	
Room:	B 414	
Topic:	President's Roles	
Goal:	Students will deeply understand what the President can and cannot do.	
Time	**You**	**Me**
9:00–9:05	Advance organizer	15-second introduction Monitor students
9:05–9:30	Quick review: The President's roles	Monitor students
9:30–9:55	Monitor students	Explain each step of nominal group technique Give students 5 minutes to complete each step Students done early can review their speeches
9:55–10:10	Clarify what President can and cannot do Monitor students	Co-construct criteria: Clarify what President can and cannot do Vote
10:10–10:25	Co-lead discussion of voting results Take control whenever it seems right	Co-lead discussion about voting results
10:25–10:30	Post-organizer	Monitor students

 Template available for download at **resources.corwin.com/impactcycle**

In the co-taught lesson illustrated in the planning form above, the instructional coach is collaborating with a ninth-grade Civics teacher who wants to increase the percentage of student talk in her class. The coach and teacher agree to try to increase student talk during the ninety minutes the teacher has them for block lessons and that they will try to hit the goal by having the students use dialogue structures such as the nominal group technique from *High-Impact Instruction* (Knight, 2007, pp. 287–288). The nominal group technique is depicted in the following checklist. Although the coach knows the dialogue structure inside out, she doesn't know US social studies content, so coach and teacher decide to co-teach.

✔ CHECKLIST: NOMINAL GROUP TECHNIQUE

	✔
Teacher presents a question or problem.	
Students (on their own or in pairs) write down their ideas about how to respond to the question or problem.	
All ideas are recorded by the teacher or student discussion host[2] (if students are meeting in groups).	
The teacher or student discussion host directs students' attention to each idea and asks for comments.	
Students vote privately to identify best ideas. Sometimes students generate criteria for voting before they vote.	
Teacher presents a question or problem.	
Students (on their own or in pairs) write down their ideas about how to respond to the question or problem.	

 Available for download at **resources.corwin.com/impactcycle**

As the co-teaching form shows, coach and teacher have broken down exactly how they will collaborate throughout the lesson. The teacher will introduce the lesson and provide a mini-lecture. The coach will introduce the nominal group technique and move students through the process step-by-step. The coach will initiate the debrief after the activity, but the content teacher will jump in to lead the discussion to the extent she feels comfortable. Finally, the content teacher will wrap the lesson up with a post-organizer. Throughout the lesson, both teachers will monitor students to make sure they understand the activity they are doing and the content they are learning.

When coaches model through co-teaching, they are engaging in a special form of collaboration, so I spoke with co-teaching and collaboration expert Suzanne Robinson, from the KU Department of Special Education, to get her insight into how instructional coaches should conduct themselves when they are co-teaching. Suzanne and I agreed that a coaching relationship

---

2. For more information on student discussion hosts, see *High-Impact Instruction* (Knight, 2007, p. 285).

differs from a more traditional co-teaching relationship, but that partnership, which Suzanne refers to as *parity*, is very important in both. Suzanne told me,

> In a co-teaching relationship, the idea of parity is really important. That doesn't mean they have to know the same thing, but they have an equal and shared responsibility. It can be defined by literally "your turn–my turn" or it can be defined by differing expertises that are blended together, etc.

Since co-teaching is a sustained relationship, Suzanne told me, "Parity works itself out over time as the teachers' different expertise comes to the fore to make learning happen for kids," but since coaching has a shorter timeline, establishing that parity is more difficult. Suzanne pointed out, "One of the things I have discussed with teachers who don't have time to build that parity is to make sure they carry themselves as guests, always willing to defer to the teacher in charge to maintain the relationship. You really want a respectful relationship so that the teachers can learn from each other."

VISITING ANOTHER TEACHER'S CLASSROOM

Another way for teachers to see new teaching strategies in practice is to observe teachers in their school who are already teaching the strategies effectively. Visiting a colleague's classroom can help teachers master all kinds of strategies, such as asking open-ended questions and promoting classroom dialogue, managing classroom procedures such as handing out assignments, using a learning map as an advance organizer for the class, setting up learning activities such as dialogue structures or cooperative learning, and many other practices.

Visiting other teachers' classrooms can also help teachers understand how to implement broader approaches to learning, such as the gradual release of responsibility framwork described by Doug Fisher and Nancy Frey in *Better Learning Through Structured Reading: A Framework for Gradual Release of Responsibility* (2008). Similarly, it can be very helpful for teachers to observe other teachers when they are asked to implement instructional programs such as Lucy Calkins's *A Guide to The Writing Workshop, Grades 3–5* (2006).

Ideally, coach and teacher visit a model teacher together and then meet afterward to talk about what they saw, preferably with the model teacher as well. However, sometimes the only way a teacher will be able to visit a class is if the coach covers her class so that she will be free to visit.

The reason for visiting another teacher's class is to get better at implementing a specific teaching strategy. I suggest that coaches clarify that the visit is just to see a particular strategy, so that teachers can get the most out of their visit by focusing on that particular strategy, usually with a checklist in hand. Trying to take in everything that happens in a class can be overwhelming, but focused attention can lead to genuine growth.

Since learning is the purpose of the visit, everything we know about learning from modeling applies. When possible, coach, collaborating teacher, and model teacher should get together before the visit and review a checklist for the teaching strategy that will be modeled. Also, when possible, everyone should get together after the lesson to discuss the new teaching strategy. When time permits and the model teacher doesn't mind, there can be great value in video recording the lesson so that it can be reviewed during a post-lesson conversation and again by the collaborating teacher before she implements it herself.

Coaches need to consider carefully which teachers they will propose as model teachers. The ideal model teachers are able to masterfully demonstrate the strategies that are being learned. They are confident about their skills and at ease discussing what happens in their classroom. Teachers who are unwilling to be video recorded, for example, might be the same ones who would be uncomfortable with an open discussion about their lessons. Finally, the ideal model teachers are positive and emotionally intelligent people who put teachers at ease and encourage them in their learning.

Schools around the world are now addressing the need for model teachers by identifying teachers to lead model classrooms intended to be open all the time for visiting teachers. To help create model classrooms, at the start of the year, instructional coaches work intensively with model classroom teachers to ensure that they master the teaching strategies they will be modeling. Coaches likely would meet with model teachers at least daily and sometimes multiple times to help them become masters at the strategies they will demonstrate.

Once model teachers are confident that they have mastered the strategies, coaches can start encouraging others to visit the classroom to see the strategies in action. Coaches or model teachers can post a schedule listing when each teaching strategy will be demonstrated. In the best situations, teachers visit the model classroom after they have set a goal and are getting ready to implement a new strategy to hit the goal. Video recordings of model lessons can also be made available for teachers to watch when they are unable to visit the model classroom.

WATCHING VIDEO

Watching a video of a lesson is not the ideal way to see a new teaching strategy in action, but it still can be a useful aid for learning new strategies. In some schools, coaches and other leaders are creating libraries of videos demonstrating specific teaching strategies available to teachers.

In schools that have created an instructional playbook, videos that demonstrate the teaching practices in the playbook could be very helpful. Of course, those in charge of the videos need to ensure that the model lessons that are recorded are exemplary. Teachers naturally implement what they see others do, so it is important that what others do is best practice.

Coaches can also search for online video of teachers implementing teaching strategies. The Teaching Channel (teachingchannel.org), for example, has more than 1,000 videos of teachers teaching and talking about teaching. I used my videos on the Teaching Channel, from my program *Talking About Teaching*, to illustrate the teaching strategies in *High-Impact Instruction* (Knight, 2007).

For most teaching practices, modeling is critically important. And when it comes to learning new teaching practices, in general, more is better than less. If time permits, there is great value in seeing a model lesson carried out in different ways. For example, a coach might share a video with a teacher, model in the classroom without students (so that coach and teacher can break down a new strategy), and then model the strategy in the classroom with students. Some coaches like to practice a kind of coaching gradual release consisting of modeling a practice, then co-teaching, and then watching the teacher implement the practice.

What matters with modeling is that the teachers learn what they need to learn so that they can confidently implement a new teaching strategy. Coaching doesn't start to have an impact until teachers change the way they teach and students improve how they learn.

MAKING IT REAL

One of the major themes that surfaced when we interviewed instructional coaches for this book was the importance of having a professional learning community of other coaches to help them deepen their knowledge and skills. That community can be an especially powerful way for coaches to deepen their knowledge of teaching strategies and improve their ability to describe and model those strategies.

Creating checklists with a team of colleagues can quickly deepen coaches' knowledge of practices. I suggest when coaches come together to create checklists, they develop one checklist at a time, with each coach creating his or her own checklist, sharing it with the group, and then discussing with the group what should and should not be on the checklist. Inevitably, people identify different elements, and the ensuing discussion around what is and is not essential for the checklist compels everyone to think deeply about what matters most for a given teaching strategy.

Coaches can improve their ability to describe strategies by video recording themselves using checklists to describe strategies and then analyzing the video to check the simplicity, clarity, and completeness of their explanations. Again, this activity may work best with a team. Everyone can be paired up with a partner, video record themselves describing a strategy to their partner, review their video, and then discuss their video with their partner and the group. Of course, it can be extremely valuable for coaches to review video of themselves explaining strategies to teachers in real coaching sessions.

Finally, teams can be great settings for improving how to model teaching practices. Coaches can video record themselves modeling teaching practices in triads, review their video, and then discuss what they saw on the video with their group. Again, coaches can bring real video of modeling to their team to share the video and ask for feedback. My book *Focus on Teaching: Using Video for High-Impact Instruction* (Knight, 2014) contains many suggestions for how to set up effective video learning teams, and forms that teams can use can be downloaded for free at corwin.com/focusonteaching.

TO SUM UP

- Instructional coaches need to understand a number of high-impact teaching strategies that address many different aspects of teaching.

- Many coaches benefit from creating instructional playbooks that summarize the teaching strategies they share with teachers.

- Instructional playbooks contain (a) a one-page list of all the teaching practices in the playbook, (b) one-page summaries of each of the teaching strategies, and (c) checklists coaches may use with teachers when explaining teaching strategies.

- Instructional coaches should be precise but provisional when they share strategies with teachers.

- Teachers get deeper understanding of teaching strategies when they see them modeled.

- Modeling can be done (a) in teachers' classrooms with their students present, (b) in teachers' classrooms without their students present, (c) co-teaching, (d) visiting another teacher's classroom, and (e) watching video.

GOING DEEPER

As mentioned earlier, the most thorough discussion of the power of checklists is Atul Gawande's *The Checklist Manifesto: How to Get Things Right* (2010). You can read a shorter description of Gawande's ideas about checklists by searching online for Gawande, checklists, *New Yorker*. To read Gawande's article about coaching, "Personal Best," see *The New Yorker* (2011, October 3).

Joseph Grenny, Kerry Patterson, David Maxfield, and Ron McMillan's *Influencer: The New Science of Leading Change,* 2nd Edition (2013) provides a great explanation of the importance of modeling as a part of change and learning.

Thousands of books about instruction may be used to create instructional playbooks. I will mention a few that I have found to be especially helpful. John Hattie's research provides the most comprehensive assessment of the research on teaching, and I find his *Visible Learning for Teachers: Maximizing Impact on Learning* (2012) to be his most accessible book. While Robert Marzano's many books on instruction are very helpful, I have found his *The Art and Science of Teaching: A Comprehensive Framework for Effective Instruction* (2007) to be especially helpful. Finally, John Saphier, Mary Ann Haley-Speca, and Robert Gower's *The Skillful Teacher: Rebuilding Your Teaching Skills*, 6th Edition (2008) is a tremendously valuable resource for any teacher.

Randy Sprick has been a long-term partner with the Instructional Coaching Group, and all of his books are very useful for coaches wanting to learn about classroom management. His book *CHAMPS: A Proactive and Positive Approach to Classroom Management*, 2nd Edition (2010) is a great introduction to his work. Grant Wiggins and Jay McTighe's *Understanding by Design* (2005) is the classic work on designing curriculum. Finally, Jan Chappuis's *Seven Strategies of Assessment for Learning*, 2nd Edition (2014) is a great introductory work on formative assessment, which she, along with her longtime colleague Rick Stiggins, refers to as *assessment for learning*.

Video 4.5

Crysta's Learn Stage—Complete

Video 4.6

Cat's Learn Stage—Complete

resources.corwin.com/ impactcycle

5

Is about

Making adjustments until a goal is met

By

By

By

By

Confirming direction

Reviewing process

Inventing improvements

Planning next actions

- Breaks the ice
- Ensures teachers and coaches share the same expectations

- Goal is essential
- Data can be:
  - ○ Student achievement
  - ○ Observations
  - ○ Video

- Determine date/time for next meeting
- Identify actions that have to happen
- Identify when
- Re-confirm commitment

Possible adaptations:
- Teaching strategy
- The way a strategy is taught
- Goal
- Progress measure

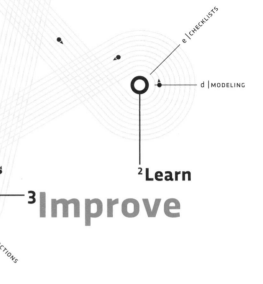

IMPROVE

¹**Identify**

GOAL | b

a | CURRENT REALITY

TEACHING STRATEGY | c

e | CHECKLISTS

d | MODELING

²**Learn**

³**Improve**

DIRECTION | f

PROGRESS | g

IMPROVEMENTS | h

i | ACTIONS

> *You gotta set your course, but when you arrive . . . it doesn't always happen like you planned.*
>
> **—John Coltrane**
> quoted in *Ashley Kahn, A Love Supreme: The Story of John Coltrane's Signature Album*
> (2002, p. 18)

Jacee Martinez came from a family of teachers. Her grandmother was a first-grade teacher, and following her, Jacee's mother taught first grade for thirty-five years. Jacee's sister teaches fifth grade. Her brother teaches at a university. When Jacee chose teaching over law, few people were surprised; she really was carrying on a family tradition.

Having lived with educators all her life, Jacee had seen firsthand the difference teaching could make, and she entered the field of education deeply committed to making a significant, positive impact on children's lives. She took her job very seriously, and she felt that teaching fourth-grade students in Othello, Washington, was especially important because her students had a lot of needs. As Jacee told me during an interview, in her school, "A lot of students come to school with no language skills. They deal with poverty on a daily basis, and many come to school hungry. So when they come to us, we might be the one smiling face and the only meals they receive that day."

Since teaching was in her blood and because her students really needed her help, Jacee felt frustrated and anxious when she wasn't meeting her students' needs. Jacee was highly effective when teaching math, but she knew she had to learn more about writing. During her writing lessons, when she saw her students struggle, Jacee usually just moved on, not knowing what to do to help them. When we talked, Jacee admitted, "My anxiety would just rage because they would ask me a question, or they would be struggling with something, and I would have no idea how to help them. As a teacher, that helpless feeling put me in their shoes because they were sitting there not knowing what to do and asking me for help, and I was sitting there not knowing what to tell them. I hated that. I would dread writing because I didn't want to get to the point where I couldn't help them."

Jacee knew how important writing would be in her students' futures, but she didn't know how to help them learn. "I wanted to fix it," she said, "but I just didn't know how." Feeling overwhelmed and anxious, Jacee turned to Marci Gonzalez for help. Marci was her instructional coach.

Marci was a participant in our University of Kansas (KU) study of instructional coaching, and as a member of that study, she received weekly coaching on the Impact Cycle from Dr. Marti Elford, a coach-of-coaches and project director on the research project. To support Marci, Marti, who had been an instructional coach before she received her PhD and became a researcher at KU, had weekly FaceTime coaching conversations with Marci. "My role," Marti explained, "was not only to support Marci as she supported the teachers she worked with, but also to support her as she moved toward her own goals as a coach." As a result of their work together, Marti said, "We became very good friends. Reciprocity reigned. I learned as much from Marci as I could ever have hoped to share with her."

THE IMPROVE STAGE OF THE IMPACT CYCLE

As Jacee's instructional coach, Marci laid the groundwork for change in the Identify and Learn stages of the Impact Cycle by helping Jacee get a clear picture of reality, set a goal, identify teaching strategies, and then learn those teaching strategies. However, it was during the Improve stage of the Impact Cycle that real change happened in Jacee's classroom.

The Improve stage is where ideas turn into action, where real improvement either does or doesn't occur. Improve is the most challenging stage of coaching—translating research into action—and also often the most exhilarating stage since it demands a high level of imaginative brainpower from teacher and coach, who think together to improve students' learning and well-being. The foundation for coaching is laid during Identify and Learn, but learning gets real during Improve.

During the Improve stage of the Impact Cycle, instructional coach and collaborating teacher move through a four-step process. They (a) Confirm Direction, by ensuring that they have a shared goal for each coaching conversation; (b) Review Progress, by looking at data related to implementation of a new teaching strategy or strategies and student progress toward a goal; (c) Invent Improvements, by determining what needs to be changed so that students will reach their goal; and (d) Plan Next Actions, by identifying what next steps have to be taken, when they will take place, and who will do them.

In the rest of this chapter, I describe each of these steps and suggest questions coaches can ask as they move through the four steps. Through all four steps of the Improve stage, coach and teacher conversations primarily focus on one question but in different ways: "Did we hit the goal?" How a coach and teacher move forward is determined by their answer to that simple question.

Did you hit the goal?

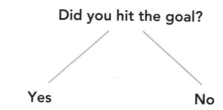

Yes

Do you want to

- Continue to refine your use of the practice?
- Choose a new goal?
- Take a break?

No

Do you want to

- Change the goal?
- Change the way you measure progress toward the goal?
- Stick with the strategy as it is?
- Revisit how you teach the new strategy?
- Choose a new strategy?

STEP 1: CONFIRM DIRECTION

To ensure they are on the same page as their collaborating teachers, coaches should start every coaching conversation by asking the teacher about her most pressing concerns. This is true of all coaching conversations, but it is especially true during the Improve stage. Teachers are busy people doing emotionally complex work, and coaches should take a minute or two just to make sure their expectations for the conversation are the same as those of the collaborating teacher. On some occasions, I have gone into a coaching conversation with a set of expectations and then discovered quickly that my collaborating teacher had other pressing issues that needed to be discussed before he could talk about progress toward the goal.

When I asked one elementary teacher whom I was coaching what was on her mind, she told me that one of her students who was living in foster care had been moved away from the community to another town. She had spent the year developing a relationship with the boy, watching him build confidence and grow, and naturally, she felt affection and concern for him, especially since she knew neither his mom nor his dad was a part of his life. She didn't get to say goodbye, and she didn't know what the future held for him, so at the start of the coaching conversation, we talked about her worries and feelings. After that, we were ready to turn to the Impact Cycle.

Here are some questions that I've found helpful for confirming direction.

Given the time we have today, what's the most important thing for us to talk about? I learned this question from communication expert Susan Scott during one of her workshops, and it has become one of the questions I ask most frequently. I find it very helpful because it positions the collaborating teacher as the one who sets the agenda for the day. It is a simple way to ensure teachers know that they have at least equal status in the coaching conversation and that coaching is for them and their students, not for the coach. The question also ensures that coach and teacher address any issues that may be at the front of the teacher's mind. For example, if a teacher is worried about a new student who has just been placed in her class and whose behavior may upset the class routines, that worry has to be addressed before anything else can be discussed in a meaningful way.

What's on your mind? Michael Bungay Stanier, mentioned earlier in this book, provides an alternative simple question for setting the direction of the coaching conversation, "What's on your mind?" which he calls the "kick-starter question." According to Michael,

Because it's open, it invites people to get to the heart of the matter and share what's most important to them . . . And yet the question is focused, too. It's not an invitation to tell you anything or everything. It's encouragement to go right away to what's exciting, what's provoking anxiety, what's all-consuming, what's waking them up at 4 a.m., what's got their hearts beating fast. (2016, p. 39)

Usually coach and teacher are able to confirm direction quickly, whereupon the conversation moves naturally into the second step, Review Progress. When that transition takes longer than one or two minutes, coach and teacher are probably talking about something very important. A teacher who feels overwhelmed by planning, thrilled about student progress, worried about a new program, or excited about plans for her class, frequently just wants to reflect on those ideas with a trusted colleague for a few minutes. Often that trusted colleague is a coach.

When Jacee and Marci met for coaching conversations, Marci frequently took time at the start of the coaching conversation to ensure that she and Jacee were indeed on the same page about what they needed to discuss. Sometime after Marci and Jacee were no longer at the same school, I wrote Jacee to ask how important she felt it was for Marci to take the time to confirm direction. Jacee wrote back the following:

> Marci and I had a variety of conversations about our lives and my students' lives on many occasions. Every student has unique needs. The year I worked with Marci I had students facing domestic violence, a variety of behavioral diagnoses, complicated home lives and even anxiety. Looking back, we had many conversations about how overwhelming it was to carefully respect each individual student's need while still achieving the goal. I remember how good it felt to have someone listen. Marci would listen and sometimes empathize, sympathize or give advice. I often felt like I needed to put her on a payroll for being my counselor or cheerleader. Sometimes we weren't actually talking about coaching, but they were some of the most important and pivotal conversations in my journey as a teacher.

After Marci and Jacee confirmed direction, they inevitably ended up discussing how students were doing as they progressed toward their goal. This meant that Jacee and Marci naturally ended up talking about the students' progress, the second step in the Improve stage of the Impact Cycle: Review Progress.

Questions for Step 1: Confirm Direction

Given the time we have today, what's the most important thing for us to talk about?

What's on your mind?

STEP 2: REVIEW PROGRESS

During the Improve stage of the Impact Cycle, the coach and teacher gather data for at least two reasons: (a) to assess how close a teacher's students have gotten to the goal and (b) to measure how the teacher is implementing the new strategy.

When I was coaching Cat Monroe, one of the two teachers featured in the videos that accompany this book, her goal was that 85 percent of her students would be authentically engaged, so we naturally gathered data on students' engagement. Additionally, since Cat was trying to increase engagement by asking more open-ended, opinion questions,[1] we also gathered data on that. So I video recorded Cat's lessons, and then Cat reviewed the video to identify how many of her questions were open/opinion questions vs. closed/right-or-wrong questions.

Video 5.1

Cat Reviews Data to Monitor Progress

resources.corwin.com/ impactcycle

Data reveal how close students and teachers have progressed toward their goals and help teachers and coaches partner to identify next steps. When students and teachers have met their goals, the coach and teacher plan next actions. When goals have not been met, the following questions have proven to be most helpful by pointing to a way forward. The coach usually asks only a few of these questions, depending on the teacher and the students.

What has gone well? Beginning with successes, coach and teacher keep motivation high by starting on a positive note, which, as I explain, is especially important when otherwise teachers might be tempted to give up hope that they will reach their goal. Even under the best of circumstances, reaching a goal usually requires some adjustments, so

---

1. For more information on questioning and student engagement, see *High-Impact Instruction: A Framework for Great Teaching* (Knight, 2013).

teachers may need to be reminded of the successes they have already experienced so as not to focus on what might feel like lack of progress, or failure. Knowing what went well also serves a practical purpose because coach and teacher may want to amplify that success by applying it to other aspects of the lesson. Other ways to word this question include, "What are you seeing that shows this strategy is successful?" "What progress has been made toward the goal?"

What did you learn? This is an open question that still provides focus to the coaching conversation, which may or may not be warranted at the time. The question calls attention to the experimental and creative nature of the work the coach and teacher are doing together. Teacher and coach are trying out new ways of reaching out to students, and they should be learning all the time. A slightly different way to ask this question is to ask, "What surprised you?"

What roadblocks are you running into? Of course, knowing what is going well is not enough. Teacher and coach also have to talk about what is keeping the teacher and students from meeting the goal. This question is open enough that teachers are free to identify whatever comes to mind. Sometimes with this question, the coach feels a need to reframe the conversation by narrowing the focus, away from complaint to commitment. For example, if a teacher says, "My biggest roadblock is that these students don't care about learning at all," the coach might ask, "What would it look like if your students did care about learning?" Then, after the teacher has explained that, the coach could ask, "What could we do that might move the students in that direction?"

As mentioned above, one important role the coach plays while reviewing progress is to provide support when teachers start to doubt that they will hit their goal. As change experts James Prochaska, John Norcross, and Carlo DiClemente (1994) have found, when people experience change, "linear progression is a . . . relatively rare phenomenon" (p. 47). Most changers "slip up at some point" (p. 47). Smokers require three or four serious attempts before actually changing, and New Year's resolutions stick only after at least five consecutive years. "Relapse remains the rule rather the exception when it comes to solving most common problems" (p. 47).

Brian Moran and Michael Lennington, authors of *The 12-Week Year* (2013) who draw on Don Kelley and Daryl Connor's classic emotional cycle of change, offer a similar perspective, suggesting that when people make changes, they move through five phases: (a) uninformed optimism, (b) informed pessimism, (c) the valley of despair, (d) informed optimism, and (e) success and fulfillment. Most problematic, of course, is the valley of despair. The authors write:

The valley of despair . . . is when most people give up. All of the pain of change is felt and the benefits seem far away or less important—and there is a fast, easy way to end the discomfort: Going back to the way you used to do things. After all, you rationalize that it wasn't so bad before. (p. 99)

Michael Fullan (2000), after decades of studying educational change initiatives around the globe, describes a similar phenomenon: People attempting to change usually experience what he refers to as an "implementation dip," "literally a dip in performance or confidence as one encounters an innovation that requires new skills and new understandings" (p. 41). During change, Fullan writes, "People feel anxious, fearful, confused, overwhelmed, deskilled, cautious, and—if they have moral purpose—deeply disturbed" (p. 41).

Anxious, disturbed, a valley of despair? These are not warm and fuzzy words and phrases. No wonder teachers sometimes want to give up. But, that is all the more reason why coaches can be extremely helpful. An effective coach understands, as Michael Fullan says about leaders, "that their job is to help people get through the dip" (2000, p. 72).

Marci confidently and calmly helped Jacee get through the rough waters and ambiguous times of the dip by keeping a focus on the goal, pointing out the gains that had already occurred and reminding Jacee that change is almost always messy. At the same time, while actively providing support, Marci never took control of the learning process but always positioned Jacee as the decision maker.

Jacee's first decision was whether or not she would be coached. Jacee didn't choose to be coached until January when she came to Marci for help with writing. Together Marci and Jacee worked out a writing goal and identified that they needed to work on Content Planning from *High-Impact Instruction* (Knight, 2013) as the starting point for their work. Marci told me, "She just wanted to work in the area of writing, so I suggested the process and the strategy. But, from there she was able to state the goal. We kind of shared ideas about the strategies."

After she and Marci reviewed her students' writing, the goal Jacee identified was that 80 percent of her students would be able to independently write a well-organized paragraph three times in a row and that the other 20 percent of the students would be able to write paragraphs with some support. Jacee with Marci developed a paragraph-writing checklist that they used to assess student writing, and they determined that Jacee would try to meet her goal using guiding questions to identify learning outcomes, learning maps to depict the content, and formative assessment to measure progress.

For Jacee and Marci the goal was essential. Coach and teacher would not have been able to monitor progress if they hadn't first identified a destination—they had to know what they were progressing toward if they were going to measure progress. The checklist they created also functioned as an easy and powerful way to see how close they were to the goal. Marti Elford, our project director and Marci's coach, told me, "The goal was essential. Without the goal, I really think they would have just spun in circles for months."

Another way Jacee monitored progress was to watch herself on video. Reviewing video recordings of her lessons helped Jacee see more clearly when she was and was not meeting students' needs, and what she learned from the recordings helped her learn a lot more during her conversations with Marci:

> I guess there are two sides to watching myself on video. Sometimes I would watch my lessons and think about all the things I am stressing out about. I would think, "Wow. I wish they could hear my thinking." Sometimes I would see the students' needs and I would have to change what I was doing. All the things that a student sees, I could see in the videos. I could see the difference between the perceptions I wanted the students to have vs. what it really looked like—it was right there. It was very telling.

Once the goal was set, everyone was deeply committed to helping Jacee's students hit their goal of writing well-organized paragraphs. Jacee told me, "Working with these kids from poverty, you really want them to hit the goal—you want to take them under your wing and coddle them. You want to do it for them, but they have to do it for themselves. They need to learn how to get the tools they need so they can do this when I am not here."

The people who set out to make it through the Dip—the people who invest the time and the energy and the effort to power through the Dip—those are the ones who become the best in the world. They are breaking the system because, instead of moving on to the next thing, instead of doing slightly above average and settling for what they've got, they embrace the challenge. For whatever reason, they refuse to abandon the quest and they push through the Dip all the way to the next level.

—Seth Godin
The Dip: A Little Book That Teaches You When to Quit (and When to Stick)
(2007, pp. 23–24)

What has gone well?

What are you seeing that shows this strategy is successful?

What progress has been made toward the goal?

What did you learn?

What surprised you?

What roadblocks are you running into?

STEP 3: INVENT IMPROVEMENTS

In many ways, this step, Invent Improvements, is at the heart of the Impact Cycle. To move through this step, coach and teacher must work through the roadblocks they encounter on their journey and discover what they need to do so that they can reach their destination. Usually, this involves seeing and building upon what is working, as well as identifying false steps that have to be taken back. Invent Improvements is the most important, most creative, and, ultimately, the most rewarding part of coaching.

The reality of improvement is that teachers usually don't hit their goal after one attempt at a new strategy. This means that coach and teacher may have to step outside of their comfort zones. It also means that coach and teacher often have to look at the classroom from multiple perspectives—seeing the classroom through students' eyes, looking at different forms of data, and modifying teaching strategies until they make the difference both teacher and coach are hoping for.

In part because of the complexity of the challenge, Invent Improvements can be the most challenging part of instructional coaching. On the one hand, coaches at times have to share their knowledge about effective instruction. Often, an instructional coach's primary job is to help teachers learn and implement powerful, proven teaching strategies so teachers' students can hit their goals. Teaching is often so demanding and complex that it would be foolish for coaches not to share what they know to help teachers meet their goals.

On the other hand, coaches need to resist the temptation to tell teachers what to do and resist giving in to what, as I described earlier in the book,

Michael Bungay Stanier (2016) refers to as the "advice monster." According to Bungay Stanier, we are often tempted to give advice whether or not the advice is actually helpful.

> Even if it's the wrong advice—and it often is—giving it feels more comfortable than the ambiguity of asking a question. You have the best intentions to stay curious and ask a few good questions. But in the moment, just as you are moving to that better way of working, the Advice Monster leaps out of the darkness and hijacks the conversation. Before you realize what's happening, your mind is turned toward finding The Answer and you're leaping in to offer ideas, suggestions, and recommended ways forward. (p. 60)

This is the fundamental paradox faced by every instructional coach. Research provides the answers to many of the challenges teachers face, but giving advice is often unhelpful, unheeded, and disempowering for teachers. What is a coach to do?

The answer is: Share answers dialogically rather than directly. When coaches embrace a dialogical approach, they share what they know when it is appropriate, being careful not to offer suggestions before they are necessary. Then, when they do share ideas or strategies, they share them provisionally, ensuring that their collaborating teachers remain the decision makers in the coaching process.

Many who write about this topic suggest that the way to foster dialogue is to do what Chris Argyris has referred to as "balancing advocacy with inquiry." For example, in *Dialogue and the Art of Thinking Together* (1999), William Isaacs summarizes Argyris's ideas.

> Advocacy means speaking what you think, speaking for a point of view. Inquiry means looking into what you do not yet know, what you do not yet understand, or seeking to discover what others see and understand that may differ from your point of view . . . Balancing advocacy and inquiry means stating clearly and confidently what one thinks and why one thinks it, while at the same time being open to being wrong. It means encouraging others to challenge our views and to explore what might stop them from doing so. (pp. 188–189)

When instructional coaches embrace a dialogical stance, they let go of the need to be right—to do what is right. This means that coaches always position their collaborating teachers as decision makers, offering suggestions only when necessary, and then, when sharing strategies, asking teachers how they would like to modify them to take advantage of their strengths as teachers along with the strengths and weaknesses of their students.

When instructional coaches take the dialogical approach, they begin conversation with questions, questions that will foster inquiry and enable teacher and coach to think together, brainstorm, share, and invent solutions together. When coaches give in to the Advice Monster, coaching conversations often lack energy and seem more like an argument than a dialogue. But when coaches start by humbly asking good questions, listening effectively, valuing their collaborating teachers' ideas, and communicating respect, the Inventing Improvements conversation becomes energizing, highly engaging, fun, and extremely helpful.

The following questions help coaches foster dialogue as they partner with instructional coaches to Invent Improvements that will help teachers help their students move closer to the goal.

Do you want to keep using the strategy as it is? Often a coach and teacher have identified a great goal and an appropriate strategy that should move the class to the goal, only to find that the strategy doesn't have much impact when it is first implemented. The teacher may be tempted to change the strategy, but often the best plan is to wait for the strategy to start to have an impact. The reality is that when students have developed counterproductive habits of behavior, such as frequent disruptions or lack of engagement, it will take time for any change to reverse these habits to have an impact since habits are reasonably entrenched. Furthermore, some strategies simply take a while to have an impact.

When Wendy Reinke coached teachers to increase positive attention to decrease disruptions, she eventually saw pretty dramatic changes in student behavior. However, those changes didn't happen immediately; in fact, in some cases, student behavior got worse before it got better (Sprick, Knight, Reinke, Skyles, & Barnes, 2010).

When I worked with Cat Monroe, Cat changed from asking a lot of closed, right-or-wrong questions to asking more open, opinion questions. Eventually, the change had an impact, but students were so used to answering closed questions that it took a while for them to become more engaged. The bottom line here is that before a teacher changes her strategies midstream, she should ask whether or not the strategy just needs more time to have the desired impact.

Do you want to revisit how you use the strategy? During the Learn stage of the Impact Cycle, the coach and teacher determine how a strategy will be used in the classroom by going through a checklist (or a few checklists) and modifying it until it describes the selected teaching strategy in the way that the teacher expects will have the most powerful impact on students' learning and/or well-being. Once the strategy is used in the classroom, however, it often becomes clear that adaptations have to be made for the strategy to have maximum impact.

At least three kinds of modifications can be made to teaching strategies with the goal of having more impact.

First, teachers may feel they have to tighten up the way they are using the strategy. If a teacher watches her lesson on video, for example, she may realize that she skipped some items on the checklist and that she will have more impact if she uses the teaching strategy in a way that is closer to what is on the checklist. I have found that it sometimes takes me several attempts before I am able to use a new teaching strategy fluently.

Second, teachers may feel that the changes they made to the original strategy decreased its effectiveness. For example, a teacher who used learning maps to increase student achievement, but who didn't think students needed to write their own notes on the maps, may decide that the maps would be more powerful if students did write on them.

Finally, teachers may decide that more changes have to be made to a strategy to increase its impact. When Cat and I worked together, we came to the conclusion that the open, opinion questions would have more impact if we used them with powerful thinking prompts. We agreed that the open questions were not having the impact we hoped for and that Cat might be able to increase their impact if she shared provocative thinking prompts that dealt with issues students would want to discuss because they found them personally relevant.

Video 5.2

Crysta Changes How She Assesses Engagement

resources.corwin.com/impactcycle

Do you want to choose a new strategy? The Improve stage of the Impact Cycle always involves some experimentation, as it is often difficult to predict whether or not a teaching strategy will work until teacher and coach see how students react to it. Frequently, teacher and coach identify a strategy that works, but sometimes a strategy simply misses the mark. For example, a teacher might use a cooperative learning strategy to increase student engagement and then discover that before cooperative learning can have an impact, she needs to implement some classroom management strategies.

On those occasions when teachers decide to change a new teaching strategy, coach and teacher will need to repeat most parts of the Learn stage of the Impact Cycle. Thus, the coach will have to explain the strategy to the collaborating teacher using a checklist, and then ask the teacher how she would like to adapt it to meet the needs of her students and her own teaching style. Also, in our experience, most teachers greatly benefit from seeing the teaching strategy demonstrated in one or more of the ways described in Chapter 4.

Do you want to change the way we measure progress toward the goal? Just as coach and teacher may find that they need to modify the way a teaching strategy is implemented, they may also discover that they need to modify how they measure progress toward the goal. An effective measure, as researchers say, should be valid—measuring what it is supposed to measure—and reliable, yielding the same score when used correctly by different people.

When I worked with Cat, we started off measuring progress by asking the students to complete an exit ticket ranking their level of engagement from 1 to 4, with 4 being authentically engaged. But we soon realized that our measure was not giving us valid data because we could see that the students were strategically compliant at best (going through the motions but not excited about learning), yet ranked themselves as authentically engaged. We switched to using experience sampling to gather data (see the Instructional Coaches' Toolkit at the end of this book for more information on experience sampling), and from that point forward we got much more valid data.

Do you want to change the goal? Often teacher and coach set a goal fairly quickly. We have found that even an imprecise, general goal can provide a rough target to get the Impact Cycle started. However, once teacher and coach start to implement changes in the classroom, they may realize that the goal needs to be refined.

For example, a coach and teacher may set a goal without considering the standards that exist for the teacher's class and, after reviewing the standards carefully, decide they need a more or a less challenging goal. Additionally, after coach and teacher watch students try to hit the goal, they may decide that students will hit the goal quickly and, therefore, choose to set a more challenging goal, or they may decide that the goal is too challenging and, therefore, make the goal more reachable.

A word of caution: Coach and teacher must resist the temptation to choose a less challenging goal until they are sure that the goal needs to be modified. If teachers and coaches water down their goals too quickly, they will never know what their students would have been capable of achieving—this is very important given that the goal of coaching is to help students and teachers achieve their best.

One important aspect to remember about the Impact Cycle is that although it involves clearly described stages and steps, the cycle itself is designed to adapt to the unique strengths and needs of teachers and students. That is, the cycle prescribes stages and steps, but it is a different process every time. This is especially true when teachers and coaches meet to Invent Improvements. Indeed, its very adaptability makes the Impact Cycle especially helpful when used for the complex situation of the classroom. In fact, coaches will struggle to be effective if they do not recognize the complexity of teaching and the need for adaptive responses to that complexity.

We can get some insight into the need for adaptive responses by considering the writing of two researchers from Toronto, Sholom Glouberman and Brenda Zimmerman, who published a work in 2002 that described the different complexities of work. Although their report referenced health care workers, their explanations help us understand the complexity of coaching.

The authors identified three types of tasks: simple, complicated, and complex. A simple task, like baking a cake, involves a simple set of steps, like a recipe, that will produce the same results each time when the steps are followed. A complicated task, like putting a person on the moon, involves much more complicated work, but it still involves formulas and recipes that, when they are followed, should produce predictable outcomes. Finally, a complex task, like raising a three-year-old, cannot be broken down into a set of steps because every day and every child are different. Within complex tasks, the authors explain,

> Although expertise can contribute to the process in valuable ways, it provides neither necessary nor sufficient conditions to assure success. To some extent this is because every child is unique and must be understood as an individual. As a result there is always some uncertainty of the outcome. (p. vi)

Different types of challenges require different types of responses. Ron Heifetz, founding director of the Center for Public Leadership at Harvard University, along with Alexander Grashow and Marty Linsky, describes the kinds of challenges presented by simple and complicated tasks as technical challenges. According to these authors, technical challenges "have known solutions that can be implemented by current know-how. They can be resolved through the application of authoritative expertise" (2009, p. 19).

Heifetz and his colleagues view the challenges presented by complex tasks as adaptive challenges. The authors write that "adaptive challenges can only be addressed through changes in people's priorities, beliefs, habits, and loyalties. Making progress requires going beyond any authoritative expertise to mobilize discovery, shedding certain entrenched ways, tolerating losses, and generating new ideas to thrive anew" (p. 19). Put another way, there is no simple recipe for the complex task of raising a child, for example.

If raising one child is complex, educating and inspiring a room full of children must be especially complex, and certainly anyone who has taught recognizes how many variables are at play in the classroom. Teaching and coaching require adaptability. In *Guiding Lights: The People Who Lead Us Toward Our Purpose in Life* (2004), Eric Lui describes why all educators, including coaches, need to demonstrate adaptability:

> Teaching is not one-size-fits-all; it's one-size-fits-one. So before we transmit a single thing, we must tune in to the unique and ever-fluctuating frequency of every learner: his particular mix of temperament, skills, intelligence, and motivation. This means, as teachers, putting aside our own egos and preconceptions about what makes this particular lesson so important . . . It means letting go of the idea of control. (p. 47)

"Most problems," Heifetz and his colleagues write, "come mixed with the technical and adaptive elements intertwined" (2009, p. 19). In schools, technical solutions are appropriate for simple and complicated tasks like organizing a seating chart or teaching basic procedures such as how to hand out assignments, but most of teaching is complex work, and technical solutions will not work. Indeed, the authors write, "The most common failure in leadership is produced by treating adaptive challenges as if they were technical problems" (p.19). The same is true for coaching. A one-size-fits-all model for coaching will not lead to improvements and may actually make things worse.

For these reasons, coaches need to be quick to respond to the real opportunities presented by teachers and students. To be responsive, they need to have valuable expertise to share with teachers, and they need to be open to exploring many different pathways toward a goal. Effective interactions involve what I refer to as an "informed, adaptive response."

Part of the reason Marci was such as an effective coach was that her responses were truly informed and adaptive. To be informed, she had to understand effective instruction—the central task of an instructional coach, after all, is partnering with teachers to improve instruction. As a participant in our study, Marci gained a deep understanding of the effective teaching strategies described in *High-Impact Instruction* (Knight, 2013). She fully understood the Impact Cycle described in that book, and she was a National Board Certified Teacher who had taught every grade from second through to twelfth. In addition, she was a certified trainer for Charlotte Danielson's *Framework for Teaching* (1996) and had a deep understanding of many other resources for teachers.

Marci's knowledge about coaching was essential, but just as essential was the fact that she used that knowledge to make sure that her coaching was not "one size fits all," but "one size fits one." Thus, Marci partnered with

Jacee to adapt the learning maps described in *High-Impact Instruction* so that Jacee could more clearly describe the elements of an effective paragraph. She also guided Jacee to use formative assessment to monitor student progress toward the goal and helped her use the gradual release model of "I do it, We do it, You do it" to ensure students were exposed to sufficient modeling and practice to learn how to develop effective paragraphs.

As Marci and Jacee moved through the Impact Cycle, Marci was ready to help Jacee move through roadblocks. For example, when Jacee wasn't sure how to help her students understand the difference between main ideas and details, Marci asked some questions that helped Jacee come up with an instructional plan. Similarly, when Jacee felt overwhelmed with grading, and was close to giving up, Marci helped her come up with the strategy of having students give each other peer evaluations to lessen the burden on Jacee.

Marci's ability to adapt was something that Marti Elford especially noticed:

> Marci and Jacee met every week, and every day Jacee would say, "This is where we are," and "I think this is going really well." Or, "This is not going so well. What do you think we should do differently?"

Marci and Jacee would talk it through. Often Marci would go to the meeting prepared with some ideas. When that happened, Jacee wouldn't just accept it at face value. She would look at it. She would think, *OK, that might work, but it might be even better if we did this*. So, Marci's idea would give Jacee something to go on. It would spark her own thinking. They were even adaptive about the goal. Marci told me:

> The goal was something that we adjusted, came back to, and worked on for a long time, and she persisted through it. I think the support I was able to give her . . . for example, we looked at some research, the content planning process was pretty eye-opening to help her see how complex writing is. There were many times I positioned myself in the class as a co-teacher. I might not have been modeling, but I was there to bounce ideas off if she got stuck in the middle of a lesson. I remember one time she said, "When things get really, really hard in the middle of a classroom, my default is to stop everything and do something totally different." So, one of the reasons why I positioned myself as a co-teacher in the classroom was that when they hit a hard spot in the students' writing, when it was kind of messy and all over the place, and she did not know what to do, I could just offer a question or two to get us thinking about how we could keep going with writing and not quit. Don't stop the lesson. Let's push through it.

Video 5.3

Crysta Discusses the Progress She Has Made

resources.corwin.com/impactcycle

Do you want to keep using the strategy as it is?

Do you want to revisit how you use the teaching strategy?

Do you want to choose a new strategy?

Do you want to change the way we measure progress toward the goal?

Do you want to change the goal?

STEP 4: PLAN NEXT ACTIONS

All of the work teachers and coaches do together—watching video, setting goals, learning new teaching strategies, and so on—will not mean anything unless teachers actually implement the new strategies, monitor progress, and make adaptations, as necessary, until goals are met. For that reason, Plan Next Actions is a crucial step when coaches partner with teachers to help them help their students hit goals.

Numerous books have been written about how to plan, manage time, and be more productive (several are listed at the end of this chapter). When the collective body of studies on productivity is reviewed, certain steps and themes occur repeatedly. Instructional coaches, who want to see real change happen, may find these suggestions help them have an unmistakable positive impact in their schools.

Set goals that produce great work. As I've written throughout this book, instructional coaching is propelled forward by a powerful, emotionally compelling goal, and when there is no goal, there is a real likelihood that no meaningful action will occur. Planning for each week begins only when there is a goal—one that teachers are willing to work hard to achieve. Michael Bungay Stanier writes that we need to set goals that inspire great work, and he distinguishes between bad work and great work. "Bad work," Stanier writes, "is a waste of time, energy, and life. Doing it once is one time to many" (2010, p. 4). On the other hand, "Great work . . . is the work that is meaningful to you, that has an impact and makes a difference. It inspires, stretches, and provokes. Great work is the work that matters" (p. 5). The first step in being productive, then, is to set goals that produce great work.

Write down and organize what has to be done. In large part, being productive can happen only when the ambiguous aspects of our action are translated into action steps that can actually be taken. As David

Allen, probably the most influential productivity author writing today, has said, "We have to transform all the 'stuff' we're trying to organize into actionable stuff we need to do" (2002, p. 17). Simply put, Allen says, we need to identity the important parts of a project, sort those parts, and break everything down to an appropriate level of detail.

Almost every productivity author I reviewed agrees that, as Scott Belsky writes, change leaders must have "a relentless bias toward action" (2012, p. 25). This means that change leaders (in our case, teachers and coaches) must clearly describe what actions need to take place and then identify when those actions will occur and who will carry them out.

Ensure that actions are done. Plans only matter when they are turned into actions, so a big part of a relentless focus on action is to commit to doing what you plan to do. There are many ways to do this, but I find Leo Babauta's (2009) book to be most powerful. Babauta suggests that to implement an action, we should identify no more than three Most Important Tasks (MITs) we have to do each day to move toward our goal. Our MITs, he writes, "are the tasks you want or need to get done today" (p. 58).

> Here's the beauty of MITs: Usually the small, unimportant tasks that we need to get done every day (emails, phone calls, paperwork, errands, meetings, internet browsing, etc.) will get in the way of our important longer-term tasks—but if you make your MITs your top priorities each day, the important stuff will get done instead of the unimportant. (p. 58)

Simplicity boils down to two steps: Identify the essential. Eliminate the rest.

—Leo Babauta
The Power of Less (2009, p. ix)

Every person plans differently, and some people are more comfortable with what I like to call improvisational planning than others. As a general rule, when it comes to coaching, however, I've found it is better to do too much planning than too little. When coach and teacher maintain a "relentless focus on action," they usually do three things: (a) identify the date and time for the next coaching meeting, (b) identify tasks to be done prior to the meeting, and (c) estimate when the tasks will be completed. The coaching planning form on the next page is designed to help coaches and teachers track and help students in hitting their goals.

NEXT STEPS PLANNING FORM

GOAL	PROGRESS	NEXT ACTIONS	WHEN	COMMITMENT LEVEL (1–5)

Available for download at **resources.corwin.com/impactcycle**

Using the coaching planning form. The coaching planning form is designed to be used when coaches and teachers meet to plan next actions. Completed from left to right, coaches may want to complete the form as they move through the four steps of the Improve questions or complete it as a closing activity for planning next actions.

As they prepare to use the form, teacher and coach begin by discussing whether or not they need to modify the goal at all. After the teacher decides whether or not she wants to modify the goal, the goal is written on the form. Then, coach and teacher record the latest data on progress toward the goal. For example, a coach working with a teacher whose goal is to increase time on task to 95 percent would simply write down the most recent score on measures of time on task. Teacher and coach then turn to identifying next actions by completing the form and answering a few questions.

When should we meet next? By answering this question, teacher and coach establish an ending point for planning. I suggest teacher and coach meet at least once each week. Meeting within one week maintains everyone's focus and provides for a quick response when strategies are not successful. If teacher and coach let two weekends pass before they meet, there is a real danger that ground may be lost.

What tasks have to be done before we meet again? When will they happen? Who will do them? I suggest that coach and teacher first write down next actions on sticky notes, trying to write down all actions that are to be completed. Then, they can organize the notes chronologically, double-checking to make sure they have written down all of the important tasks. The next step is to write down the tasks on the form in a way that also identifies who will do what. Finally, the teacher, guided by the coach, determines when each task will be completed, and the coach writes the date on the form.

On a scale of 1–5, how committed are you to this goal now? Before concluding, I think it is a good idea to ask the collaborating teacher whether his level of commitment to the goal is changing. Sometimes, small successes help teachers to see that their goal is attainable, and, if so, coaches can respond by sharing that enthusiasm. At other times, teachers, especially at first, feel overwhelmed by the roadblocks they are encountering, and, in such case, the coach can be a big help just by reinforcing that the goal is worthwhile and achievable. However, when a teacher's commitment truly

Video 5.4

Crysta Makes Plans for Next Actions

Video 5.5

Cat Makes Plans for Next Actions

resources.corwin.com/impactcycle

Video 5.6

Crysta's Improve Stage—Complete

Video 5.7

Cat's Improve Stage—Complete

resources.corwin.com/ impactcycle

drops, coach and teacher should explore whether a different goal or different strategies might foster a higher level of commitment.

To help Jacee plan each next action for coaching, Marci met with her at least once every week. In these meetings, Marci helped Jacee break down the standards, set short-term goals, and give sound feedback to her students. With Marci's help, Jacee stayed focused and persevered, in part because the goal was so important to her, to Marci, and, ultimately, to Marti. Eventually, Jacee's students hit their goal.

Looking back on the coaching process that Marci and Jacee experienced, Marti told me that one reason they succeeded was that:

None of us was willing to give up; Jacee was so invested in her students, and Marci was so invested in Jacee, I was so invested in Marci, so when those students succeeded, when they reached their goal and when they understood what a great thing they had done and how important it was—that was the reward. If I never do anything else in my career, the work we did is some of the most rewarding work I've ever done.

Everyone was thrilled when Jacee's students hit the goal of writing effective paragraphs at least three times in a row, and when I talked with Jacee, she described how Marci had supported her and helped her plan for success. "She was very patient with me, and she was able to know my personality and keep moving me forward. She was able to get me back to our objective and our goal when I got impatient."

Jacee also talked about what it felt like to go through the Impact Cycle.

I have always been reflective, but the process encouraged me to be reflective in a different way. It took the subjectivity out of a lot of things. The video showed me that what I thought was happening and what was really happening were two different things. It changed my perception of some things. In a lot of ways, it helped me feel better about what I was doing vs. me just beating myself up, and that encouraged me to keep going. The process taught me to not be afraid when I don't know how to do something. It taught me I can make modifications and change; I can become a better teacher when my students need me to be. That is something I still work hard on every day—to be the teacher my students need, not the teacher I want to be.

Marti, who watched the coaching proceed from a distance, was impressed and moved by what she saw unfold as the coach and teacher moved through the Impact Cycle until they hit the goal:

> I think there are teachers who are born with a teacher's heart. Those people realize they have a limited amount of time to pour knowledge and confidence and the right amount of challenge into the students that come into their classroom. I think Jacee is one of those people. I think she's predisposed to be concerned. She had a diverse group of children. She had students who would have succeeded without a lot of instruction and support but she also had a couple who might never have succeeded. I really believe that this goal and Marci and Jacee working together was huge in the success of those students who really never had success. It may make all the difference in their lives because now they know they can succeed.

Video 5.8

Crysta's Entire Impact Cycle—Complete

Video 5.9

Cat's Entire Impact Cycle—Complete

resources.corwin.com/impactcycle

Questions for Step 4: Plan Next Actions

When should we meet again?

What tasks have to be done before we meet?

When will those tasks be done?

Who will do them?

On a scale of 1–5, how committed are you to this goal now?

TO SUM UP

The Improve stage of the Impact Cycle can be the most complex because during this stage coach and teacher often have to invent adaptations and solutions so that teachers and students can hit their goals. When coaches guide teachers through this stage, they usually move through four steps.

- During the Confirm Direction step, coaches ask questions to make sure that their conversation is focused on what is most important to collaborating teachers.

- During the Review Progress step, coaches review data and ask questions so that they and the collaborating teacher can identify how close they are to the goal.

- During the Invent Improvement step, coaches and teachers collaborate to identify what needs to be changed, if anything, so that the goals can be met.

- During the Plan Next Actions step, coaches and teachers identify when they will meet again, what has to happen before that meeting, when those actions will happen, and who will do them.

MAKING IT REAL

As is usually the case, a powerful way for coaches to improve their coaching skills is to video record coaching conversations and watch the video to see how frequently they had to fight the urge to give advice. If collaborating teachers don't mind, it can be especially helpful to watch teachers' facial expressions during coaching conversations to see how teachers respond when they are asked questions and given advice. Coaches can learn a lot by watching a video recording of a conversation several times to get a clear picture of the impact the questions and statements they make during coaching conversations.

Coaches can also use video to see how dialogical they are in their conversations with teachers. When coaches watch video of their lessons, they can consider a few simple questions:

- Who is doing most of the talking?
- Who is doing most of the thinking?

- Is the collaborating teacher genuinely problem-solving or just agreeing with my thinking?
- Was the solution primarily made by me, my collaborating teacher, or both of us?

When coaches are truly engaged in dialogue, their collaborating teachers should be doing most of the talking and thinking and should be authentically engaged in problem solving, not just agreeing with their coach. During effective coaching sessions, the collaborating teacher usually comes up with the solution or does so in partnership with the coach.

One final way coaches can deepen their understanding is through what we call coaching fishbowls:

1. Coach and teacher set up a role-play or real coaching situation (e.g., a coach might bring in an actual scenario, and another coach could role-play being the teacher, or if it is possible to get a substitute teacher, the real teacher could come to the session).

2. Coach and teacher move through the Invent Improvements step of the cycle (or some other part of the cycle). The coach can push the "pause" button at any point to get advice or to ask the teacher for his or her perspective on the process. Consider video recording the session and then reviewing the session.

Different coaches can do this at different times throughout a year, and other steps and stages can be studied—such as identifying a goal or explaining a strategy using a checklist.

GOING DEEPER

About one week after our research team realized we had to find a way to help our coaches ask better questions, I was lucky enough to see Susan Scott give a presentation on having "fierce conversations," and thanks to her, I began to see the power in a well-asked question. Susan's books, *Fierce Conversations: Achieving Success at Work and in Life One Conversation at a Time* (2002) and *Fierce Leadership: A Bold Alternative to the Worst "Best" Practices of Business Today* (2009), come from a slightly different theoretical grounding than my work, but they are both packed with communication strategies that can help any coach.

Three books, in particular, have influenced my understanding of dialogue. David Bohm's *On Dialogue* (2004), which is actually a presentation that was transcribed and turned into a short book, has influenced a generation of authors writing about dialogue, and I have found the book to be profound, wise, and very helpful. William Isaacs is one of many authors who were deeply influenced by Bohm. Isaac's *Dialogue: The Art of Thinking Together* (1999) is an almost encyclopedic description of its topic, a comprehensive, theoretical book that nevertheless contains many practical suggestions for anyone interested in fostering dialogue. Finally, Paulo Freire's *Pedagogy of the Oppressed* (1970), which I first read as an undergraduate in a second-year Philosophy of Education class, has probably influenced me more than any other book I've ever read. The book is not an easy read, at least it wasn't for me; sometimes it reads more like a poem than a treatise, but it is nevertheless a compelling manifesto for engaging in dialogue to honor the humanity of everyone we encounter.

I am a little compulsive about trying to plan and use my time effectively, so I read time management books the way a world traveler might pore over maps. Several books have especially shaped the way I plan my life these days. David Allen's *Getting Things Done: The Art of Stress-Free Productivity* (2002) is an incredibly influential book to which practically every other productivity author owes a debt. His time management approach has been implemented by thousands, and even if you don't implement the model exactly as described by Allen, you will inevitably adopt some of his ideas if you read his book. Other books that have been very helpful for me include Scott Belsky's *Making Ideas Happen: Overcoming the Obstacles Between Vision and Reality* (2012), blogger Leo Babauta's *The Power of Less: The Fine Art of Limiting Yourself to the Essential . . . in Business and Life* (2009), and a special favorite, Michael Bungay Stanier's *Do More Great Work* (2010).

Instructional Coaches' Toolkit

Strategies for Enrolling Teachers

We see instructional coaching as a partnership, not a top-down program. As the table below illustrates, this means that teachers work with coaches because they are committed to student success, not because they are doing what they are told to do. Coaching is guided by teachers' knowledge about their students and adapted through dialogue between teacher and coach to meet the unique needs of each group of students and each classroom. Taking the partnership approach means that teachers do most of the thinking, and coaches and teachers work together equally toward the goal of making a powerful, positive difference in children's lives.

Top-Down	Partnership
Compliance	Commitment
People *outside* the classroom know what students need	People *inside* the classroom know what students need
One size fits all	One size fits one
Constructive feedback	Dialogue
Coach does most of the thinking	Teacher does most of the thinking
Judgmental	Non-judgmental
Teachers have lower status than coaches	Teachers have equal status with coaches
Accountable to leaders	Accountable to students

When leaders make coaching compulsory, they ignore one important fact: Whether teachers are told they have a choice about coaching or not, the reality is that they do have a choice. A teacher who doesn't see the value of coaching can find all kinds of ways to sidestep the coaching process. Indeed, asking coaches to spend a large amount of time trying to convince teachers that they must collaborate is a poor use of such a valuable resource.

Instructional coaching, done well, should be rewarding, worthwhile, and enjoyable and save teachers' time. Therefore, if a large number of teachers in a school do not want to be coached, most likely something is out of sync in the school culture or the coaching provided. Coaching helps teachers do what they want and need to do, and if teachers don't want coaching, the solution isn't to force it onto them; the solution is to find out why they don't want it.

The following strategies represent ways coaches and administrators can enroll teachers while also respecting teachers' need to have a voice in what they learn.

PRINCIPAL REFERRAL

If principals ignore the importance of partnership, they may unintentionally damage coaching relationships before the coaching even begins. When teachers are told they have no choice but to participate in coaching, they may be inclined to see coaching as a punishment more than a support and, therefore, resist (see William R. Miller & Stephen Rollnick's *Motivational Interviewing: Helping People Change,* 3rd Edition (2012) for a deep discussion of change and choice).

A better strategy is to make coaching optional but improvement compulsory. We refer to this as being firm on the standard and flexible on the process. In other words, a principal articulates a goal for improvement (e.g., increasing student engagement) but offers teachers the freedom to

Firm on the Standard; Flexible on How to Get There—an Example

After a school agrees that 95 percent time on task is a school-wide goal for improvement, a principal observes a classroom and sees that 63 percent of students are on task. When the principal meets with the teacher who taught the lesson for a post-observation discussion, the principal shares the data and says, "You're at 63 percent time on task, and our goal is 95 percent. The good news is, there are many things you can do. I can loan you Phil Schlecty's book *Engaging Students* if you'd like to borrow it. There are videos at the district library on how to increase engagement, and I'm sure you can also find information online about engaging students. Another option is that you could work with Kristin, our instructional coach. Kristin knows a lot about engagement, and working with her would probably be a really easy way to increase engagement. I can email Kristin if you like. But the bottom line is, how you increase engagement is up to you. All I'm concerned about is that time on task goes up, and I know you'll make it happen."

decide how they will work to improve. Ideally, teachers should also be involved in identifying the goals.[1]

Coaching flourishes in settings where administrators communicate their expectation that everyone will be engaged in some sort of improvement. Indeed, when teachers are recognized as professionals, a high expectation around improvement is a natural outcome because continuous improvement is an ever-present characteristic of professionalism. Professionals, by definition, are people who work at getting better, and anything less can only be called unprofessional. However, another equally important characteristic of professionalism is autonomy. If we want teachers to act like professionals, we need to treat them like professionals, and that starts with autonomy.

STRATEGIES FOR ENROLLING TEACHERS INTO COACHING

ONE-TO-ONE CONVERSATIONS

Often teachers are enrolled into coaching through one-to-one conversations with coaches. For this to happen, the coach schedules a time for an informal conversation with each teacher about what coaching is and how it works. Such conversations may be over in as little as fifteen minutes or last more than forty-five minutes, depending on the number of questions a teacher might have and the amount of time that is available.

To help clarify what coaches do, we suggest coaches create a simple one-page document that describes instructional coaching. The document can include a summary of the teaching practice a coach can share (see the Instructional Playbook description later in this book), a description of the coaching cycle, information about the relationship between coach and teacher, and whatever else a coach might choose to share.

Coaches may also want to confirm whether or not the teacher wishes coaching to be confidential, and explain that teachers make all the major decisions about the coaching cycle (what the goal is, which teaching strategy or strategies will implemented, when the goal is met). Some coaches believe

---

1. For more information on how to involve teachers in identifying instructional improvement goals, see *Unmistakable Impact: A Partnership Approach for Dramatically Improving Instruction*, Chapter 3 (Knight, 2011).

INSTRUCTIONAL COACHING

Instructional coaching is a confidential partnership entirely focused on making it easier for teachers to meet the needs of their students. If coaching isn't a valuable and worthwhile activity for you, I haven't done my job well.

COACHING AND MY PD PLAN

Instructional coaching is an easy and powerful way you can complete your My PD Plan.

What Can We Do Together?

All teachers identify the focus for their coaching cycle; often goals relate to student behavior (such as increasing engagement), achievement (as measured by, for example, formative assessment), and attitude (for example, encouraging students to read for pleasure).

Many of the teaching practices we might use in pursuit of your goal may be drawn from the Big Four described in Jim Knight's *High-Impact Instruction*:

Content Planning

Guiding Questions

Learning Maps

Formative Assessment

Specific Proficiencies

Checks for Understanding

Modifications to
Teaching and Learning

Instruction

Thinking Prompts

Effective Questions

Cooperative Learning

Stories

Authentic Learning

Community Building

Learner-Friendly Culture

Power With vs. Power Over

Freedom Within Form

Expectations

Witness to the Good

Corrections

Contact Information:

Wayne Gretzky: Room 99   Extension 2857 it is important to explain their own teaching experiences. Professional development expert Sue Woodruff, whom I interviewed for *Instructional Coaching: A Partnership Approach to Improving Instruction* (2007), told me that having a one-to-one conversation like this allows her to communicate that "I have had experiences in schools with real kids and real teachers." Sue explains, "I want them to see that I've been in the trenches like they are. I want them to see that the real reason I do this is because I believe in it. I have a passion for it. I'm not doing it as a job."

SMALL- OR LARGE-GROUP PRESENTATIONS

One-to-one conversations are extremely powerful but not always necessary for enrolling teachers in coaching. In settings where teachers feel a great deal of psychological safety and where there is strong enthusiasm for professional development and professional learning, coaches may want to enroll teachers through large- or small-group presentations.

In both instances, large or small groups, we have found that it is best to keep the presentations short—the presentation shouldn't be used to explain every nuance of coaching and every aspect of every teaching practice that a coach can share. The goal is simply to enroll teachers in coaching. For that reason, we suggest that coaches limit the presentation to less than thirty minutes.

During the presentation, a coach should give a simple explanation of what coaching is, and if the coach has developed a one-page document, she can share it during the presentation. Whether or not the coach has a one-page document, she should consider describing some of the nuts and bolts of coaching along with the partnership perspective that lies at the heart of the process.

During any kind of enrollment conversation, but perhaps especially during group presentations since clarity of communication goes down when the size of a group goes up, it is extremely important to communicate a deep respect for the profession of teaching. Respect is manifested in the conciseness of the presentation, the clear message that coaching is adaptive and not compulsory, and respectful comments about teaching. Coaches also need to ensure that whoever introduces or thanks them for the presentation (if that occurs) communicates a deep respect for teachers. If a person finds it difficult to communicate a deep respect for teachers, he or she probably shouldn't be coaching.

At the end of the presentation, the coach should hand out a simple form where teachers can communicate whether or not they would like to

ARE YOU INTERESTED?

Name: _____

Email Address: _____

Date: _____

I am most interested in:

_____

_____

_____

_____

_____

Times that are good for me:

_____

_____

Maybe some other time: _____

Available for download at **resources.corwin.com/impactcycle**

participate in coaching. We have found that if coaches ask people to email them to indicate if they are interested in coaching, that simple extra task limits the number of volunteers (sometimes to zero). However, if a coach shares a simple form like the one included on the previous page, then 25 percent to 75 percent of teachers usually sign up for coaching.

WORKSHOPS

Workshops introduce ideas into a system, but they rarely change practice. For practice to change, teachers likely need someone to help them implement whatever new practice is being shared. There are many reasons for this, but perhaps the main reason is that in most cases a few days after a workshop, most participants don't recall all of the finer points of a new practice, making the prospect of implementing whatever was learned overwhelming.

Fortunately, coaches can serve as teachers' memory. Workshops can introduce teachers to new practices, and the coach can help teachers put the ideas into practice. For this reason, workshops should always provide teachers with a chance to get coaching if they want to implement new practices. In truth, if coaching is not provided, attending the workshop likely won't be worthwhile. When teachers are given time to plan how to partner with a coach following a workshop, a form such as the one on the next page may be used.

INFORMAL CONVERSATIONS

A final way in which coaches can enroll teachers is through informal conversations throughout the school year. It is essential here not to make every encounter about coaching. Otherwise, teachers may start to feel they are being sold to and will start to avoid conversations with the coach. However, if during an informal conversation a teacher expresses a concern and a coach can offer some genuine support, there is a great likelihood that teachers will sign up for coaching.

The strategies suggested here give coaches many ways to enroll teachers. In most cases, coaches will find it most powerful to combine some or all of the strategies. For example, a coach might give a large-group presentation to the school and then follow up with one-to-one conversations with individual teachers. Ultimately, the most powerful way to enroll teachers is through word of mouth. If coaches help some teachers reach more students or save time, others will seek out coaching assistance for themselves.

COACHING PLANNING FORM

ACTIVITY	DATE	LOCATION	TIME
Film the class			
Identify a goal			
Explain the new teaching practice			
Model			
Film/observe the class			
Explore			

Available for download at **resources.corwin.com/impactcycle**

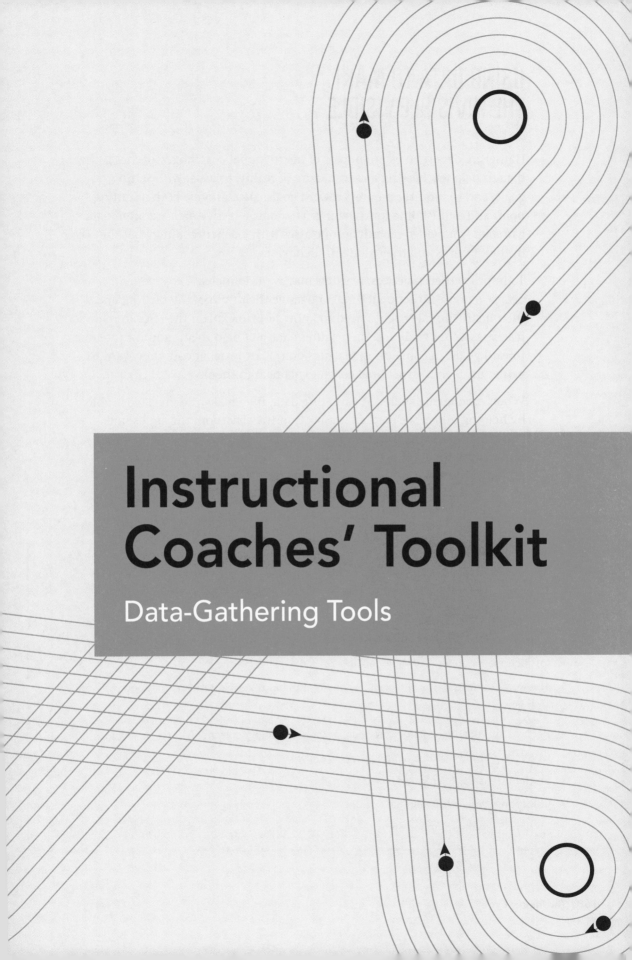

Instructional Coaches' Toolkit

Data-Gathering Tools

USING DATA TO MAKE THE INVISIBLE VISIBLE

Gathering data is an essential part of instructional coaching. Coaches gather data to help teachers get a clear picture of reality, to assist with setting goals, and to monitor progress toward goals. Data provide both a starting point and a finish line for coaching. The most effective data are often data gathered from video recordings of classes with teachers coding what they see in their lessons and their students' behavior.

To improve their practices, teachers may want to increase engagement, decrease non-instructional time, or change their ratio of interaction, and their instructional coaches need to know how to explain the relevant data so teachers can set goals and then gather data that help them monitor progress toward goals. In some cases, teachers do not know what data they want to gather until an instructional coach explains it to them.

When coaches are skilled at gathering data, they make the invisible visible by helping others see particular aspects of the classroom through some particular data focus. For example, when a coach gathers data on non-instructional time, teachers are often surprised to learn how much potential there is for more learning time in their classrooms.

Data in the Toolkit

- Student Engagement
  - Measured through time on task
  - Measured through experience sampling
- Instructional and Non-instructional Time
- The Real Learning Index (a global measure combining time on task and instructional time)
- Teacher vs. Student Talk
- Ratio of Interaction (describing reinforcing and correcting comments)
- Correcting Students (observing for consistency)
- Student Behavior (disruptions; respectful interactions)
- Questions: Type, Kind, and Level
- Student Responses (opportunity, variety, correctness)

This toolkit contains a summary of what data coaches should gather. A more comprehensive and in-depth description of how to observe teachers and students, including a summary of the relevant research for each data focus, is included in my upcoming book with Michael Faggella-Luby, *Observing for Impact* (in press). Some of what I include here was previously presented in my books *High-Impact Instruction* (Knight, 2013) and *Focus on Teaching* (Knight, 2014).

STUDENT ENGAGEMENT

When my colleagues and I conducted interviews with teachers and coaches for the book *Focus on Teaching: Using Video for High-Impact Instruction* (Knight, 2014), we found that about half of the teachers who set goals after watching video of their lessons wanted to increase student engagement during their lessons. Engagement is important; if students aren't listening, they aren't learning. However, engagement is a nuanced concept. To better describe engagement, I've slightly adapted the three levels of engagement identified by Phil Schlechty in *Engaging Students: The Next Level of Working on the Work* (2011): authentic engagement, strategic compliance, and off task.

Students who are *authentically engaged* are doing tasks because they find them inherently worthwhile, meaningful, or enjoyable. When the bell sounds to end a class, students who are authentically engaged would like to continue doing whatever they are doing.

Students who are *strategically compliant* are doing tasks because they have to do them, not because they want to do them. Such students want to finish tasks as quickly as possible so that they can spend their time on other activities that they find authentically engaging.

Finally, students who are *off task* are simply not doing the tasks they have been asked to do. They might be having side conversations, doing work for another class, texting, reading books or other publications that are unrelated to the course, or just looking out the window. Whatever they are doing, it is not what their teacher wants them to do.

TIME ON TASK

Measuring time on task is a way of taking a snapshot of how many students are doing the learning that is proposed for them at a given point in time and how many are not. Thus, if the teacher is asking students to write a paragraph, students who are on task (doing the task given them) are writing the paragraph. If the teacher is leading classroom discussion, the students who are on task are listening, asking questions, or responding to questions. As a general rule, a teacher's goal should be 90 percent time on task or higher.

Time on task is the simplest and most objective measure of engagement, but it is not a sensitive measure—that is, when you measure time on task, you don't distinguish whether students are authentically engaged or strategically compliant; you simply measure whether they are doing what they are supposed to be doing. Time on task, therefore, is an especially valuable measure in classrooms when students clearly are not on task, and even though it lacks sensitivity, it is useful because it is reliable. Different people who have had adequate training and practice time should get more or less the same results when they observe for time on task.

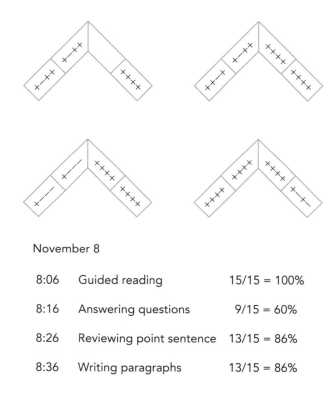

November 8

8:06	Guided reading	15/15 = 100%
8:16	Answering questions	9/15 = 60%
8:26	Reviewing point sentence	13/15 = 86%
8:36	Writing paragraphs	13/15 = 86%

The easiest way to note time on task is to record your observations on a seating chart for the students in the class. The data may be recorded in many different frequencies (every five or ten minutes, for each different activity, once or twice a class, etc.). I prefer to record data every ten minutes during a class. To do this, I watch the class for exactly ten minutes, and then at the ten-minute point, I count how many students are on task. I put a + on the seating chart under the name of every student who is on task and a – under the name of every student who is off task. I then calculate a total on-task percentage by dividing the number of students on task by the number of students in class. If twenty of twenty-five students are on task, for example, then the time on task percentage is 80 percent. Once I have assessed each student, I repeat the process after another ten minutes have passed.

Assessing Time on Task

When you are gathering time on task data, you are taking a snapshot of students' behavior at the moment you look at the students. Your observation is a sample of that moment, and it should reflect exactly what you see only at the moment of observation.

More than anything else, "time on task" means that students are engaged in the learning activity proposed for them by the teacher. Thus, if the teacher is asking students to write a paragraph, students who are on task (doing the task given them) are writing paragraphs. If the teacher is leading classroom discussion, on-task students are listening, asking questions, or responding to questions. As a general rule, a teacher's goal should be 90 percent time on task or higher.

What It Looks Like

Time on task may include some of the following student behaviors:

- Doing the assigned task, which could include (but is by no means limited to) conducting an experiment, reading, working on a cooperative learning project, writing in their notebook, engaging in classroom debate, or completing a learning sheet
- Making eye contact with the teacher or other students engaged in the assigned learning
- Responding verbally and nonverbally to teacher prompts, which could include (but is by no means limited to) smiling, doing assigned tasks, asking questions, engaging in hands-on activities, or taking out materials needed to work on a task

What It Doesn't Look Like

Time on task usually does not include some of the following student behaviors:

- Doing something other than the assigned task, such as
  - Sleeping,
  - Not taking out materials,
  - Texting,
  - Engaging in side conversations,
  - Reading unassigned reading material, or
  - Touching or bothering other students

A more sensitive but less reliable measure is assessing how many students are authentically engaged. A well-planned lesson that keeps all students authentically engaged is one that should lead to learning. Unfortunately, it is hard to know just by watching whether a student is authentically engaged or strategically compliant. Any measure of authentic engagement, therefore, is fairly subjective. We have found that the best way to determine a level of authentic engagement is to ask the students to describe their level of engagement.

Students can describe their level of engagement in different ways. In *Focus on Teaching* (Knight, 2014) I suggested that students could complete exit tickets ranking their level of engagement on a scale from 1 (not engaged) to 4 (authentically engaged). Unfortunately, we have found that students often assess themselves as being authentically engaged when we can see during the lesson that, in fact, they are mostly strategically compliant or off task.

We have found that a more accurate way of measuring authentic engagement is to use experience sampling. To do this, set a timer (such as a common kitchen timer) to go off every ten minutes in class and give every student a copy of the Engagement Form (see the facing page). Ask students to circle their level of engagement every time the bell rings. If teachers audio or video record their lessons, they can slide their recording up to just below each ten-minute point and then listen to the recording to see what students were doing when they filled in the Engagement Form. In this way, a teacher can get a picture of how students are responding to various learning activities during a lesson.

INSTRUCTIONAL VS. NON-INSTRUCTIONAL TIME

During any period of instruction, there will be times when students are engaged in activities that promote learning (such as working on a project, listening to direct instruction, cooperative learning, classroom discussion, reading, or writing) and times when they are doing things that do not directly lead to learning (transition activities such as settling in at the start of class, getting textbooks or other curriculum materials out, taking roll, or lining up to leave class at the bell).

Obviously, the more students are engaged in learning activities, the more they will learn, so increasing the amount of time students are engaged in learning is a worthy goal. You can keep track of instructional and non-instructional time by using the stopwatch function on your smartphone (or

ENGAGEMENT FORM

Date: _____

Instructions: Each time you hear the bell, please rate how engaging the learning activity is in which you are involved. You are only to rate whether or not the learning activity is engaging for you.

NONCOMPLIANT			COMPLIANT		ENGAGED	
1	2	3	4	5	6	7
1	2	3	4	5	6	7
1	2	3	4	5	6	7
1	2	3	4	5	6	7
1	2	3	4	5	6	7
1	2	3	4	5	6	7
1	2	3	4	5	6	7
1	2	3	4	5	6	7
1	2	3	4	5	6	7
1	2	3	4	5	6	7
1	2	3	4	5	6	7
1	2	3	4	5	6	7
1	2	3	4	5	6	7

 Available for download at **resources.corwin.com/impactcycle**

Data-Gathering Tools

INSTRUCTIONAL VS. NON-INSTRUCTIONAL TIME

INSTRUCTION	NON-INSTRUCTIONAL
Total Time _____	Total Time _____

Available for download at **resources.corwin.com/impactcycle**

use a stopwatch). Regardless of the tool used, the first step is to time each transition. Then subtract the total transition time from the total time of the class to see how much time was spent on learning activities (see the facing page). For example, in a forty-five-minute class, if transition time was fifteen minutes, then thirty minutes would be spent on learning activities.

THE REAL LEARNING INDEX

One of the most powerful combinations of data coaches can gather in teachers' classrooms is what we refer to as the Real Learning Index (RLI). The RLI combines time-on-task data (the percentage of students who are doing the learning activity presented to them) with instructional time data (the percentage of time focused on learning during a lesson), two very useful forms of data.

To calculate RLI, the coach (a) calculates the percentage of students who are on task at different points in a lesson (perhaps every ten minutes), (b) calculates the percentage of instructional time, and (c) multiplies one number by the other to see how much of the potential for learning has been realized.

In a class where every second is focused on instruction and every student is engaged 100 percent of the time, the RLI would be the highest possible score, 1.00 time on task × 1.00 instructional time equaling a score of 1.00 or expressed as a RLI 100. In reality, even the smoothest run, most engaging class will get a score less than 100. There will always be some non-instructional time, and likely there will always be moments when students drift off task. However, the closer a score is to 100, the more time and attention are dedicated to learning.

Let's consider a simple example to better understand the RLI. Imagine a classroom in which 78 percent of the time is instructional time. For sake of illustration, I'll depict that instructional time in the pie chart included below.

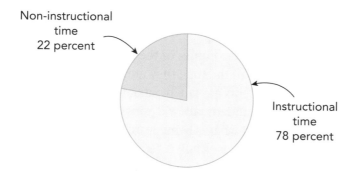

Already, we are only realizing 78 percent of the potential for learning, but the next question is how many students actually took advantage of the opportunity to learn during instructional time. As depicted in the diagram below, if 73 percent of students are on task during instructional time, the RLI is 57 (0.78 × 0.73). Thus, the RLI shows us that close to half of the potential for learning in this class is not being realized. In other words, the teacher could have a big impact on learning simply by increasing student engagement or decreasing non-instructional time.

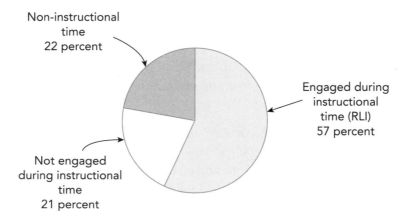

Non-instructional
time
22 percent

Engaged during
instructional
time (RLI)
57 percent

Not engaged
during instructional
time
21 percent

As with any form of targeted observation, the RLI suffers from significant limitations. Targeted observation focuses on specific areas for growth, but such a focus always leaves out other aspects of instruction that are important. For example, RLI does not address what students are learning or even if students are learning at all. For this reason, teachers may choose to set student achievement goals rather than student behavior goals. In my opinion, however, when the RLI is very low that should be addressed first before addressing other aspects of instruction.

TEACHER VS. STUDENT TALK

When teachers watch video recordings of their lessons, they are often surprised to see how much of the time they are doing the talking and how little of the time their students are talking about what they are learning. The correct ratio of teacher to student talk will vary depending on what kind of learning is occurring and what is being learned. Each teacher, therefore, needs to judge how much student talk is "enough." Overall, chances are that in many classrooms, the amount of student talk is not enough.

TEACHER VS. STUDENT TALK

TEACHER	STUDENT
Total Time _____	Total Time _____

Data-Gathering Tools

Instructional coaches and teachers can record teacher and student talk data in much the same way as they record instructional and non-instructional time. That is, the teacher notes the start and end of the class to determine the total time, records when students are talking about learning, and subtracts student time from total time to determine the amount of time the teacher talked.

RATIO OF INTERACTION

Teacher attention is a major motivator for students. Effective teachers encourage students by letting them know that they see them acting in ways that will help them learn. Teachers can learn a lot about the way they guide learning by watching how often they praise students for appropriate behavior and how often they correct students for inappropriate behavior. The ratio of times teachers let students know they see them doing what they are supposed to be doing vs. the number of times teachers correct students is usually referred to as ratio of interaction (Reinke, Herman, & Sprick, 2011; Sprick, 2010).[2]

The easiest way to score ratio of interaction is to use the seating chart for the students in the lesson you are observing, putting a plus under the name of a student who receives reinforcing, positive comments or nonverbal gestures from the teacher and a minus under the name of a student who receives corrective feedback. Reinforcing and corrective comments that are directed at the whole class can be noted as pluses and minuses on the side or bottom of the seating chart. When video-recorded lessons are reviewed, observers may want to replay some parts of the video to confirm that they have coded the data correctly.

When I observe a lesson, I find it helpful to think of teacher attention as a flashlight. When teachers shine their flashlights—their attention—on a student who is acting appropriately, record a plus on the appropriate spot on the seating chart. When teachers shine their flashlight—their attention—on students who are acting inappropriately, put a minus on the paper. After watching the complete video thoroughly, add up the pluses and minuses and

---

2. Randy Sprick and Wendy Reinke taught me about ratio of interaction and many other forms of data collection when I collaborated with them to write *Coaching Classroom Management: Strategies and Tools for Administrators and Coaches* (Sprick, Knight, Reinke, Skyles, & Barnes, 2010).

Ratio of Interaction

When you are gathering ratio of interaction data, you are observing how often teachers reinforce students for appropriate behavior and how often they correct students for inappropriate behavior. As a general rule, we suggest that teachers pay five times as much attention to appropriate behavior as they do to inappropriate behavior.

Ratio of interaction is not a measure of a teachers' "niceness." Rather, it is a measure of how a teacher directs her attention. Indeed, even if a teacher speaks very positively while attending to a student who is acting inappropriately, that teacher's action must still be recorded as a correction because the student is getting attention because he is acting in ways that are counterproductive to learning.

What It Looks Like

Attention to appropriate behavior can be expressed verbally or nonverbally and can be directed to an entire class or an individual student. Teachers' verbal attention to students is usually perceived with a teacher calling attention to what is going well.

Some examples of verbal positive attention include the following:

"Your effort on this assignment really paid off."

"The way you're paying attention is going to help you learn."

"This is what I'm talking about, class; this is the way a great team learns together."

"Thank you for getting ready so quickly."

"Keep it up. This is the way winners behave."

Some examples of nonverbal positive attention include the following:

Thumbs up

Nodding yes

Smiling in the direction of the student receiving your attention

High-fiving a student

Some examples of verbal negative attention include the following:

"You need to get working."

"What are you supposed to be doing now?"

"John, that's not acceptable."

(Continued)

(Continued)

"In this class, we raise our hands before talking."

"Eyes up here."

Some examples of nonverbal negative attention include the following:

Moving over to be close to a student who is off task (proximity control)

Staring at a student until she stops the inappropriate behavior (the evil eye)

Frowning at a student

Taking a student's book out and pointing to the task the student should be doing

estimate a ratio of interaction. A general guideline is to strive for an average of five praises for every one correction.[3]

Ratio of interaction should not be considered the same as positive feedback, especially inauthentic feedback for student work. When coaches observe for ratio of interaction, they are observing how and to what extent teachers pay attention to students and communicate that they are paying attention. The core idea here is that if teachers communicate only that they see students when they misbehave, they should not be surprised if that is what students do.

A final point: Behavior that interrupts learning or violates norms or expectations must be corrected, so trying to change ratio of interaction by decreasing corrections is not a good plan. The best strategy is to increase positive attention.

CORRECTING STUDENTS

If teachers increase positive attention but fail to correct students, chances are students will not act the way they hope to see them acting. Praising student behavior without correcting when appropriate is a bit like planting and

3. The 5:1 ratio is not a hard-and-fast rule. I suggest that ratio based on Gottman and Silver's (1999) research, which showed that a 5-to-1 ratio is typical in healthy relationships (*The Seven Principles for Making Marriage Work*).

CONSISTENT CORRECTIONS CHART

Data-Gathering Tools

	OBSERVED	CORRECTED

$$\frac{\text{Corrected}}{\text{Observed}} = \underline{\hspace{3cm}} \text{ percent}$$

online resources ⟍

Available for download at **resources.corwin.com/impactcycle**

watering a garden but not pulling the weeds. Eventually, the weeds take over. If teachers want to create a learner-friendly culture in their classrooms, they must correct students consistently.

When teachers issue corrections inconsistently (e.g., allowing side conversations to go unchecked one day and correcting them the next), students become confused about what they can and cannot do, and, as a result, complain that their teacher is being unfair. In short, using corrections consistently is just as important as knowing what to correct, maybe even more important.

One thing teachers can observe, then, is how consistently they correct students. To develop the habit of effective corrections, teachers first need to clarify what behaviors need to be corrected. For example, they may want to correct students when they engage in side conversations, speak or act rudely, text during class, bother other students, move around the room when they are supposed to be in their seats, ridicule others, swear, or exhibit off-task or other disruptive behaviors. Once a teacher and students have established behavioral expectations, the teacher must consistently correct anyone who violates those expectations; otherwise, they will be expectations in name only.

The easiest way for instructional coaches and teachers to assess how consistent teachers are with corrections is to video record and later review lessons in the classroom to see how often students should be corrected and how often they corrected. To gather these data, teachers should note every time they see a correctible behavior and every time they correct the behavior.

Educators may find it helpful to use the Consistent Corrections chart on the previous page. To use the chart, note the kind of behavior to be corrected in the left-hand column and then put a tally on the chart every time the behavior is observed and every time it is corrected. As a general rule, corrections should be consistent at least 90 percent of the time.

STUDENT BEHAVIOR

Frequently, teachers choose goals that focus on student behavior because they know that students who aren't listening to their teacher or their classmates aren't learning. Two variables that can be observed to measure student behavior are disruptions and respectful interactions.

DISRUPTIONS

When you are measuring disruptions, you are tallying each time a student disrupts another student's learning or the teacher's instruction. Such data are easily gathered by watching a video recording of a class or observing a class and putting a tally on a piece of paper each time a student is disruptive. If two students are disruptive at the same time, score that as two disruptions. Coaches and teachers find it especially helpful to use a seating chart to keep track of which students are disruptive. You can find many suggestions on how to reduce the number of disruptions in *High-Impact Instruction* (Knight, 2013), Part III, "Community Building."

RESPECTFUL INTERACTIONS

Another easy-to-measure but important data focus is respectful interactions. Simply put, when you observe respectful interactions, you are determining whether students are treating others in ways that are appropriate and acceptable in your classroom. Often this means you are observing whether students are *not* doing something—not shouting, swearing, touching, interrupting, and so forth. As with disruptions, you can watch a video recording of a class or observe a class and put a tally on a piece of paper each time a student says or does something that is not respectful. If two students are not respectful at the same time, score that as two disruptions.

KIND, TYPE, AND LEVEL OF QUESTIONS

One of the easiest and most powerful adjustments that teachers can make is to reconsider the kind, type, and level of questions they ask. As I explain in *High-Impact Instruction* (Knight, 2013), it is important to choose the right questions for the kind of learning teachers wish to foster in the classroom.

KIND

Questions can be either open or closed. I define open questions as those that have an infinite number of responses. For example, if I ask you, "What do you think of Hemingway?" you might not say much or you might go on for hours. There is no limit to what you could say, and that is why this is called an open question.

For closed questions, on the other hand, only a finite number of responses are possible. For example, if I ask, "What was Hemingway's first novel?" there is only one answer—*The Sun Also Rises*. Although some closed questions may produce lengthy responses such as, "What are all the novels Hemingway wrote?" the essential characteristic of a closed question is that eventually you run out of answers.

TYPE

Open and closed questions can also be opinion or right or wrong questions. Opinion questions don't have right or wrong answers. Opinions are personal and individual, so a person answering an opinion question can only answer it correctly, giving his opinion. For example, if I ask what you think of the new *Dr. Who*, your opinion can't be right or wrong; your opinion is simply your opinion.

But right or wrong questions, as the name suggests, have correct or incorrect answers. Teachers usually ask right or wrong questions to confirm whether students know the content or can demonstrate the skills they have been learning.

LEVEL

In many school districts around the world, teachers use Bloom's classification of educational goals, sorting questions into six levels—knowledge, comprehension, application, analysis, synthesis, and evaluation (Bloom, 1956). Others use taxonomies by Marzano, Erickson, Costa, or others.

We have found it helpful to sort questions into three categories: knowledge, skill, and big ideas. *Knowledge questions* prompt students to demonstrate that they can remember information. *Skill questions* prompt students to explain how to do something. *Big idea questions* prompt students to talk about the themes, concepts, ideas, and content structures that recur throughout a course.

Teachers can use the Question Chart on the next page to assess the kind, type, and level of their questions. Generally speaking, for direct instruction, teachers usually ask a lot (four per minute) of closed, right/wrong questions to confirm student understanding and ensure student engagement. For constructivist learning, teachers generally ask more open, opinion questions to prompt students to explore learning from their own perspective.

QUESTION CHART

QUESTION	KIND	TYPE	LEVEL

Data-Gathering Tools

STUDENT RESPONSES

In addition to gathering data on the kinds of questions teachers ask, coaches and teachers can gather data on how students respond to questions. In particular, coaches and teachers can observe (a) how frequently students respond to questions, (b) which students respond to questions, and (c) how often students respond correctly to questions.

OPPORTUNITIES TO RESPOND

One important variable coaches and teachers can watch for is how many times teachers give students opportunities to respond to what they are learning. Responses can include asking students to answer questions; prompting students to use checks for understanding such as white boards, response cards, or thumbs up, thumbs down (see pp. 62–65 in *High-Impact Instruction* [Knight, 2013] for a list of nineteen checks for understanding); asking students to turn to their neighbor; or other forms of response.

Increasing opportunities to respond is helpful only when teachers are engaged in what I refer to as intensive-explicit instruction—others use different terms for this type of instruction, including direct instruction (Hattie, 2012; Roehler & Duffy, 1984), explicit instruction (Archer & Hughes, 2011), explicit, direct instruction (Hollingsworth & Ybarra, 2008), and strategic instruction (Ellis, Deshler, Lenz, Schumaker, & Clark, 1991).

During intensive-explicit instruction, as John Hattie (2008) has written about direct instruction, "the teacher decides learning intentions and success criteria, makes them transparent to students, demonstrates them by modeling, evaluates if they understand what they have been told by checking for understanding, and re-telling them what they have told by tying it together with closure" (p. 206). Studies of intensive-explicit instruction have led to the recommendation that teachers maintain engagement and confirm student learning by prompting students to respond at least four times per minute.

Gathering data on opportunities to respond (OTR) is quite simple: just note the time at the start of your lesson, put a tally on a piece of paper every time you give students an opportunity to respond, note the time at the end of the lesson, count the number of OTRs, and then divide the number of OTRs by the number of minutes to determine OTRs per minute.

Offering a high number of opportunities to respond will likely not be a good teaching strategy for teachers taking a constructivist approach to learning. If the goal of questioning is to facilitate a rich classroom discussion, then too many questions may inhibit conversation. When dialogue is the goal, a small number of high-level, provocative questions will likely be more helpful than a rapid-fire series of question.

NUMBER OF DIFFERENT RESPONDERS

A high number of responses doesn't promote learning for all if the responses are all coming from the same three or four students. For that reason, when recording OTR, it is a good idea to also note who responds to prompts. This is easily done by putting tallies on the seating chart for the class being observed, so the teacher can see which students are responding and which ones are not. If the students respond to the same prompt, as in choral response, observers can simply put a tally on the side of the page. Using a seating chart, you can record the total number of responses and the total number of different students responding.

NUMBER OF CORRECT ANSWERS

Coaches and teachers can gain deeper insight into students' responses by noting how many students give correct or incorrect answers, often referred to as correct academic responses. The right number of correct answers will vary depending on your instructional goals. For example, if students have 100 percent correct academic responses, that may be because they have learned the material or because the questions are too easy.

Students can learn much by making mistakes, so some incorrect responses can be a good thing. However, when students are giving many incorrect academic responses, likely some modifications to instruction are necessary. You can find suggestions on possible modifications to teaching in *High-Impact Instruction* (Knight, 2013, pp. 73–77).

To record the number of correct responses, using the seating chart for the class, put a plus under a student's name when he or she gives a correct response and a minus when the student gives an incorrect response. Classroom management expert Wendy Reinke suggests that when students are learning new material, they should provide at least 80 percent correct academic responses. When students are reviewing content they have already learned, a reasonable goal is 90 percent correct responses (Reinke, Herman, & Sprick, 2011).

CONCLUSION

The approaches to gathering data presented in this toolkit are only suggestions, and the discussion is not comprehensive. Teacher and coach might focus their attention on other data (such as the level of student comments assessed with Bloom's taxonomy), and they may co-construct definitions that are different from the definitions provided here. What is critical is that (a) coach and teacher share a precise definition of what data will be observed so that they can have fruitful conversations about the data and (b) the data being observed really do reveal whether or not students and teacher are making progress toward the goal. Data are ways that people can identify a clear picture of reality, identify a finish line, and identify whether or not progress is being made toward that finish line. When teacher and coach work together effectively, there is a very good chance those goals will be met.

Instructional Coaches' Toolkit

Instructional Playbook

The teaching strategies described in this playbook are also included in *High-Impact Instruction: A Framework for Great Teaching* by Jim Knight (2013).

Content Planning
  Guiding Questions
  Learning Maps
Formative Assessment
  Specific Proficiencies
  Checks for Understanding
Instruction
  Thinking Prompts
  Effective Questions
  Freedom Within Form (Dialogue Structures)
  Stories
  Cooperative Learning
Community Building
  Learner-Friendly Culture
  Power With vs. Power Over
  Expectations
  Witness to the Good and Fluent Corrections

CONTENT PLANNING: GUIDING QUESTIONS

In One Sentence

- If students can answer all of the guiding questions for a unit correctly and completely, they should get an A.

The Hattie Check

- Student expectations = 1.44; Teacher clarity = 0.75.
- Students can use guiding questions to review and monitor their learning and confirm understanding.
- To develop guiding questions, teachers need to identify and clarify the knowledge, skills, and big ideas students need to learn.

What's the Point?

- Guiding questions clearly state what students need to know, do, and understand to be successful in a unit.
- Guiding questions are necessary for formative assessment and differentiation because teachers need to know what they are going to teach before they assess or differentiate.
- Guiding questions can and should be used as points of departure for many classroom discussions.

How Are Guiding Questions Used by Teachers?

- To develop guiding questions, teachers need to unpack standards and carefully identify the knowledge, skills, and big ideas students are to learn in a unit.
- Teachers report that they find it very valuable to create questions by collaborating with others teaching the same unit.
- Teachers should prompt students to write down part or all of each question on their own at the start of a unit.
- Guiding questions can be shared with students when learning maps are shared.
- Guiding questions can be posted in the classroom during each unit.

How Are Guiding Questions Used by Students?

Students use guiding questions:

- to keep the main goals of the unit in mind,
- to frequently review and clarify their learning, and
- as points of departure for classroom dialogue.

CHECKLIST: EFFECTIVE GUIDING QUESTIONS

	✔
Address the standards.	
Identify the knowledge students need to learn.	
Identify the skills students need to learn.	
Identify the big ideas students need to learn.	
Address meaningful and/or important topics.	
Address personally relevant topics.	
Use the most appropriate words.	
Keep language easy to understand.	
Prompt students to use learning strategies.	
Prompt students to use technology.	
Prompt students to use communication skills.	

online resources ▶ Available for download at **resources.corwin.com/impactcycle**

CONTENT PLANNING: LEARNING MAPS

In One Sentence

- A graphic organizer depicting the essential knowledge, skills, and big ideas students are to learn in a unit.

The Hattie Check

- Student expectations = 1.44; Teacher clarity = 0.75; Concept mapping = 0.75.

- Students can use learning maps to review and monitor their learning and confirm understanding.

- Learning maps are a form of concept map teachers can use to ensure their lessons are clear.

What's the Point?

- Learning maps are powerful because their visual depiction of a unit keeps students and teachers on track.

- The map is an accommodation for students who struggle to take notes, and it structures the beginning and ending of lessons.

- Learning maps are living study guides that make connections explicit and support repeated review.

How Are Learning Maps Used by Teachers?

- Teachers should spend twenty-five to forty minutes to introduce the unit through an interactive discussion of the map on the first day of a unit.

- Throughout the unit, the maps may be used as visual prompts for conversations around advance and post-organizers.

- Teachers should prompt students to record new information on their maps as it is learned.

- At the end of the unit, maps can be integrated into the unit review.

How Are Learning Maps Used by Students?

Students use learning maps:

- to take note of key information,

- to frequently review and clarify their learning, and

- as points of departure for classroom dialogue.

CHECKLIST: LEARNING MAP

A QUALITY LEARNING MAP:	✔
Answers all the guiding questions.	
Has a starting map with only the core idea, paraphrase, and subtopics.	
Has a complete ending map on no more than one page.	
Shows connections through line labels.	
Is organized according to the sequence of the learning in the unit.	

 # CHECKLIST: CREATING LEARNING MAPS

	✔
Identify the knowledge, skills, big ideas, and other information that needs to be in the map.	
Display everything by transferring information to sticky notes and putting it out where it all can be seen.	
Organize information into a map.	
Connect information using line labels.	
Refine the map by adding, subtracting, combining, and simplifying.	

 # CHECKLIST: INTRODUCING THE LEARNING MAP AND GUIDING QUESTIONS

	✔
The teacher spends twenty-five to forty-five minutes to thoroughly introduce the unit.	
Students complete their personal map in their own handwriting (at least partially).	
The teacher co-constructs the map with students.	
The teacher provides many opportunities for students to respond to learning so that learning is highly interactive.	
Students store their map in a place where it will be easy for them to retrieve it.	

✔ CHECKLIST: DAILY USE OF THE LEARNING MAP AND GUIDING QUESTIONS

	✔
Students have their map open on their desk when the bell rings to start the class.	
Class begins with a review of the content covered up until the current point in the unit.	
The learning map is used to introduce the day's lesson.	
Students record new content learned on the learning map.	
Each day ends with a review of the material depicted on the learning map.	

✔ CHECKLIST: END-OF-UNIT REVIEW WITH LEARNING MAP AND GUIDING QUESTIONS

	✔
Teacher and students have created a complete learning map by the end of the unit.	
Learning map should be integrated into the end-of-unit review.	
Teacher should prompt students to use the map to study for the end-of-unit test (when there is a test).	
Teacher should prompt students to keep their maps stored in an orderly, easy-to-find place in their notebooks.	
When returning students' tests, the teacher should clearly explain how the map would have helped them prepare for the test.	

 Available for download at **resources.corwin.com/impactcycle**

Instructional Playbook

FORMATIVE ASSESSMENT

- Teachers and students monitor student learning so that both can make adjustments until students succeed.

The Hattie Check

- Student expectations = 1.44; Providing formative evaluation = 0.90; Feedback = 0.75.
- Students must know how well they are doing to assess their performance against expectations.
- Teachers can't use formative evaluation to adjust their learning unless they know how well students are learning.
- Teachers can't provide feedback unless they know how well students are learning.

What's the Point?

- Formative assessment might be the single most powerful intervention teachers can employ to increase learning.
- Formative assessment isn't possible unless teachers are really clear on their learning targets.
- Most teachers won't know how well students are learning unless they employ some form of formative assessment.
- Formative assessment increases student engagement and student learning.

How Are Learning Maps Used by Teachers?

- Teachers should use formative assessment frequently, ideally whenever students learn new knowledge, skills, or big ideas.
- Teachers can use checks for understanding, checklists, or rubrics to assess student learning.
- Whatever teachers do doesn't become formative assessment until they modify either the way they teach or what students do to increase learning.

How Are Learning Maps Used by Students?

Students use learning maps:

- to identify their strengths,
- to identify areas where they can improve,
- to make adjustments to increase learning, and
- to be motivated by seeing their growth and success.

CHECKLIST: SPECIFIC PROFICIENCY

THE SPECIFIC PROFICIENCY IS:	✔
Targeted: A partial answer to a guiding question.	
Focused: Contains one idea.	
Complete: Written as a complete sentence.	
Short: As concise as possible.	
Accessible: Easily understood by students.	
Comprehensive: In combination with all other specific proficiencies, represents a complete answer to the question.	

online resources ⌕ Available for download at **resources.corwin.com/impactcycle**

CHECKS FOR UNDERSTANDING: A LIST

Exit Tickets: Exit tickets are short tasks students hand in at the end of class, completed on small pieces of paper or index cards and may include a writing assignment, a short quiz, or a single question.

White Boards: Teachers ask all students to answer a question on their individual white boards, then hold up them up at the same time. Teachers can then lead a clarifying discussion if there are conflicting answers.

Response Cards: Response cards include index cards with a "Yes" on one side and a "No" on the other side, or cards with the colors red, yellow, and green on them. Teachers ask students to answer a question by holding up the appropriate card for their answer at the same time as their classmates.

Clickers: Various companies sell electronic devices that enable students to respond to questions and send their responses directly to a teacher's computer or tablet. Teachers can immediately see which students answered correctly and incorrectly and display tallies of the answers.

Thumbs Up, Thumbs Down, Thumbs Wiggly: Students respond to questions through their thumbs: *Thumbs up* means they understand/agree, *thumbs down* means they don't understand/agree, and *holding thumbs horizontally and wiggling* means they're not sure if they understand/agree.

(Continued)

(Continued)

Turn-To-Your-Neighbor: After students complete a learning task, teachers can ask them to compare their answer or idea with a neighboring student to see if they have the same answer. If yes, students give the teacher a thumbs up. If no, students give the teacher a thumbs down.

Hot Potato: The teacher asks a student a question to test his or her understanding of content. If the student gets the answer right, he or she gets to ask another question that tests another student's understanding. The student asking the question must know the answer so he or she can confirm whether or not the new student gave the correct answer.

Soccer, Hockey, Basketball: The teacher organizes the class into two teams and draws a playing field on the white board with a puck or ball drawn at the center. If a team gets a correct answer, the teacher moves the ball or puck closer to the other team's goal. If a member of a team gets an answer wrong, the ball or puck moves toward their own goal. If the ball or puck gets in their zone, and they get a wrong answer, or the other team gets a right answer, a goal or basket is scored.

Graphic Organizers: Asking students to create graphic organizers is a good check of student understanding because in most cases students won't be able to create correct graphic organizers unless they understand the content.

Game Shows: With a little effort, teachers can develop their own version of popular game shows such as *Jeopardy, Who Wants to Be a Millionaire, Wheel of Fortune,* or *Family Feud.* Teachers should divide the class into teams and give each team review time prior to the game.

Jigsaw or Gallery Walk: Students are organized into groups to create a poster on chart paper that they can display in the room. The poster should demonstrate the students' knowledge of content covered. Once the groups have finished, new groups are formed that include a member from each initial group. The groups then walk around the room, stopping at each poster. Whoever created the poster explains it to the rest of their new group.

Four Corners: Students move to a corner of the room based on their answer to a question. For example, a teacher might pose a multiple-choice question and designate each different corner as *a, b, c,* or *d.*

Quizzes or Tests: Multiple-choice, true-or-false, fill-in-the-blanks, and short-answer quizzes and tests are used frequently to gauge student performance. Quizzes or tests can be used with many of the above assessment techniques.

Paraphrasing: Teachers can assess student understanding by ask students to retell in their own words what they have learned.

Group Answers: Teachers use this strategy to check student understanding by putting students in groups and giving them a task to complete, a question to answer, a term to memorize, or some other assignment. They should explain that in groups everyone is responsible for everyone's learning and that they'll check for understanding with one group member. Thus, all students need to ensure that everyone knows whatever is being learned.

Writing: Students' understanding can be assessed using numerous writing assessments. Students can be prompted to write a response to a passage they've read, write a letter to an author, write a short story to illustrate a concept that has been learned, and so forth.

✔ CHECKLIST: QUALITY ASSESSMENT

THE INFORMAL ASSESSMENT:	✔
Clearly tells students how well they are performing.	
Clearly tells teachers how well all students are performing.	
Is easy to use.	
Takes little time to implement.	

✔ CHECKLIST: USING ASSESSMENTS EFFECTIVELY

WHAT TO DO:	✔
Ensure all students respond.	
Develop a group response ritual.	
Ask students to explain their responses.	
Repeat assessments to ensure clarity.	
Reinforce students using assessment results.	
Use effective questioning techniques.	

 Available for download at **resources.corwin.com/impactcycle**

✔ CHECKLIST: REVISITING AND REFINING THE ASSESSMENTS

QUESTIONS:	✔
Did my questions effectively address the key learnings and standards?	
Should I change my questions in any way to make them more effective?	
Did the assessments address the right things?	
Was I able to monitor all students' progress?	
Did students have a clear understanding of their progress?	
Were the assessments fun?	

 Available for download at **resources.corwin.com/impactcycle**

INSTRUCTION: THINKING PROMPTS

In One Sentence

- A thinking prompt is a device (a video clip, photo, work of art, case, newspaper clipping, song, poem, word, etc.) presented to students to promote productive conversations in class.

The Hattie Check

- Classroom discussion = 0.82; Teacher-student relationships = 0.72; Questioning = 0.48.

- Teachers spend 30–50 percent of their time asking questions. Thinking prompts are used in conjunction with effective questions.

What's the Point?

- Thinking prompts
  - promote dialogue,
  - increase student engagement,
  - provide background knowledge, and
  - help students make connections.

How Are Thinking Prompts Used by Teachers?

- Thinking prompts are often used at the beginning of a lesson or unit to engage students or to promote thought and dialogue.

- Thinking prompts may be used for open or closed learning.

- To be most effective, thinking prompts should be paired with effective questioning (a small number of open-ended, opinion questions for open learning; a large number of closed-ended, right/wrong questions for closed learning).

What Is an Effective Thinking Prompt?

The most effective thinking prompts are:

- Provocative (students feel a strong desire to respond)
- Complex (they can be analyzed from many different perspectives)
- Personally relevant
- Positive and inspirational (fostering a learner-friendly classroom culture)
- Short (leaving ample time for classroom discussion)
- Appropriate for the content without being "lame"

CHECKLIST: EFFECTIVE THINKING PROMPTS

	✔
Provocative	
Complex	
Personally relevant	
Positive and inspirational	
Short	
Appropriate for the content	

online resources ➤ Available for download at **resources.corwin.com/impactcycle**

✔ CHECKLIST: CREATING A SAFE ENVIRONMENT FOR CLASSROOM DISCUSSION

	✔
Establish norms for classroom discussion.	
Use the most effective kind, type, and level of question.	
Listen with empathy to every student.	
Promote dialogue by listening for students' key ideas and restating them clearly when students' comments lack focus.	
Encourage students by frequently offering authentic praise.	
Suggest connections between ideas offered by students.	
Keep the conversation short enough to maintain student engagement and long enough to prompt meaningful reflection.	

 Available for download at **resources.corwin.com/impactcycle**

Instructional Playbook

INSTRUCTION: EFFECTIVE QUESTIONS

In One Sentence

- Effective questions are the right questions for the kind of learning students are to experience.

The Hattie Check

- Classroom discussion = 0.82; Teacher-student relationships = 0.72; Questioning = 0.48.
- Teachers spend 30–50 percent of their time asking questions. Thinking prompts are used in conjunction with effective questions.

What's the Point?

- Asking questions that are appropriate for the intended learning increases engagement and learning.

What Are the Different Types of Questions?

- Type of question
  - **Open-ended** questions have an unlimited number of responses (If you were mayor, what would be some things you would do?)
  - **Closed** questions have a finite number of responses (What are the capitals of Canada's provinces?)
- Kind of question
  - **Opinion** questions do not have right or wrong answers and are usually used as catalysts for conversation (Are you persuaded by this TV commercial? Why? Why not?)
  - **Right or wrong** questions have correct and incorrect answers, and they are used to determine whether or not students understand something that has been taught or learned (What is a pentagon?)
- Level of question
  - **Knowledge** questions prompt students to demonstrate that they can remember information they have learned (What are the parts of a cell?)
  - **Skill** questions prompt students to apply their knowledge to new situations or settings (How should you multiply fractions?)
  - **Big idea** questions explore the themes, concepts, overarching ideas, and content structures that recur throughout a course (Why is it important to be able to identify and decode propaganda?)

What Is the Central Idea for Effective Questioning?

- Open learning usually requires open-ended, opinion, and often big idea questions.
- Closed learning usually requires closed, right or wrong, knowledge, and skill questions.

Which Question to Use for Closed vs. Open Learning

Closed Learning	Question	Open Learning
Closed	Kind	Open
Right or wrong	Type	Opinion
Knowledge or skill	Level	Big idea
Many: up to more than four per minute	Number of questions	Few: As few as one to five per lesson

✔ CHECKLIST: USING QUESTIONS EFFECTIVELY WITH STUDENTS

	✔
Ask questions of all students.	
Use repeat, rephrase, reduce, and reach out.	
Celebrate mistakes.	
Avoid giving away the answers.	
Provide sufficient wait time.	

 online resources — Available for download at **resources.corwin.com/impactcycle**

INSTRUCTION: FREEDOM WITHIN FORM (DIALOGUE STRUCTURES)

In One Sentence

- Dialogue structures are classroom activities that promote student freedom and autonomy by providing a structure for interaction.

The Hattie Check

- Classroom discussion = 0.82; Teacher-student relationships = 0.72; Questioning = 0.48.

- Teachers spend 30–50 percent of their time asking questions. Thinking prompts are used in conjunction with effective questions.

What's the Point?

- Dialogue structures shape students' activities so that they can explore what they are learning from different perspectives and in different ways. They are similar to cooperative learning in that they are mediated by students, but different in that their main point is to foster autonomy and dialogue.

What Are Some Examples of Dialogue Structures?

- **Brainstorming:** A simple process that guides a group of students to list ideas or thoughts about a particular topic.

- **Affinity diagram:** A way for students to organize a large quantity of information by (a) writing down ideas related to a topic on sticky notes or slips of paper, (b) attaching the notes to a wall or laying them out on a table or desks, and (c) sorting the notes into groups, usually without talking.

- **Labovitch method:** A three-step process for structuring analysis and writing developed by Ben Labovitch at Humber College in Toronto, Canada. It involves asking students to (a) identify important information (such as their favorite scene in a movie), (b) group the information in ways that make sense, and (c) identify big ideas that the groupings surface, which can become thesis statements for writing.

- **Open space:** A group conversation process that is driven entirely by the interests and choices of participants.

- **Nominal group technique:** A simple structure that students can use to make a decision.

CHECKLIST: BRAINSTORMING

DURING BRAINSTORMING:	✔
Focus on quantity by coming up with as many ideas as possible.	
Put criticism on hold to encourage students to make many suggestions.	
Encourage students to produce more and more ideas.	
Encourage unconventional ideas.	

 # CHECKLIST: AFFINITY DIAGRAM

DURING AFFINITY DIAGRAM:	✔
First, students pick a topic to be discussed and write down their ideas on sticky notes.	
Second, students affix all the sticky notes to a surface (a white board, wall, table top, or floor).	
Third, students (usually without talking) sort the notes into groups that are related.	

 # CHECKLIST: LABOVITCH'S THREE-FOLD METHOD OF ANALYSIS

DURING LABOVITCH'S THREE-FOLD METHOD OF ANALYSIS:	✔
First, ask students to identify their favorite scene in a work everyone has read or watched and list all the scenes on the board.	
Second, ask students to group the scenes in ways that seem to make the most sense to them.	
Third, identify big ideas, which can become a thesis statement for an analysis of the work.	
Fourth, prompt students to use the grouping to organize the topics for the paragraphs in their essays.	
Fifth, prompt students to use the scenes as details for their paragraphs.	

CHECKLIST: NOMINAL GROUP TECHNIQUE

DURING NOMINAL GROUP TECHNIQUE:	✔
The teacher presents a question or problem.	
Students (on their own or in pairs) write down their ideas about how to respond to the question or problem.	
All ideas are recorded by the student discussion host (if students are meeting in groups).	
The teacher or student discussion host directs students' attention to each idea and asks for comments.	
Students vote privately to identify best ideas. Sometimes, students generate criteria for voting before they vote.	
Teacher presents a question or problem.	
Students (on their own or in pairs) write down their ideas about how to respond to the question or problem.	

CHECKLIST: OPEN SPACE

DURING OPEN SPACE:	✔
Students create a list of topics they want to discuss.	
Each student who proposes a topic agrees to host a discussion.	
Students choose which topic group they want to join for a discussion.	
According to the "Law of Two Feet," students can move to another group if they're not learning in the group they initially chose.	
Students may be asked to create a product (such as a brainstormed list or graphic organizer) and share it with the rest of the class at the end of the lesson.	

 Available for download at **resources.corwin.com/impactcycle**

INSTRUCTION: STORIES

In One Sentence

- Stories engage students, provide background information, and help students connect with and remember what they are learning.

The Hattie Check

- There are not enough studies of stories for Hattie to conduct a meaningful calculation of effect size.

- Existing studies show that students are more engaged and learn more in science, history, and mathematics classes when stories are told.

What's the Point?

- Stories have been used for teaching and communication since human beings first began to communicate. Chances are that the teachers you have known who used stories effectively left their mark on you.

What Is the Purpose of a Story?

- Stories can be used to (a) anchor new knowledge, (b) build prior knowledge, (c) prompt thinking and dialogue, (d) generate interest, (e) inspire hope, and (f) offer new perspectives.

How Should Stories Be Structured?

- Frequently used structures for stories include escalation, hero-conflict-resolution, building or upsetting expectations, and self-revelation epiphanies.

How Are Stories Used Within Open and Closed Learning?

- Closed: When stories are used for closed learning, teachers explicitly show the connections between stories and the content being learned.

- Open: When stories are used for open learning, students are encouraged to build their own understanding of the story.

How Should Stories Be Told?

- Effective stories are (a) planned ahead of time, (b) conversational, (c) simple, (d) short, (e) appropriately paced, and (f) spontaneous.

CHECKLIST: PURPOSES FOR STORIES

Anchoring new knowledge	
Building prior knowledge	
Prompting thinking and dialogue	
Generating interest	
Inspiring hope	
Offering new perspectives	
Describing epiphanies	
Building community	

CHECKLIST: EFFECTIVE STORIES

EFFECTIVE STORIES ARE:	✔
Not Lame: Is the story of interest to students or just the teacher?	
Concise: Have you cut out every word that you can? Generally, shorter stories are more powerful.	
Vivid: Have you included enough details to paint a rich picture?	
Emotional: Will the story touch students' hearts?	
Surprising: Can you make the story more effective by including a surprise ending?	
Humble: Stories that celebrate a teacher's successes can be off-putting to students.	

CHECKLIST: TELLING STORIES

WELL-TOLD STORIES ARE:	✔
Planned ahead of time.	
Spontaneous.	
Conversational.	
Simple.	
Short.	
Appropriately paced.	

 Available for download at **resources.corwin.com/impactcycle**

Instructional Playbook

INSTRUCTION: COOPERATIVE LEARNING

In One Sentence

- Cooperative learning is learning that is mediated by students whereby students work in groups of various sizes and control their very own learning.

The Hattie Check

- Classroom discussion = 0.82; Cooperative vs. individualistic learning = 0.59; Cooperative vs. competitive learning = 0.54; Cooperative learning = 0.42.

- Johnson and Johnson reviewed 150-plus research articles and reported a high effect size for time on task comparing individualistic learning to cooperative learning (1.17) and achievement (0.67); see co-operation.org/what-is-cooperative-learning

What's the Point?

- Cooperative learning helps teachers accomplish many goals in the classroom. It increases engagement and provides opportunities for formative assessment and differentiated instruction.

- Cooperative learning also allows for the collaborative construction of knowledge, provides an opportunity for students to develop and practice communication skills, and prepares students for working on teams when they leave school to join the workforce.

What Are Some Examples of Cooperative Learning?

- **Turn-To-Your-Neighbor:** Teacher organizes students into pairs and then, at various points throughout the class, prompts students to turn to their partner and have a conversation about what they are learning.

- **Think, Pair, Share:** Students write down their thoughts in response to a prompt, share with another student what they have written, and then share some of their conversation with the larger class.

- **Jigsaw:** Students are divided into small groups; each group learns a portion of content being learned in class, and then, after the teacher reassigns students to other groups, each student explains to their new group what they have learned.

- **Value Line:** Teacher presents an issue, topic, or question and then assigns a value to each possible response and asks students to form a line based on how they have responded. After students line up, the teacher guides a discussion about the topic.

- **Round Table:** In groups, students each write down a question on a piece of paper and then pass the paper to the student next to them and keep going so that every student gets a turn at answering the question.

CHECKLIST: COOPERATIVE LEARNING SUCCESS FACTORS

SUCCESS FACTORS:	✔
The teacher clearly understands the learning structure.	
The teacher has created a psychologically safe environment.	
The teacher has written expectations for how students should act, talk, and move while they perform the cooperative learning activity.	
Students have learned the expectations for how to act, talk, and move during the cooperative learning activity.	
Students have learned and use appropriate social skills to ensure they interact positively and effectively during the activity.	
The teacher has carefully considered the optimal makeup of each group of students.	
The teacher has given students sufficient time for each activity, without providing so much time that the learning loses intensity.	
Students have additional activities they can do if they finish their tasks before others.	
The teacher has planned additional activities to use during the class if activities take less time than planned.	
The teacher has planned how to adjust the lesson plan if activities take more time than planned.	
The teacher uses an effective attention signal.	

 online resources Available for download at **resources.corwin.com/impactcycle**

Instructional Playbook

CHECKLIST: TURN-TO-YOUR-NEIGHBOR

STUDENTS KNOW:	✔
Who their learning partner will be before they start.	
What tasks, if any, they need to do before they turn to their neighbor.	
What tasks they need to do with their partner (e.g., confirm their understanding, compare answers, share an opinion).	
The outcome they need to produce for the class (e.g., a written product, a comment to share with the class, thumbs up) at the end of the conversation.	
How they should communicate with each other (in particular, how they should listen and talk).	

CHECKLIST: THINK, PAIR, SHARE

STUDENTS KNOW:	✔
Who their learning partner will be before they start.	
Exactly what the thinking prompt is to which they are responding.	
How much time they will have to write their response.	
That they are to use all the time they are given to think and write about their response.	
The outcome they need to produce for the class (e.g., a written product, a comment to share with the class, thumbs up) at the end of the conversation.	
How they should communicate with each other (in particular, how they should listen and talk).	

CHECKLIST: JIGSAW

STUDENTS KNOW:	✔
What group they will be in for the first activity (perhaps by writing down the number for their group).	
What group they will be in for the second activity (again, perhaps by writing down the number for their group).	
How they are to work together to learn and summarize what they are learning.	
The product they need to create to share with the second group.	
Before moving to the second group, that what they have created has received their teacher's stamp of approval.	
How they should communicate with each other in both groups (in particular how they should listen and talk).	
How they will record (usually take notes or fill out a learning sheet) what they learn from their fellow students in their second group.	

 # CHECKLIST: VALUE LINE

STUDENTS KNOW:	✔
The question that they are considering.	
How much time they have to consider the question.	
Where the numbers for the value line are located in the room.	
Why they are being asked to line up in a value line.	
When they should move and how quickly.	
What they should talk about and how loudly they should talk.	
What they should do when they get to their spot on the number line.	

 Available for download at **resources.corwin.com/impactcycle**

 # CHECKLIST: ROUND TABLE

STUDENTS KNOW:	✔
Each question they are responding to.	
How much time they have to consider the question.	
Where they are to pass the paper.	
How they will sum up what they have learned or discovered.	
How they will share what they have learned with the rest of the class.	

 Available for download at **resources.corwin.com/impactcycle**

COMMUNITY BUILDING: LEARNER-FRIENDLY CULTURE

In One Sentence

- Culture is the invisible force that shapes behavior in a classroom. Teachers should do everything in their power to create a culture that will have the greatest positive impact on student learning and well-being.

The Hattie Check

- Teacher-student relationships = 0.72; Classroom behavioral = 0.68; Classroom management = 0.52.

- While the overall effect size for classroom management is 0.52, it should be noted that in classrooms where there is a great need for management strategies, the impact could be much higher.

What's the Point?

- When cultural norms promote hard work, kindness, openness, and respect, those norms can help all students be more productive, supportive, and respectful, but when norms guide students to make fun of hard work, be rude, or promote silence, those norms can inhibit learning, support, and respect.

What Can Teachers Do to Shape Culture?

- Teachers should co-construct norms with students.

- Teachers should reinforce and correct students.

- Teachers should spread learner-friendly emotions.

- Teachers should design a learner-friendly environment.

- Teachers should walk the talk.

How Can Students Have a Say in Culture?

- Students can be asked
  - To help with the design of the classroom and to bring in toys, quotations, works of art, music, or other artifacts that might shape a learner-friendly culture.
  - To frequently review and clarify their learning, and
  - As points of departure for classroom dialogue.

✔ CHECKLIST: CREATING LEARNER-FRIENDLY CULTURES

TO CREATE LEARNER-FRIENDLY CULTURES:	✔
Co-construct norms with students.	
Reinforce students when they act consistently with cultural norms.	
Spread learner-friendly emotions.	
Design a learner-friendly learning environment.	
Walk the talk.	

 Available for download at **resources.corwin.com/impactcycle**

LEARNER-FRIENDLY ENVIRONMENT SURVEY

ORDER	1	2	3	4	5
Good lighting (natural, soft)					
Comfortable and inviting (temperature, furniture)					
Everything has its own place					
Expectations/norms/targets posted					

CLEANLINESS	1	2	3	4	5
Clutter-free					
Smells nice					
Clean floor/carpets					
Clean desks/furniture					

SIGNS OF LIFE	1	2	3	4	5
Colorful walls/posters/photos					
Student work displayed					
Print-rich environment					
Personality of students/teacher reflected					
Plants/flowers/class pets					
Class library					

LAYOUT/ACCESSIBILITY	1	2	3	4	5
Easy to move around					
Students can easily access books, materials, supplies					
Easy to do teamwork					
Age-appropriate furniture/materials					

Source: This survey was developed in partnership with educators from Hazelwood and Riverview Garden School Districts.

online resources 🔍 Available for download at **resources.corwin.com/impactcycle**

Instructional Playbook

POWER WITH VS. POWER OVER

In One Sentence

- Each time we exert power over students, we move a little closer to becoming the dictator we always vowed we would never become.

The Hattie Check

- Teacher-student relationships = 0.72; Classroom behavioral = 0.68; Classroom management = 0.52.
- While the overall effect size for classroom management is 0.52, it should be noted that in classrooms where there is a great need for management strategies, the impact could be much higher.

What's the Point?

- Few people have more direct power over others than teachers.
- Power can poison our ability to see the world through others' eyes.
- Students are not served well when a teacher's need for control runs up against a student's need for autonomy.
- "Power with" is an alternative to "power over," involving authentic power developed with students.

What Is Power Over?

- Power over shows up in psychological bullying, asserting there is only one truth (the teacher's), and the constant reminder to students that they have inferior status.
- Power over can surface when teachers subtly ridicule students in front of their peers, lecture students to show who is boss, glare at students who are out of line, or use their much greater knowledge and experience to show up a student in a classroom debate.
- In worst-case scenarios, students feel impotent when confronted by a dominating teacher, and, feeling powerless or hopeless, they lose the desire to learn.

What Is Power With?

- Power with begins with the simple desire to empathize with students, to deeply understand how they are experiencing your class and the school, and how they think and feel about what is important in their lives.
- Build power with by
  - Asking every day in every class what each student is experiencing right now in class.
  - Having students try a program like Possible Selves to uncover their goals, strengths, and weaknesses, and to make an action plan for growth.
  - Connecting with students through one-to-one conversations.
  - Asking your instructional coach to interview your students.

CHECKLIST: POWER WITH

WHILE WATCHING YOUR STUDENTS, DID YOU:	✔
Give your students you full attention when they were talking?	
Affirm students for their contribution (either verbally or nonverbally)?	
Refrain from interrupting students when they are talking?	
Avoid sarcasm, singling students out, power-tripping, and other actions that communicate a lack of respect?	
Make bids for connection and appropriately turn toward students' bids for connection?	
Communicate the same degree of respect to all students?	

 Available for download at **resources.corwin.com/impactcycle**

Instructional Playbook

CHECKLIST: DEMONSTRATING EMPATHY

USE SOME OR ALL OF THE FOLLOWING STRATEGIES TO DEMONSTRATE EMPATHY:	✔
Prepare yourself to demonstrate empathy by considering how your self-interest, need for control, habits, biases, or other ways of seeing the world might interfere with your ability to demonstrate empathy toward your students.	
Think deeply to identify every student's needs.	
Think deeply to identify every student's emotions.	
While teaching, ask "What is this student or what are these students experiencing right now?"	
Look at photos of your students while planning your lessons.	
Give students the student survey available online at studysites.corwin.com/highimpactinstruction/toolkit.htm.	
Prompt students to write about their needs, thoughts, feelings, and experiences in notes, exit tickets, or other ways.	
Schedule one-to-one conversations with all students.	
Get insight into being a student by enrolling in a difficult class.	

 Available for download at **resources.corwin.com/impactcycle**

COMMUNITY BUILDING: EXPECTATIONS

In One Sentence

- If we want students to demonstrate certain behaviors, we need to clarify in our own minds what that behavior looks like, and then clearly communicate to students how they should demonstrate that behavior.

The Hattie Check

- Teacher-student relationships = 0.72; Classroom behavioral = 0.68; Classroom management = 0.52.

- While the overall effect size for classroom management is 0.52, it should be noted that in classrooms where there is a great need for management strategies, the impact could be much higher.

What's the Point?

- If teachers don't clarify and teach expectations, the students will be unclear on how they are to act, talk, and move.

- Teachers should approach teaching expectations just as seriously as they approach teaching content.

- Students need to learn expectations if they are going to have an impact on their behavior.

- Clear expectations provide a solid foundation for teacher interactions with students around behavior.

- Clear expectations increase the psychological safety of the classroom by providing guidelines within which behavior occurs.

Act, Talk, Move Expectations

- Expectations may be written about any behaviors, but three areas especially seem important:
  - **Act:** Explaining the activity and what students have to do.
  - **Talk:** Explaining what kind of talking, if any, can take place.
  - **Move:** Explaining what kind of movement can and cannot take place in the classroom.

How Teachers Should Develop and Teach Expectations

- List all of the learning activities and transitions.
- Identify expectations by answering the ATM questions (Act, Talk, Move).
- Teach the expectations using other Big Four teaching practices, such as role playing and exit tickets.
- Continually assess how students are doing with respect to acting consistently with expectations.

✔ CHECKLIST: CREATING AND TEACHING EXPECTATIONS

	✔
List all learning activities and transitions.	
Identify your expectations by answering the ATM questions (Act, Talk, Move).	
Teach the expectations using other high-impact teaching practices such as role playing and formative assessment.	
Continually assess the extent to which students are acting consistently with expectations.	

online resources ↖ Available for download at **resources.corwin.com/impactcycle**

✔ CHECKLIST: ACT, TALK, MOVE EXPECTATIONS

QUESTIONS FOR DEVELOPING "ACT" EXPECTATIONS FOR STUDENTS:	✔
What learning goal should students be working toward?	
What does excellent work look like?	

QUESTIONS FOR DEVELOPING "TALK" EXPECTATIONS FOR STUDENTS:	✔
Can students talk during this activity?	
What topics are appropriate for conversation?	
What topics are not appropriate for conversation?	
How loudly can students talk (library voice, inside voice, conversational voice, hockey game voice)?	

QUESTIONS FOR DEVELOPING "MOVE" EXPECTATIONS FOR STUDENTS:	✔
For what reason, if any, can students leave their seat?	
Do students need permission to leave their seat during those times?	
How should students act when they leave their seat? (How quickly should they move? May they talk with anyone? How many times can they repeat the process?)	

 Available for download at **resources.corwin.com/impactcycle**

COMMUNITY BUILDING: WITNESS TO THE GOOD AND FLUENT CORRECTIONS

In One Sentence

- To create a positive environment for learning, teachers need to reinforce constructive and correct destructive student behavior when they see it.

The Hattie Check

- Teacher-student relationships = 0.72; Classroom behavioral = 0.68; Classroom management = 0.52.
- While the overall effect size for classroom management is 0.52, it should be noted that in classrooms where there is a great need for management strategies, the impact could be much higher.

What's the Point?

- If teachers inconsistently correct and reinforce behavior, students will not know what learning is acceptable or encouraged, and that may lead to off-task student behavior and a psychologically unsafe classroom environment.
- Teacher attention is a significant motivator for students, and if teachers direct their attention only to inappropriate behavior by correcting students, they may unintentionally reinforce the behavior they are trying to extinguish.

How Should Teachers Be a Witness to the Good?

- Most fundamentally, being a witness to the good is about taking the time to see and comment on student actions that foster personal or group learning.
- Teachers should strive for a 5:1 ratio of reinforcing attention (verbal and nonverbal) vs. correcting attention.
- One strategy is for teachers to make a list of behaviors they especially want to see and then reinforce students when students demonstrate them.

How Should Teachers Fluently Correct Students?

- Randy Sprick's correction strategy:
  - Identify the behaviors that always must be corrected.
  - Identify how the behavior will be corrected, the first, second, third, and fourth time it is observed.
  - Video record lessons to see whether or not you correct behavior when you see it.
  - Work on one behavior at a time until all correctible behavior is consistently seen and corrected.

Strategies for Increasing Positive Attention

- Commit to saying hello to every student as he or she enters the classroom (put special emphasis on kids with whom you may have had a recent negative interaction).

- Seek out positive (appropriate) interactions that are not contingent on behavior.

- Find the little things that make kids tick (activity, team, interest, etc.) and talk about them with them.

- Catch the good behavior by drawing attention to it (thanking students, commenting, etc.).

- Focus praise or attention on effort rather than attributes (talk about a student's hard work rather than a student's intelligence).

- Pay attention to both academic and behavioral opportunities for praise.

- Post reminders to yourself to praise (sticky note to yourself on the projector, poster in the class, on your lesson plans).

- Set specific praise goals (today every student who gets the book out will be praised).

- Set goals based on irrelevant prompts (every time a teacher enters my room, I'll praise three kids).

- Double up on praise by naming all students who are doing something appropriate (Michelle, Lea, Susan, and Jenny, thanks for getting your books out so quickly).

- Vary your methods of praise.

- Call (or email) the parents of children who are doing well.

- Send home postcards (or email) to parents to praise kids.

- Prominently display student work in the classroom.

- Ignore minor misbehavior if the behavior is attention seeking.

CHECKLIST: FLUENT CORRECTIONS

TO CREATE FLUENT CORRECTIONS:	✔
Identify behaviors that must be corrected by reviewing ATMs and/or video(s) of students in class.	
For each behavior, identify how you will correct students the first, second, third, and fourth time you observe them engaging in the behavior.	
Identify an initial target behavior for which you want to develop the habit of consistent corrections.	
Video record a lesson.	
Watch the video and tally how often students engage in the target behavior and how often you correct it.	
Keep video recording lessons and tallying behaviors and corrections until you consistently correct the target behavior.	
Repeat the process with other behaviors that need to be corrected until you consistently correct all inappropriate behaviors.	

Source: I learned this strategy during a conversation with Randy Sprick. For more information about Randy's excellent work on classroom management, see his website: http://www.safeandcivilschools.com.

 Available for download at **resources.corwin.com/impactcycle**

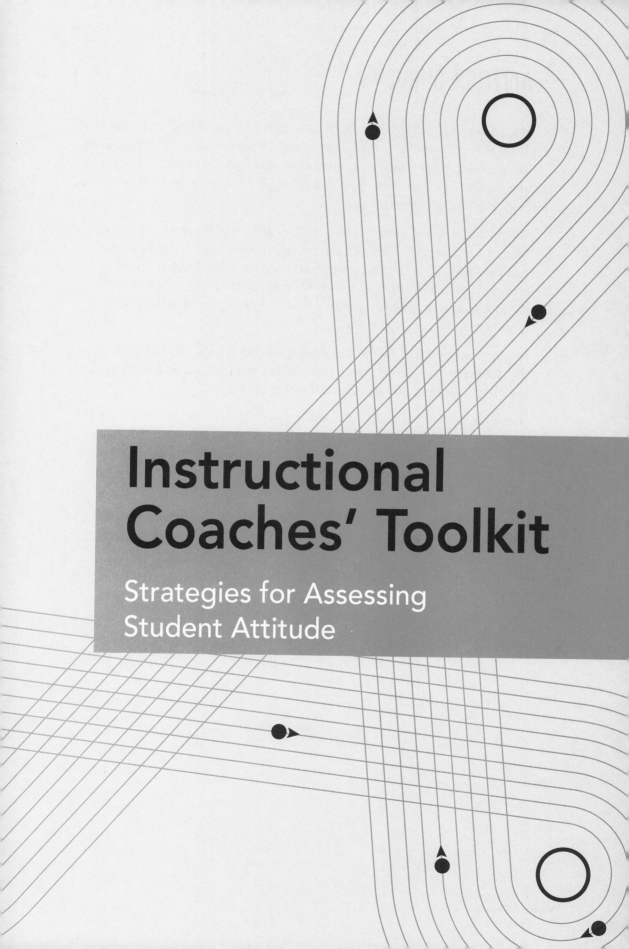

Instructional Coaches' Toolkit

Strategies for Assessing Student Attitude

ATTITUDE SURVEYS

Many teachers working with coaches are interested in setting goals related to student attitude rather than engagement or achievement. For that reason, the following mini-assessments are included as possible forms that might be used, modified, or perhaps serve as inspiration for coaches and teachers who wish to assess student attitude.

Several books served as inspiration for the creation of these simple forms. First, in his book *Flourish: A Visionary New Understanding of Happiness and Well-Being* (2012), Martin Seligman introduced the PERMA acronym for considering well-being, based on his belief that well-being involves the following five variables: positive emotion, engagement, relationships, meaning, and accomplishment.

For an assessment for the PERMA framework, see "The EPOCH Measure of Adolescent Well-Being" developed by Margaret Kern, Lizbeth Benson, Elizabeth Steinberg, and Laurence Steinberg (2016).

Shane Lopez's work, in particular *Making Hope Happen: Create the Future You Want for Yourself and Others* (2014), deepened my understanding of hope. Lopez explains that hope involves three factors: goals that matter, pathways to those goals, and our own confidence that we can meet those goals, which he refers to as agency.

To access Shane Lopez's hope survey, published by Gallup, please see the Gallup Student Poll described online here: http://www.gallupstudentpoll .com/171791/gallup-student-poll.aspx.

I was engaged in today's lesson.

😞 😐 😊

What would make learning more engaging?

_____

_____

_____

_____

_____

_____

_____

engagement

Strategies for Assessing Student Attitude

I was engaged in today's lesson.

| 1 | 2 | 3 | 4 | 5 | 6 | 7 |

Not at all   *Totally*

What would make learning more engaging?

_____

_____

_____

_____

_____

_____

_____

engagement

I like to talk in class.

What could be changed to make it easier
for you to speak in class?

_____

_____

_____

_____

_____

_____

openness

I feel comfortable speaking in class.

1   2   3   4   5   6   7
Never   Always

What could be changed to make it easier
for you to speak in class?

_____

_____

_____

_____

_____

_____

_____

_____

openness

 Available for download at **resources.corwin.com/impactcycle**

I feel safe at school.

I'd feel safer if:

_____

_____

_____

_____

_____

_____

_____

_____

safety

I feel safe at school.

1	2	3	4	5	6	7
Never						*Always*

I'd feel safer if:

_____

_____

_____

_____

_____

_____

_____

_____

safety

I feel happy today.

I'd feel happier if:

_____

_____

_____

_____

_____

_____

_____

_____

happiness

Strategies for Assessing
Student Attitude

I was happy today.

1   2   3   4   5   6   7

Not at all   *Totally*

What would have to change to make you happier?

_____

_____

_____

_____

_____

_____

_____

_____

happiness

I had positive experiences today.

I'd have more positive experiences if:

_____

_____

_____

_____

_____

_____

_____

_____

positivity

Available for download at **resources.corwin.com/impactcycle**

Strategies for Assessing Student Attitude

I had positive experiences in school this week.

| 1 | 2 | 3 | 4 | 5 | 6 | 7 |

Never   Always

What would help you have more
positive experiences in school?

_____

_____

_____

_____

_____

_____

_____

_____

positivity

Available for download at **resources.corwin.com/impactcycle**

How sure are you that you will learn in class this week?

What can I do to help you learn?

_____

_____

_____

_____

_____

_____

_____

_____

hope

Strategies for Assessing Student Attitude

What are your goals for this week?

_____

_____

_____

What strategies will you use to meet your goals?

_____

_____

_____

How confident are you that you
will meet your goal?

| 1 | 2 | 3 | 4 | 5 | 6 | 7 |

Not confident   *Very confident*

How can I help you to hit your goals?

_____

_____

_____

hope

How much do I want to come to school?

What could make school a place you really want to go?

_____

_____

_____

_____

_____

_____

_____

_____

value

Strategies for Assessing Student Attitude

For me, school is:

1   2   3   4   5   6   7

A waste of time   *Very important*

What could be changed to make school more important for you?

value

Would you like to do more lessons like this?

What would make this lesson better?

_____

_____

_____

_____

_____

_____

_____

_____

meaning

Today's lesson was meaningful.

1	2	3	4	5	6	7

Not at all   *Totally*

What could I change to make it more meaningful?

_____

_____

_____

_____

_____

_____

_____

_____

meaning

APPENDIX
Lean-Design Research

DEVELOPMENT OF THE IMPACT CYCLE

Since my book *Instructional Coaching: A Partnership Approach to Improving Instruction* was published in 2007, my colleagues and I at the Kansas Coaching Project at the University of Kansas Center for Research on Learning and at The Impact Research Lab have been concerned with our own improvement issue: How we can improve the effectiveness and efficiency of coaching—the impact? To that end, we have conducted studies that look at the impact of coaching on implementation following a workshop (Cornett & Knight, 2009), the impact of coaching on teaching practices (Knight, Skrtic, Knight, & Hock, in press), and other topics.[1] While

---

1. This book is a practitioner's guide, not a comprehensive discussion of all aspects of instructional coaching, so I won't describe those studies here. They will be described, however, in a forthcoming 2nd edition of *Instructional Coaching: A Partnership Approach to Improving Instruction* (in press). In addition, some of our research papers may be found at instructionalcoach.org/research.

that research has shaped our thinking about coaching, the research model that most informs the coaching cycle described in this book is a newer approach that we refer to as Lean-Design Research (LDR).

LEAN-DESIGN RESEARCH

LDR is a combination of design research (Reinking & Bradley, 2008) and Lean Startup methods (Ries, 2011). Eric Ries, the author of *The Lean Startup*, describes the essence of the lean approach as follows: "The fundamental activity of a startup is to turn ideas into products, measure how customers respond, and then learn whether to pivot or persevere" (2011, p. 26). Ries sums up the lean approach as "Build. Measure. Learn." LDR research is used to accomplish the same goals and to turn ideas into more and more effective and efficient products or processes, and it employs many of the lean methods for that purpose.

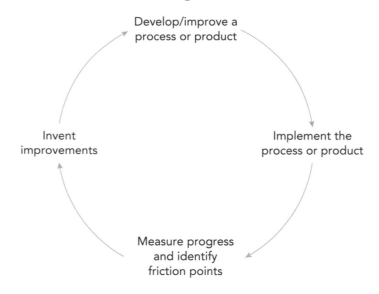

Lean-Design Research

Develop/improve a process or product

Implement the process or product

Measure progress and identify friction points

Invent improvements

DEVELOP/IMPROVE A PROCESS OR PRODUCT

The LDR model is designed to improve a product or process, so naturally it begins with the development or identification of a product or process. Whatever is being studied does not need to be perfected. It simply needs to be good enough to get the learning process moving. Eric Ries refers to this beginning product or process as a minimum viable product, or MVP. In our case, the process to be studied was instructional coaching. Instructional coaching was already much more refined than a typical MVP since we had been studying it for more than a decade. However, we co-opted The Lean Startup methods to refine instructional coaching much as a group of entrepreneurs managing a startup might refine a new iPhone app, for example.

IMPLEMENT THE PROCESS OR PRODUCT

The goal of LDR is to improve a process by learning what happens when people use it. To apply LDR to instructional coaching, we worked with two groups of coaches. First, between 2009 and 2012, we collaborated with four coaches from the Beaverton, Oregon, School District. Then, between 2012 and 2014, we collaborated with six coaches from the Othello, Washington, School District. The coaches implemented an approach to instructional coaching, identified roadblocks or friction points, collaborated with us to invent improvements, and then implemented the refined version of the Impact Cycle. In total, the coaches in Beaverton and Othello moved through the cycle eleven times, and in large part, our revisions of the model are the result of feedback from the coaches.

MEASURE PROGRESS AND IDENTIFY FRICTION POINT

When we conduct LDR, we are essentially asking, "How can we do a better job of achieving a goal?" At the start in Beaverton, Oregon, for example, our goal was to conduct coaching in a manner that clearly had an impact on teaching practice, so we measured whether or not teaching improved as a result of coaching.[2] In the last year of our work in Beaverton, and in our more recent work in Othello, Washington, we shifted our attention to student-focused goals.

After coach and teacher established a goal, we monitored how quickly and effectively the goal was reached with the intention of identifying roadblocks or friction points that slowed down the process. For example, as we moved through the many different iterations of coaching, we identified questioning, goal setting, and the use of video as areas where we needed to improve the cycle.

---

2. Teaching did improve, with each of eight teachers in our project showing significant improvement as a result of coaching (Knight, Skrtic, Knight, & Hock, in press).

Video Recordings

To measure progress and identify friction points, we gathered data in several ways. One way was by video recording most coaching interactions as well as the lessons taught by the teachers being coached. These videos provided the point of departure for the coaching of coaches and data-gathering interviews.

Interviews

A great deal of data was also gathered from interviews with the coaches. Members of our research team interviewed all Othello coaches weekly via FaceTime conversations, and research assistants on the Beaverton project interviewed instructional coaches before and after each iteration. In Othello, the interviews served two purposes. First, they were data-gathering conversations, and we used the data to make decisions about how coaching could be improved. Second, the interviews provided an opportunity for the coaches to be coached. That is, in the midst of helping the coaches do their work, we gathered important data about what worked and what didn't work.

Focus Groups

Our research team also held focus-group meetings with the coaching teams— usually following each iteration of the coaching model—to collaboratively discuss what worked and what needed to be improved within the coaching model. During these conversations, research team members and coaches reviewed video of coaching conversations and discussed other aspects of the coaching process. While our focus-group discussions were loosely structured, the main goals of each discussion were to (a) identify what was working, (b) identify friction points, and (c) invent improvements.

INVENT IMPROVEMENTS

On some occasions, we were able to identify solutions during our focus-group discussions. With some friction points, however, we had to seek out the knowledge of experts outside of our team. Sometimes, this involved interviews. For example, when our research process surfaced that the Beaverton coaches needed guidance on how to ask questions, I interviewed many experts to get their advice on how coaches should ask questions. These experts included Steve Barkley—author of *Questions for Life* (2011b) and *Instructional Coaching With the End in Mind* (2011a), Bruce Wellman—co-author of books related to cognitive coaching and school improvement, including *Data-Driven Dialogue* (2004), Joellen Killion—author of *Taking the Lead: New Roles for Teachers and*

School-Based Coaches (2006) and *Coaching Matters* (2012), Lucy West—author of *Content-Focused Coaching* (2003) and *Agents of Change* (2013), and Cathy Toll—author of *The Literacy Coach's Survival Guide* (2006) and *Lenses on Literacy Coaching* (2007b).

In addition to interviewing experts, I invented ways to resolve friction points by reviewing relevant literature. For example, when our team of researchers and coaches realized that we needed to improve our goal-setting process, I reviewed Conzemius and Morganti-Fisher's *More Than a Smart Goal* (2012), Heath and Heath's *Switch* (2010), Heidi Grant Halvorson's *9 Things Successful People Do Differently* (2012), Scott Belsky's *Making Ideas Happen* (2012), David Allen's *Getting Things Done* (2002), Daniel Pink's *Drive* (2009), Peter Senge's *Fifth Discipline* (1990), Robert Fritz's *The Path of Least Resistance* (1989), and other works that provide a comprehensive summary of research on goal setting. If you are familiar with the work of the authors above, you will see their work reflected in the goal-setting process described in this book.

LEARN FROM ITERATIONS BY REPEATED IMPLEMENTATION

During the LDR process, we learn by asking someone to try something, measuring how well it works, and making adaptations that address friction points. Then, we try it all over again to see if our improvements make a difference. As a result, the heart of LDR is to try multiple iterations of the process or product, in our case instructional coaching, to learn what does and what does not work, to make modifications between each iteration, and then to monitor whether or not the goals are met more effectively and/or efficiently.

For our study, we asked instructional coaches to move through the coaching cycle two or three times each year. After each iteration, we made refinements and then measured whether or not coaching was improving. LDR led to significant refinements to the instructional coaching process that I first described in *Instructional Coaching* (Knight, 2007). Thanks to LDR, the instructional coaching model now is described as a cycle—as opposed to a linear model—and includes the use of video cameras, implementing a small number of high-impact instructional practices, setting student-focused goals, as well as many other refinements described in the rest of this book.

DECISION MAKING

Within our LDR model, decision making occurs organically throughout the process. On some occasions, coaches and the coach of coaches make decisions as they discuss roadblocks that inevitably arise during the coaching process.

Often, decisions are made during the focus-group meetings, when our research team and coaches meet. Sometimes, I make decisions independently or with my colleagues after reviewing data, consulting with experts, and reviewing the literature, and then propose the changes to our team. Ultimately, as principal investigator, I make final decisions about modifications to the coaching cycle. The effectiveness of each decision is eventually measured through another movement through the improvement cycle.

MULTIPLE ITERATIONS TO TEST EFFECTIVENESS AND EFFICIENCY

The final test of the effectiveness of any modifications is the real-life implementation of the process, where we can discover whether or not the modifications helped us arrive at our goals more efficiently and effectively. For the past five years, we have conducted at least two and sometimes three iterations each year to test our modifications and refine the coaching cycle. The result of such study is the Impact Cycle described in this book.

INTERVIEWS

In addition to the data gathered from our LDR methods, a lot of the ideas and content for this book come from interviews with instructional coaches from the United States, Canada, Australia, Brazil, the United Kingdom, and Dubai conducted by my colleagues and me at the Instructional Coaching Group. The coaches' comments provide many of the stories, strategies, and real-life examples used here. Since this book is a kind of "how-to" book, it made sense to include comments by people who are spending most of their working time coaching.

Finally, to enrich my understanding of coaching, I interviewed many experts. This included Atul Gawande, whose *New Yorker* article about coaching, probably more than any other publication, has popularized the importance of coaching in North America. Robert Garmston, whose cognitive coaching in many ways laid the groundwork for many of the coaching models that are being developed or promoted around the world. Christian van Nieuwerburgh, the leading expert on coaching in education in the UK, and John Campbell, the leading expert on coaching in education in Australia. I used these interviews to test out ideas, and although many may disagree with me on some topics, we all agree that coaching can have a profound, positive impact on the lives of teachers and students.

REFERENCES

Adams, M. (2016). *Change your questions change your life: 12 powerful tools for leadership, coaching and life* (3rd ed.). Oakland, CA: Berrett-Koehler.

Allen, D. (2002). *Getting things done: The art of stress-free productivity.* New York: Penguin Books.

Archer, A. L., & Hughes, C. (2011). *Explicit instruction: Effective and efficient teaching.* New York: The Guilford Press.

Babauta, L. (2009). *The power of less: The fine art of limiting yourself to the essential . . . in business and in life.* New York: Hyperion.

Barber, N. (2014). *What teachers can learn from sports coaches: A playbook of instructional strategies.* New York: Routledge.

Barkley, S. G. (2010). *Quality teaching in a culture of coaching.* Lanham, MD: Rowman & Littlefield.

Barkley, S., & Bianco, T. (2011a). *Instructional coaching with the end in mind.* Cadiz, KY: Performance Learning Systems.

Barkley, S., & Bianco, T. (2011b). *Questions for life: Powerful strategies to guide to critical thinking.* Cadiz, KY: Performance Learning Systems.

Belsky, S. G. (2012). *Making ideas happen: Overcoming the obstacles between vision and reality.* New York: Penguin Books.

Berger, W. (2016). *A more beautiful question.* New York: Bloomsbury.

Block, P. (2002). *The answer to how is yes: Acting on what matters.* San Francisco: Berrett-Koehler.

Bloom, B. S. (Ed.). (1956). *Taxonomy of educational objectives, handbook 1: Cognitive domain.* White Plains, NY: Longman.

Bloom, G. S., Castagna, C. L., Moir, E., & Warren, B. (2005). *Blended coaching: Skills and strategies to support principal development.* Thousand Oaks, CA: Corwin.

Bohm, D. (1996). *On dialogue.* New York: Routledge.

Bossidy, L., & Charan, R. (2002). *Execution: The discipline of getting things done.* New York: Crown.

Bossidy, L., & Charan, R. (2004). *Confronting reality: Doing what matters to get things right.* New York: Random House.

Brown, B. (2015). *Rising strong: The reckoning. The rumble. The revolution.* New York: Penguin Random House.

Burkin, J. M. (2009). *Practical literacy coaching: A collection of tools to support your work.* Thousand Oaks, CA: Corwin.

Calkins, L. (2006). *Guide to the writing workshop, grades* 3–5. Portsmouth, NH: First Hand.

Chappuis, J. (2014). *Seven strategies of assessment for learning* (2nd ed.). Boston: Pearson Education.

Collins, J. (2001). *Good to great: Why some companies make the leap . . . and others don't.* New York: HarperCollins.

Conzemius, A., & Morganti-Fisher, T. (2012). *More than a SMART goal: Staying focused on student learning.* Bloomington, IN: Solution Tree.

Cornett, J., & Knight, J. (2009). Research on coaching. In J. Knight (Ed.), *Coaching: Approaches and perspectives* (pp. 192–216). Thousand Oaks, CA: Corwin.

Costa, A. L., & Garmston, R. J. (2002). *Cognitive coaching: A foundation for renaissance schools* (2nd ed.). Norwood, MA: Christopher-Gordon.

Danielson, C. (1996). *Enhancing professional practice: A framework for teaching.* Alexandria, VA: Association of Supervision and Curriculum Development.

Duhigg, C. (2012). *The power of habit: Why we do what we do in life and business.* New York: Random House.

Ellis, E., Deshler, D. D., Lenz, B. K., Schumaker, J. B., & Clark, F. (1991). An instructional model for teaching learning strategies. *Focus on Exceptional Children, 23*(6), 1–24.

Ellis, E. (2001). *The framing routine.* Lawrence, KS: Edge Enterprises, Inc.

Fisher, D., & Frey, N. (2008). *Better learning through structured reading: A framework for gradual release of responsibility.* Alexandria, VA: Association of Supervision and Curriculum Development.

Fisher, R., & Shapiro D. (2005). *Beyond reason: Using emotions as you negotiate.* New York: The Penguin Group.

Freire, P. (1970). *Pedagogy of the oppressed.* New York: Continuum.

Fritz, R. (1989). *The path of least resistance: Learning to become the creative force in your own life.* New York: Ballantine Books.

Fullan, M. (2000). *The new meaning of educational change* (3rd ed.). New York: Teachers College Press.

Gawande, A. (2010). *The checklist manifesto: How to get things right.* New York: Metropolitan.

Gawande, A. (2011, October 3). Personal best: Top athletes and singers have coaches. Should we? *The New Yorker.* Retrieved from http://www.newyorker.com/magazine/2011/10/03/personal-best

Godin, S. (2007). *The dip: A little book that teaches you when to quit (and when to stick).* New York: Penguin.

Goldsmith, M. (2015). *Triggers: Creating behavior that lasts—becoming the person you want you be*. New York: Random House.

Gottman, J., & Silver, N. (1999). *The seven principles for making marriage work: A practical guide from the country's foremost relationship expert*. New York: Three Rivers Press.

Grenny, J., Patterson, K., Maxfield, D., McMillan, R., & Switzler, A. (2013). *Influencer: The new science of leading change* (2nd ed.). New York: McGraw-Hill Education.

Halvorson, H. G. (2010). *9 things successful people do differently*. Watertown, MA: Harvard Business Review Press.

Halvorson, H. G. (2015). *No one understands you and what to do about it*. Watertown, MA: Harvard Business Review Press.

Hattie, H. (2008). *Visible learning: A synthesis of over 800 meta-analyses relating to achievement*. New York: Routledge.

Hattie, J. (2011). *Visible learning for teachers: Maximizing impact on learning*. New York: Routledge.

Heath, C., & Heath, D. (2010). *Switch: How to change things when change is hard*. New York: Broadway Books.

Heifetz, R., Grashow, A., & Linsky, M. (2009). *The practice of adaptive leadership: Tools and tactics for changing your organization and the world*. Boston: Harvard Business Press.

Hollingsworth, J., & Ybarra, S. (2009). *Explicit direct instruction: The power of the well-crafted, well-taught lesson*. Thousand Oaks, CA: Corwin.

Horowitz, A. (2013). *On looking: Eleven walks with expert eyes*. New York: Simon & Schuster.

Isaacs, W. (1999). *Dialogue: The art of thinking together*. New York: Random House.

Isaacson, W. (2011). *Steve Jobs*. New York: Simon & Schuster.

Jackson, P., & McKergow, M. (2013). *The solutions focus: Making coaching and change simple*. London, UK: Nicholas Brealey International.

Jackson, P., & Waldman, J. (2011). *Positively speaking: The art of constructive conversations with a solutions focus*. London, UK: The Solutions Focus.

Jensen, B. (2000). *Simplicity: The new competitive advantage in a world of more, better, faster*. Cambridge, MA: Perseus Publishing.

Kahn, A. (2002). *A love supreme: The story of John Coltrane's signature album*. New York: Penguin Books.

Kahneman, D., & Tversky, A. (2011). *Thinking fast and slow*. New York: Norton & Company.

Kern, M. L., Benson, L., Steinberg, E. A., & Steinberg, L. (2016). The EPOCH measure of adolescent well-being. *Psychological Assessment, 28*(5), 586–597.

Killion, J., & Harrison, C. (2006). *Taking the lead: New roles for teachers and school-based coaches*. Oxford, OH: National Staff Development Council.

Killion, J., Harrison, C., Bryan, C., & Clifton, H. (2012). *Coaching matters*. Oxford, OH: Learning Forward.

Kise, J. (2006). *Differentiated coaching: A framework for helping teachers change*. Thousand Oaks, CA: Corwin.

Knight, J. (2007). *Instructional coaching: A partnership approach to improving instruction*. Thousand Oaks, CA: Corwin.

Knight, J. (2008). *Coaching: Approaches and perspectives*. Thousand Oaks, CA: Corwin.

Knight, J. (2011). *Unmistakable impact: A partnership approach for dramatically improving instruction*. Thousand Oaks, CA: Corwin.

Knight, J. (2013). *High-impact instruction: A framework for great teaching*. Thousand Oaks, CA: Corwin.

Knight, J. (2014). *Focus on teaching: Using video for high-impact instruction*. Thousand Oaks, CA: Corwin.

Knight, J. (2015). *Better conversations: Coaching ourselves to be more credible, caring, and connected*. Thousand Oaks, CA: Corwin.

Knight, J., Skrtic, T., Knight, J. R., & Hock, M. (in press). Evaluation of video-based instructional coaching for middle school teachers: Evidence from a multiple-baseline study. *The Educational Forum*.

Koestenbaum, P., & Block, P. (2001). *Freedom and accountability at work: Applying philosophical insights to the real world*. San Francisco, CA: Jossey-Bass.

Lewis, M. (2017). *The undoing project: A friendship that changed our minds*. New York: Norton & Company.

Lipton, L., & Wellman, B. (1994). *Mentoring matters: A practical guide to learning focused relationships* (2nd ed.). Arlington, MA: MiraVia.

Lopez, S. (2014). *Making hope happen: Create the future you want for yourself and others*. New York: ATRIA

Love, N. B. (2008). *Using data to improve learning for all: A collaborative inquiry approach*. Thousand Oaks, CA: Corwin.

Lui, E. (2004). *Guiding lights: The people who lead us toward our purpose in life*. New York: Random House.

Maeda, J. (2006). *The laws of simplicity (Simplicity: Design, technology, business, life)*. Cambridge, MA: MIT Press.

Marquardt, M. (2014). *Leading with questions: How leaders find the right solutions by knowing what to ask*. San Francisco: Jossey-Bass.

Marzano, R. (2007). *The art and science of teaching: A comprehensive framework for effective instruction*. Alexandria, VA: Association for Supervision and Curriculum Development.

McKeown, G. (2014). *Essentialism: The disciplined pursuit of less*. New York: Crown Publishing.

Miller, W. R., & Rollnick, S. (2012). *Motivational interviewing: Helping people change* (3rd ed.). New York: Guilford Press.

Moran, B., & Lennington, M. (2013). *The 12 week year: Get more done in 12 weeks than others do in 12 months*. Hoboken, NJ: John Wiley.

Moran, M. C. (2007). *Differentiated literacy coaching: Scaffolding for student and teacher success*. Alexandria, VA: Association for Supervision and Curriculum Development.

Patterson, K., Grenny, J., Maxfield, D., McMillan, R., & Switzler, A. (2008). *Influencer: The power to change anything*. New York: McGraw-Hill.

Pink, D. H. (2009). *Drive: The surprising truth about what motivates us*. New York: Penguin.

Prochaska, J. O., Norcross, J. C., & DiClemente, C. C. (1994). *Changing for good: The revolutionary program that explains the six stages of change and teaches you how free yourself from bad habits*. New York: Avo Books.

Quaglia, J., & Corso, M. J. (2014). *Student voice: The instrument of change*. Thousand Oaks, CA: Corwin.

Reinke, W., Herman, K., & Sprick, R. (2011). *Motivational interviewing for effective classroom management: The classroom check-up*. New York: Guilford Press.

Reinking, D., & Bradley, B. A. (2008). *On formative and design experiments: Approaches to language and literacy research (an NCRLL volume)*. New York: Teachers College Press.

Ries, E. (2011). *The lean startup: How today's entrepreneurs use continuous innovation to create radically successful businesses*. New York: Crown Business.

Roehler, L. R., & Duffy, G. G. (1984). Direct explanation of comprehension processes. In G. G. Duffy, L. R. Roehler, & J. Mason (Eds.), *Comprehension instruction: Perspectives and suggestions* (pp. 265–280). New York: Longman.

Saphier, J., Haley-Speca, M., & Gower, R. (2008). *The skillful teacher: Building your teaching skills*. Acton, MA: Research for Better Teaching.

Schlechty, P. (2011). *Engaging students: The next level of working on the work*. San Francisco: Jossey-Bass.

Scott, S. (2002). *Fierce conversations: Achieving success at work and in life, one conversation at a time*. New York: Berkley.

Scott, S. (2009). *Fierce leadership: A bold alternative to the worst "best" practices of business today*. New York: Random House.

Seidman, I. (2013). *Interviewing as qualitative research: A guide for researchers in education and the social sciences*. New York: Teachers College Press.

Seligman, M. (2011). *Flourish: A visionary new understanding of happiness and well-being*. New York: Simon & Schuster.

Seligman, M., & Csikszentmihalyi, M. (2000). Positive psychology: An introduction. *American Psychologist, 55*(1), 5–14.

Senge, P. (1990). *The fifth discipline: The art and practice of the learning organization* (revised and updated ed.). London, UK: Random House.

Sprick, R. S. (2010). *CHAMPS: A proactive and positive approach to classroom management* (2nd ed.). Eugene, OR: Pacific Northwest Publishing.

Sprick, R. S., Knight, J., Reinke, W., & McCale, T. (2007). *Coaching classroom management: A toolkit for coaches and administrators*. Eugene, OR: Pacific Northwest Publishing.

Sprick, R. S., Knight, J., Reinke, W., Skyles, T., & Barnes, L. (2010). *Coaching classroom management: Strategies and tools for administrators and coaches* (2nd ed.). Eugene, OR: Pacific Northwest Publishing.

Stanier, M. B. (2010). *Do more great work*. New York: Workman Publishing Company.

Stanier, M. B. (2016). *The coaching habit: Say less, ask more and change the way you lead forever*. Toronto, CA: Box of Crayons.

Stone, D., & Heen, S. (2015). *Thanks for the feedback: The science and art of receiving feedback well*. New York: Penguin Books.

Stotzfus, T. (2008). *Coaching questions: A coach's guide to powerful asking skills*. Redding, CA: Coach22 Bookstore.

Sweeney, D. (2010). *Student-centered coaching: A guide for K–8 coaches and principals*. Thousand Oaks, CA: Corwin.

Sweeney, D. (2013). *Student-centered coaching at the secondary level*. Thousand Oaks, CA: Corwin.

Toll, C. (2006). *The literacy coach's survival guide: Essential questions and practical answers*. Urbana, IL: NCTE.

Toll, C. (2007a). *The literacy coach's desk reference*. Urbana, IL: NCTE.

Toll, C. (2007b). *Lenses on literacy coaching*. Norwood, MA: Christopher-Gordon Publishers.

Walsh, J., & Sattes, B. (2010). *Leading through quality questioning: Creating capacity, commitment, and community*. Thousand Oaks, CA: Corwin.

Wellman, B., & Lipton, L. (2004). *Data-driven dialogue: A facilitator's guide to collaborative inquiry*. Thousand Oaks, CA: MiraVia.

West, L., & Cameron, A. (2013). *Agents of change: How content coaching transforms teaching and learning*. Portsmouth, NH: Greenwood Publishing.

West, L., & Staub, G. (2003). *Content-focused coaching: A foundation for renaissance schools*. Norwood, MA: Christopher-Gordon.

Whitmore, J. (2002). *Coaching for performance: GROWing people, performance, and purpose*. Boston: Brealey.

Wiggins, G., & McTighe, J. (2005). *Understanding by design*. Alexandria, VA: Association for Supervision and Curriculum Development.

INDEX

CORWIN
A SAGE Publishing Company

Helping educators make the greatest impact

CORWIN HAS ONE MISSION: to enhance education through intentional professional learning.

We build long-term relationships with our authors, educators, clients, and associations who partner with us to develop and continuously improve the best evidence-based practices that establish and support lifelong learning.

Solutions you want. Experts you trust. Results you need.